Beyond the Spanish State

Beyond the Spanish State

Central Government, Domestic Actors and the EU

Rachel Jones

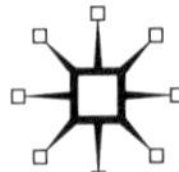

First published 2000 by
PALGRAVE
Houndmills, Basingstoke, Hampshire RG21 6XS and
175 Fifth Avenue, New York, N. Y. 10010
Companies and representatives throughout the world

PALGRAVE is the new global academic imprint of
St. Martin's Press LLC Scholarly and Reference Division and
Palgrave Publishers Ltd (formerly Macmillan Press Ltd).

Outside North America
ISBN 0–333–92125–9 hardback

In North America
ISBN 0–312–23571–2 hardback

This book is printed on paper suitable for recycling and made from fully managed and sustained forest sources.

A catalogue record for this book is available from the British Library.

Library of Congress Cataloging-in-Publication Data
Jones, Rachel, 1969–
    Beyond the Spanish state : central government, domestic actors and the EU / Rachel Jones.
        p. cm.
    Includes bibliographical references and index.
    ISBN 0–312–23571–2 (cloth)
    1. Spain—Politics and government—1975– 2. European Union—Spain.
    I. Title.

    JN8210 .J66 2000
    337.4604—dc21
                                                    00–038234

10   9   8   7   6   5   4   3   2   1
09   08   07   06   05   04   03   02   01   00

Printed and bound in Great Britain by
Antony Rowe Ltd, Chippenham, Wiltshire

To D and M

Contents

List of Tables

List of Figures

Acknowledgements

I am particularly grateful to Mike Smith for his constructive comment, and Linda Hantrais for her constant help and guidance, during the thesis on which this book is based. Others have helpfully commented on draft chapters, in particular Nacho Molina, Ian Bache and Uli Sedelmeier. A European Commission research fellowship in 1996 allowed me to carry out fieldwork in Spain which was facilitated by staff and officials at a number of institutions, libraries and government ministries, including Charles Powell, Martha Peach and Paz Fernández. Thanks are also due to my interviewees in Madrid, Seville, Brussels and the village of Barbate; among them, I am especially grateful to Luis Atienza, Ramón Rivera, Carmen Marfil, Luis Ortúzar and Miguel Ángel García. Many others have been supportive throughout. Special mention should go to Graeme Cameron, and the help of Diana Wallace and Huw Owen in the final stages was invaluable. Finally, for unwavering support and encouragement at every step of the way, I am for ever indebted to my parents.

List of Abbreviations

AEB	Asociación Española de Banca Privada (Spanish Banking Association)
ARPEBAR	Asociación de Armadores de Buques de Pesca de Barbate (Association of Shipowners of Barbate)
ASEMAR	Asociación Profesional de Empresas Armadores de Buques de Pesca de Cádiz (Professional Association of Shipowners' Firms of Cadiz)
BOE	*Boletín Oficial del Estado* (Official State Gazette)
CAP	Common Agricultural Policy
CCAA	Comunidades Autónomas (Autonomous Communities)
CCOO	Comisiones Obreras (Workers' Commissions)
CEA	Confederación de Empresarios de Andalucía (Confederation of Andalusia Business Organizations)
CEOE	Confederación Española de Organizaciones Empresariales (Spanish Confederation of Employers' Organizations)
CEPYME	Confederación Española de Pequeñas y Medianas Empresas (Spanish Confederation of Small and Medium-sized Enterprises)
CFP	Common Fisheries Policy
CiU	Convergència i Unió (Catalan Nationalist Party)
CNAG	Confederación Nacional de Agricultores y Ganaderos (National Farming and Livestock Confederation)
COAG	Coordinadora de Organizaciones de Agricultores y Ganaderos (Coordinated Farming and Livestock Organizations)
CSF	Community Support Framework
DG	Directorate-General
EAGGF	European Agricultural Guidance and Guarantee Fund
EC	European Community
ECU	European Currency Unit
EFTA	European Free Trade Association
EMU	European Monetary Union
ERDF	European Regional Development Fund
ESF	European Social Fund
ETUC	European Confederation of Trade Unions

EU	European Union
FCI	Fondo de Compensación Interterritorial (Interterritorial Compensation Fund)
FETCOMAR	Federación Estatal de Transportes, Comunicaciones y Mar (Federation of Transport, Communications and Fisheries)
FIFG	Financial Instrument for Fisheries Guidance
GDP	Gross Domestic Product
IFA	Instituto de Fomento de Andalucía (Development Agency for Andalusia)
IGC	Intergovernmental Conference
INI	Instituto Nacional de Industria (National Institute of Industry/state holding company)
IU	Izquierda Unida (United Left)
MEP	Member of the European Parliament
MP	Member of Parliament
NATO	North Atlantic Treaty Organization
OP	Operational Programme
PM	Prime Minister
PNV	Partido Nacionalista Vasco (Basque Nationalist Party)
PP	Partido Popular (Popular Party)
PSOE	Partido Socialista Obrero Español (Spanish Socialist Workers' Party)
RDP	Regional Development Plan
SEA	Single European Act
SME	Small and Medium-sized Enterprises
SPD	Single Programming Document
SPR	Spanish Permanent Representation
SSEU	Secretariat of State for Foreign Policy and the EU
UCD	Unión de Centro Democrático (Union of the Democratic Centre)
UGT	Unión General de Trabajadores (General Workers' Union)
UNICE	Union of Industrial and Employers' Confederations of Europe
VAT	Value Added Tax

Introduction

This book examines the role of the Spanish central state or government and its relations with other key domestic actors in the European Union (EU) policy-making process. Although literature on European integration has moved beyond the traditional state-centred perspective and increasingly adopted diverse approaches, new angles or different 'conceptual lenses'[1] (Allison, 1971, p. 253), the role of the central state, and many unanswered questions about its relations with other actors, remains a key focus. This book adopts a dynamic approach which centres neither wholly on the central government nor on other domestic actors, but on the changing interaction between the two.

Few studies have previously applied such an approach to the case of Spain. The generally state-centric focus of the literature reflects Spain's historical legacy, namely its relatively late transition to democratic, participative society due to the imposition of the authoritarian Francoist state until 1975. Michael Keating (1993, p. 337) highlights the fact that 'Spain has long been notable for the relative weakness of its civil society, that is the network of organized groups and institutions outside the state apparatus. This is reflected in the small number and membership of interest groups and the weakness of most of them'. Policy networks and communities have been slower to develop in Spain during EU membership than in other EU countries. However, considerable changes in relations between central government and other key domestic actors during the negotiations for accession to the European Community (EC) and membership cannot be adequately analysed by using the statist emphases of existing literature. This book provides a fuller picture of the Spanish policy-making process.

Despite the wealth of studies of EU policy-making in key member states, relatively few analyses exist in the case of Spain. The strongly pro-European position of central government, and the highly positive public attitudes to incorporation into the Community framework, may have tended to minimize discussion about Spain's integration into the European framework. Three key aspects which distinguish the Spanish case are:

- its relatively late incorporation into the EC and its rapid adaptation to membership: the Spanish government learned quickly how to 'play the game' within the Community, as illustrated by its successful first EC Presidency in 1989 and its skilful negotiation of EC/EU funding for its economically underdeveloped regions;
- the scale of change in Spanish society given the simultaneous processes of democratization, Europeanization and decentralization occurring during the period studied: the unscrambling of the autonomous effects on Spanish society of each of these processes represents a considerable challenge to the researcher, but also offers an important area for further study;
- the development of relations between central government and other domestic actors: it is likely that domestic actors will be relatively weak in a newly established democratic society.

The starting point for this book is the beginning of a new democratic era for the Spanish state after the death of Franco in 1975. It centres on Spain's attitude to Europe, the long, protracted EC accession negotiations from 1979 to 1986, and Spain's EC/EU membership between 1986 and 1996. In March 1996, and again in March 2000, the main opposition party, the Partido Popular (Popular Party, PP)[2] won the elections after 14 years of rule by the Partido Socialista Obrero Español (Spanish Socialist Workers' Party, PSOE). The focus of the book is on the period up to this turning point in the Spanish political landscape in 1996. It is for future studies to continue the analysis of the relations between central government and other key actors in Spain.

Objectives

Many studies of Spanish politics have highlighted the lack of research on policy networks and communities, even if they are less developed in Spain than in other EU member states; this book is a contribution towards filling this gap in the literature. Through viewing Spanish policy-making from a different angle, it seeks to enrich the debate on decision-making in Spain which has tended to rest on the assumption of a fixed, unequal distribution of resources between central government and other domestic actors.

The main objective is to examine the impact on the key role and autonomy of Spanish central government of potentially greater involvement of other domestic actors in the changing EU policy process. While acknowledging that it is impossible to separate the autonomous effects of processes at EU and domestic level, important factors are considered to be: the level of access to policy-making for domestic groups, their capacity to exploit available opportunities for participation, and central government's ability to control the level of domestic input, thus highlighting the key issues of access, resources and control. Rather than a pure examination of objectives and achievements at the European level, the analysis also highlights how the central state ratifies policy decisions in the domestic arena; despite its predominant role in the policy process, the central state is expected to be increasingly obliged to obtain the approval of other domestic actors for its policy decisions, and to take account of their greater input to the policy-making process. This allows an evaluation of the central state's strategies for adapting to a potentially new context.

In view of the hypothesis that policy decisions are not purely the outcome of bargaining positions formulated by central government, the study seeks to identify factors influencing relations between the central state and other domestic actors in the case of Spain. Key research questions which arise from this focus are:

- Has the level of access to the policy process for domestic actors increased during EC/EU membership?
- Have domestic actors directly affected by negotiations at EC/EU level developed the capacity to exploit opportunities for greater access to policy-making?
- To what extent has the central state retained, or even strengthened, its control of the policy process?

Addressing these key questions enables this book to evaluate the level of access to the policy process for particular groups of domestic actors, and the extent to which this has had a significant impact. Helen Wallace and Alasdair R. Young (1997) consider that the information, resources and credibility of particular groups are key factors determining access to policy-making as well as the structures of the policy process itself. The distinction they draw between participation and influence, although assuming that participation itself conveys a certain degree of influence, is a key consideration in this book. The potential for increasing involvement of non-central state actors in policy-making is expected to be influenced both by changes in the specific character of the Spanish political system and by the effects of its incorporation into the European framework. The analysis does not seek to provide a clear-cut explanation of relations between central government and other domestic actors in the EU policy-making process as a whole, but explores the potential impact of the greater involvement of a wider range of actors in the case of Spain.

Key definitions

This book distinguishes between the central state or government in Spain and non-central state actors, commonly termed other domestic actors. Regional or subnational governments are thus considered distinct from the central state. In addition to regional governments, the analysis includes the Spanish parliament (also referring to the input of key political parties where relevant to the analysis), and trade unions and employers, collectively termed socio-economic actors. The study of the trade unions focuses on the two main unions in Spain, while the examination of employers is largely based on the principal employers' confederation (see Chapter 2). The particular sector which forms a key focus of the book, namely the fisheries sector, has its own individual structure incorporating trade unions, shipowners' associations and local associations. The organization of the fishing sector is explained in Chapter 7 prior to the analysis of its relations with central government during EU-level negotiations.

Autonomy can be defined as 'the ability of a given actor to pursue its desired policy independently of, and without pressure from, another political actor' (Fioretos, 1997, p. 297). In this book, the concept mainly refers to the autonomy of the central state *vis-à-vis* other domestic actors rather than in relation to the EU, and alludes to the extent to which central government can act regardless of domestic constraints when formulating its bargaining position and implementing EU policy. The question of its autonomy also relates to issues of internal coordination between and within ministries (see analysis of institutional framework in Chapter 3). However, although central government cannot be viewed as a single, unified actor, the focus in this book is on its relations with non-central government actors rather than internal coordination mechanisms.

The term 'cohesion policy' rather than 'regional policy' is used in this book as it describes both the concept of reducing social and economic inequalities between European regions (as outlined in the Single European Act of 1986 (SEA)) and the specific Community measures to achieve that goal, including the structural funds and the Cohesion Fund (further explained in Chapters 4 and 5) for which the Spanish government vigorously fought once a member of the Community.

The term EU is used when referring to events after the enactment of the Treaty on European Union in November 1993, and to the European context more generally, whereas EC is reserved for events prior to this. EC/EU is used to refer to the whole period of Spanish membership of the Community.

Case studies

A detailed analysis of Spain's EC accession negotiations allows a series of factors to be established at the outset of this book which characterize relations between the central government in Spain and other domestic actors. While aware of the key differences between a bilateral accession process and the incorporation into a multilateral EC/EU negotiating framework once a member, the potential for a changed context in the domestic arena after Spain's EC entry is considered, given that the overwhelming consensus in favour of incorporation into a European democratic framework could not be assumed once integration had been achieved.

Cohesion policy was selected as a first policy area since its development potentially illustrated a considerable change in the roles of central state and other domestic actors. The increased participation of regional authorities in the EU policy process, particularly in the implementation of Community-funded projects, raised many fundamental questions about the changing nature of policy-making. Although the net positive effects of an inflow of EC/EU funding made the negotiation of cohesion policy for the Spanish government relatively unproblematic in the domestic arena, the distribution of funding nationally was likely to cause considerable tensions between the different administrative levels.

The study of fisheries was an area considered more likely to lead to tensions between central government and other domestic actors. The fishing sector sought to maximize its involvement in EU-level negotiations when permitted by national and Community structures. Even during the EC accession negotiations, fisheries led to considerable discontent and accusations of inadequate government support for the sector. Within the area of fisheries, the focus is on the re-negotiation of the EU–Morocco fisheries agreement in 1995 in view of its high visibility, the direct involvement of the fishing sector and strong public support for sectoral demands.

The focus of the fisheries study is the region most directly affected economically by the negotiation, namely Andalusia, which is also the main focus of the case study on cohesion policy as the principal recipient of European funding in Spain. The Spanish government has been a key protagonist in both areas during EC/EU membership, which may indicate a stronger role for central government than in other policy areas. Despite this parallel between the two case studies, a number of key factors clearly distinguish them. The case study on cohesion highlights the changing nature of the policy area during the 1989–93 and 1994–9 funding cycles, with a particular focus on subnational authorities. Cohesion policy is characterized by a series of negotiating rounds creating distributional tensions, which obliges the central state to ratify its initiatives and negotiating positions at EU level in the domestic arena. The study within the area of fisheries examines a particular episode in a specific context, although the negotiating rounds of one of the EU's most significant fishing agreements with a non-EU third country can also be located within a broader cycle of accords with Morocco, where Spain is clearly the most affected member state. In contrast to cohesion policy, the fisheries episode represents a short-term, localized crisis management issue, where high involvement of the most directly affected domestic actors at regional level would be expected. The case studies thus provide the opportunity to analyse distinct issue areas, considering different episodes and varying stages of the policy process.

Structure of the book

Chapter 1 discusses previous approaches to the study of Spain, and to the role of the central state more generally, with a view to establishing a clear framework for the case of Spain. Spain's EC accession negotiations are the focus of Chapter 2 which explores key factors influencing relations between the Spanish central state and other domestic actors during the negotiating process, and the extent to which the central state was able to retain its autonomy in the domestic arena. The focus on Spain as EC applicant in Chapter 2 forms a baseline for an analysis of Spain as EC/EU member in Chapter 3, where the development of the institutional structure established for EU policy-making and the issue of access to the policy process for domestic actors are analysed. Chapters 2 and 3 establish the broad conditions determining the nature of relations between the central state and non-central state actors in the policy process. The validity of these macro-conditions is then considered in an analysis of the micro-conditions existing in specific policy areas, namely in the two empirical case studies in Chapters 4–7, which act as tests of the assumptions made in earlier chapters.

The structure of the two case studies reflects the focus of this book on both the role of the central state and other domestic actors in the policy process. Each case is divided into two chapters, the first of which focuses on the intergovernmental level, thus putting a premium on the role of the central state, while the second focuses on the input of other domestic actors to the policy process. This structure is intended to demonstrate that an analysis going beyond a purely state-centred view explains the changing nature of the policy process more adequately. The final chapter evaluates the key findings of the book, related both to the broader framework and specific issue areas, and draws conclusions about issues which, previously, have been relatively unexplored in the Spanish case.

1
Approach to the Analysis

EU membership has raised fundamental questions about the distribution of authority and decision-making power between EU institutions and member states, and between national governments and other domestic actors. Although it could be argued that 'evidence from both the EU policy process and from major treaty negotiations has consistently reinforced … the critical role which national governments have played in the decision-making process' (Cram, 1997, p. 170), this book seeks to take into account changes in the nature of policy-making which may have an impact on the level of autonomy of the central state, and on its interaction with other domestic actors.

The issue of the role of central governments in policy-making remains problematic. In the case of Spain, Paul Heywood (1995, p. 241) refers to the policy-making process as one of the least researched elements of Spanish politics, rendering it 'difficult to locate policy-making in Spain within analytical categories familiar from the study of other west European polities'. Studies of Spain, both during the EC accession negotiations and EC/EU membership, are briefly analysed here in order to examine the way in which relations between central government and other domestic actors have previously been conceptualized.

Spain and the EC/EU

Although Spain has had close economic links with Europe since the early 1960s, its political integration into the Community did not occur until 1986. EC accession was of fundamental importance for the newly established democracy, as illustrated by the analysis of the negotiations from 1979 to 1986 in Chapter 2.

Spain during EC accession negotiations

Spain's application to join the Community tends to be discussed in terms of the reorientation of the foreign policy interests of the Spanish state, namely the shift from an isolationist policy line to a greater focus on the European context in the 1970s (Cortada, 1980; Minet et al., 1981). Although the impact of the EC on the transition of post-Franco Spain in the 1970s and 1980s is studied, the focus continues to be on Spain's overall foreign policy objectives (Preston and Smyth, 1984; Pollack and Hunter, 1987). EC accession is thus examined as a key element of Spain's modernization process alongside entry into the North Atlantic Treaty Organization (NATO), and as a global decision taken by the central state without referring to its ratification in the domestic arena. External views of Spain perhaps naturally focus on the interstate level, including the positions of key member states *vis-à-vis* Spain's application, and the overall impact of the second enlargement on the Community. Views from within Spain might be considered more likely to provide detail on the accession process and Spain's internal relationships. However, the predominantly economic focus of Spanish analysts have tended to neglect key political and institutional issues (Sampedro and Payno, 1983; Tamames, 1986). Detailed chronological accounts of each technical stage of the accession process (such as the account of government official Enrique González Sánchez from 1978 to 1986) do not analyse the broader political impact of EC entry, even when the rationale behind Spain's application for membership was largely political rather than economic.

Given that analyses of political aspects of the accession process are less common, partisan views of the Spanish government's negotiation of EC entry are used in this book to inform the analysis of the accession process. However, studies by the main opposition parties tend to reiterate key criticisms of the government's negotiating strategies, and thus limit the objective analysis of the process. For example, officials involved in the early years of the accession process attempt to counter the notion that the negotiations only commenced in 1982 when the PSOE came to power (Bassols, 1995), while Socialist politicians naturally focus on the period following their election victory in 1982, which they regard as the true starting point of the process. Many give a positive, almost self-congratulatory account of the negotiations and bargaining tactics of the Socialist government rather than an objective analysis (Morán, 1980, 1984, 1990). However, such studies also examine the acritical unanimity of all political forces in the domestic arena, thus facilitating an understanding of the pro-European consensus in

Spain during the negotiations. Frequent criticism of the minimal domestic debate of EC entry (Tsoukalis, 1981; Herrero de Miñón, 1986; Gómez Fuentes, 1986; Armero, 1989) begins to raise wider questions about relations between central government and other actors which are further explored in Chapter 2.

Analysis of interaction between the development of Spanish civil society and economic and political liberalization would be expected to form a key focus in the literature in view of Spain's historical legacy (Pérez-Díaz, 1993), as would the transition to democracy and the redefinition of its external relations (see Pridham, 1991, 1995). The focus is largely on the interstate level and the key role of the central state, although studies of central government's use of external exigencies to enforce domestic policy decisions begin to place greater emphasis on the interaction between the EU and domestic arenas, particularly during EC/EU membership (Story and Pollack, 1991; Powell, 1993; Story, 1993, 1995).

Spain during EC/EU membership

Studies of Spain as an established EU member state are relatively rare compared with the wealth of literature on Spain's transition to democracy. Although surveys of political science research (Ciavarini Azzi, 1994; Loughlin, 1993) note an important increase in both the quantity and quality of studies of Europe in Spain during its EC/EU membership, the number of political studies is small when compared to economic analyses (for example, Hudson and Rudcenko, 1988; Ruesga, 1989; Tamames, 1991; Harrison, 1992; Salmon, 1995a,b; Tovias, 1995). Similarly, evaluation of the effects of the Maastricht Treaty on Spain largely focused on its economic rather than political impact (Círculo de Lectores, 1992). Heywood (1995, p. 6) highlights the fact that the study of politics in Spain is also shaped by its location within the discipline of law, which has encouraged its focus on constitutional and legal issues (for example Mangas Martín, 1987; Remiro Brotóns, 1984). Overviews of the government and politics of Spain written in the 1990s, generally centring on the broad outlines of its political transformation, the economic and social changes in post-Franco Spanish society, and Spain's emergence as a significant voice in international affairs, are an acknowledgement of the significant gap in the literature, and an indication of a greater academic interest in Spanish politics (see Heywood, 1995; Gunther, 1996; Ross, 1997).

Existing studies of Spanish EU policy rarely provide in-depth analysis of the impact of the EU on Spain (Almarcha Barbado, 1993). The analysis of the impact of EU membership, not only on the policy process at national level but on specific sectors, by Carlos Closa (2000) is a major step forward in this regard. Studies of the institutional structure in Spain (Heywood, 1995; Newton, 1997) and the framework for EC/EU policy-making (Morata, 1996, 1997, 1998) form a firm foundation for the analysis of the changing institutional framework in this book. However, Keating (1993, p. 341) refers to views of Spanish policy-making being seen 'almost exclusively in terms of the state, which is given an exalted role in Spanish political culture'. Despite more recent attempts to focus on the role of actors other than central government in the policy process, particularly the Autonomous Communities (for example Keating, 1993; Gutiérrez Espada, 1994; Burgorgue-Larsen, 1995; Ministerio para las Administraciones Públicas, 1995; Pérez Tremps, 1995), a state-centric perspective has tended to be prevalent in studies of the key developments in Spanish politics in the 1980s and 1990s.

A key theme which emerges is that of Spain's established position in the EU as a middle-order country with considerable international prestige. The issue of EU membership is generally included as a success of the PSOE government in a wider analysis of Spain's role at international level (Alonso Zaldívar and Castells, 1992; Guerra and Tezanos, 1992; González, 1992; Guerra, 1993). The greater focus on strategies at interstate level neglects the changing relations between central government and other domestic actors; only a minority have adopted a less static approach to the changing EU policy-making process in Spain (for example Zapico Goñi, 1995). Specific sectoral studies, such as that of EMU (Heywood, 1993) have a greater focus on the potential influence on central government of domestic interests. However, outlines of key achievements at European level generally make little reference to the formulation of policies in the domestic arena (Barbé, 1996; Story, 1991a,b).

Studies of policy-making in Spain thus continue to emphasize the autonomy of the central state *vis-à-vis* other domestic actors (see Heywood, 1998; Subirats and Gomá, 1998). However, it is significant that Heywood (1998) also allows for the potential for greater diffusion of power in the future, while accepting the high degree of power concentration currently enjoyed by the central state executive. Most existing studies of the Spanish political system provide a static view of negotiations and achievements at EU level, and pay less attention to the changing domestic context. Analyses of the redefinition of Spain's external relations and the transformation of the role of the Spanish state in the international system (Gillespie et al., 1995) do not extend their dynamic view of Spain to the changing domestic arena. Given that relations between central government and other domestic actors have rarely been problematized in the case of Spain, theoretical approaches used for the analysis of relations between central government and other domestic actors in the EU policy-making process more generally are considered in the next section with a view to establishing a framework for the Spanish case.

The role of the central state

A brief consideration of different approaches to the role of the central state demonstrates that a number of key issues surrounding its role, and its relations with other domestic actors, are still being addressed in the literature. It is not the aim of this book to provide an analysis of existing theoretical frameworks, but merely to outline key approaches, both firmly state-centric and those placing greater emphasis on non-central state actors, which might help to analyse the case of Spain.

A state-centric approach

According to proponents of a realist or neorealist approach, the unitary state responds to external influences in the international system, and can make and remake the rules by which other actors operate. It is thus that a theory that denies the key role of states will be needed 'only if nonstate actors develop to the point of rivalling or surpassing the great powers' (Waltz, 1979, p. 95). Although neofunctionalists do not give the nation-state a central role in the EU policy process (for example, Lindberg, 1963, and the standard reference work of neo-functionalist thought, Haas, 1958), it is significant that Ernst Haas (1968) later acknowledged that the sovereign nation state is a distinct entity with the potential to react differently to external challenges depending on specific national factors. Contemporary versions of the statist model reflect the realist emphasis on national governments as ultimate decision-makers, but also allow for the fact that state executives are located in domestic political arenas.

A key tenet of the state-centric approach is that decision-making is determined by bargaining among state executives which has enabled the nation-state to survive as the centre of political power. Stanley Hoffmann (1982, p. 27) defines state autonomy as its capacity to resist particular pressures, to produce its own ideas and goals, and to turn its preferences into decisions. He sets out a positive-sum relationship between European integration and the maintenance of national legitimacy and autonomy, an assumption made by other key theorists (such as Milward, 1992; Mann, 1993). For example, Michael Mann (1993, p. 116) argues that 'West European weakenings of the nation-state are slight, *ad hoc*, uneven, and unique', concluding that European integration represents little threat to the state's position. The line of reasoning developed is that the EC/EU has consolidated the power and autonomy of the central state *vis-à-vis* other domestic actors. This is most evident in the work of Alan Milward (1992, pp. 2–3), who considers that the process of European integration has been 'an integral part of the reassertion of the nation-state as an organizational concept'.

One key feature clearly suggested by a state-centric approach is the importance of the influence of national leaders and their bargaining strategies in interstate negotiations. The importance of interstate bargaining between key member states in the negotiation of the Single European Act (SEA) is the focus of Andrew Moravcsik (1991) when he views the central state as the principal actor whose changing interests determine the outcomes of bargaining in the EU arena. Despite the responsibility to domestic constituencies, political leaders are considered to possess a high level of autonomy from bureaucracies, political parties and interest groups in the domestic arena. The importance of interstate bargaining is also acknowledged by Keohane and Hoffmann (1990, p. 277) who consider that 'the expansion of Community tasks depends ultimately on the bargains between major governments'. The decisive role played by national governments may be most visible in the case of the biggest leaps of integration (Milward, 1992), but the analysis of an intergovernmental negotiation, where national governments are the only negotiators with decision-making powers, can be logically viewed as validating a state-centric approach (Closa, 1995, p. 294). Although other domestic actors are considered to have a greater input to subsequent stages of the process, these are frequently seen as only the final working out of the initial interstate deal rather than a significant part of the process.

Although a purely state-centric perspective is generally considered to neglect domestic demands, reference is frequently made to the potential impact on policy preferences of the domestic arena (for example Nordlinger, 1981; Smith, 1993). However, the central state is generally assumed to be an autonomous entity with authority to determine policy preferences, even when decisions taken diverge from the demands of the most powerful groups. The inclusion of domestic interests in the analytical framework does not therefore necessarily represent a greater threat to central state autonomy. In fact, Martin Smith (1993, pp. 53–4) considers that, under certain circumstances, a close relationship between central government and domestic groups can seal off the policy process from other actors and, ultimately, increase government autonomy. Variations in domestic circumstances thus become part of the specification of the bargaining ability of the central state, and trade-offs must be made between international and domestic goals. The liberal perspective adopted by Moravcsik (1993a) represents a more systematic approach to domestic influences on decision-making. He regards the identity of domestic groups, the nature of their interests, and their influence on policy decisions as essential for a fuller understanding of the policy process, although still emphasizing the bargaining power and autonomy of national governments. However, in a later paper, he argues that 'international co-operation…tends on balance to strengthen the domestic power of executives *vis-à-vis* opposition groups' (Moravcsik, 1994, p. 7).

Moravcsik (1993a) argues that EU institutions can be used by the central state to increase its autonomy in relation to domestic interests. This is facilitated where domestic interests are weak or ambiguous, described as 'agency slack', while stronger interests may lead to a greater constraint on central government's autonomy. In Robert Putnam's (1993) two-level game framework, national governments seek to maximize their ability to satisfy domestic pressures, while minimizing any adverse consequences at the EU negotiating table. A two-level game approach thus regards negotiations at EU level as an attempt to find overlap between negotiated domestic 'win-sets' which can evolve during negotiations, where the win-set is the set of all possible agreements at inter-state level that would gain the necessary majority support domestically (that would 'win'). The central state thus retains its full role as national gatekeeper between the international and domestic arenas. Domestic constraints can result in a smaller domestic win-set which can be used in the EU arena to gain a better deal (a strategy described as 'tying hands'), illustrating the potential for central government's manipulation of domestic constraints to increase autonomy. Furthermore, international pressures may allow policies to be 'sold' domestically that would not have been feasible otherwise. The 'active state' (Ikenberry, 1986) thus retains its key role despite a greater emphasis on its need to ratify policy decisions in the domestic arena. Despite the limitations of the two-level game framework which does not specify the conditions required for different bargaining situations, nor the choice of bargaining tactics, the key questions raised about the relations between the central state and other domestic actors are significant for this analysis.

As expressed by Mark Pollack (1995, p. 385), 'the interests and tenacity of the member states, and the institutional rules they establish to govern EC policy-making, should remain at the center of the picture'. Many previous analyses of the Spanish policy process have tended to highlight the continued autonomy and initiative of central government and the relatively unproblematic ratification in the domestic arena of policy decisions. This book does not seek to prove that central government in Spain has lost this key role. It merely aims to adopt a more dynamic approach which moves away from an exclusive focus on the importance of the state executive, and considers that influence can increasingly be shared across subnational, national and supranational levels in a very fluid policy process.

Towards a less state-centric approach

The multi-level perspective goes beyond areas that are dominated by member states, and incorporates the increasing importance of actors at several territorial tiers within the EU and domestic arenas (Marks, 1993, p. 392). The multi-level governance approach has been adopted by a core group of analysts, the main advocate being Gary Marks (1992, 1993; Marks and McAdam, 1996; Marks et al., 1996a,b; Marks, 1996, 1997). Such an approach could be considered to represent the other end of the spectrum from traditional, realist frameworks as it assumes that the centre of political control no longer fully lies in central governments. A view of central government retaining full control over the domestic arena is considered one-dimensional, and in danger of failing to take sufficient account of changing networks of actors in the bargaining process (John, 1997, p. 137). While acknowledging central government's authoritative control in the policy-making process, a range of other actors are considered to have opportunities to participate. Furthermore, central government may itself agree to give up its power in specific areas, in order to reward particular constituencies, or to gain bargaining advantage in negotiations, as in the actor-centred approach proposed by Marks (1997). Kohler-Koch (1996, p. 371) describes the central state as 'no longer an actor in its own right. Its role has changed from authoritative allocation and regulation "from above" to the role of partner and mediator.'

Whereas theorists such as Moravcsik (1993a,b) argue that the central state monopolizes the interface between the separated EU and domestic arenas, multi-level theorists consider that it is no longer the exclusive channel for the representation of domestic interests. A multi-level framework would seem to be at its most convincing when focusing on regional mobilization as evidence of the potential challenge to the monopoly of central government over European policy (for example in Marks, 1992; Hooghe and Keating, 1994; Hooghe, 1995). Marks (1992, p. 214) describes the regions as 'the new interlocutors of the Commission, a role that challenges the traditional monopoly of national governments to mediate between domestic and international affairs'. The potential thus exists for the creation of 'a new political game' (Keating, 1997, p. 26) as a result of devolution of power to the subnational level. Regional involvement is considered dependent on the level of decentralization at domestic level. This has not occurred uniformly across the EU, and may be expected to be restricted to a select subset of regional actors, thus limiting the applicability of this approach. Multi-level theorists have also tended to neglect the influence of other non-governmental domestic actors, such as trade unions, business associations and interest groups, which are a key focus in this book.

Hooghe (1995) evaluates the formal and informal channels used by regional authorities to promote their interests in the European arena. She concludes that institutionalized channels are generally more effective access points to the policy process than informal mechanisms, and that these are mostly used by an elite of regional actors who have a greater capacity to exploit the opportunities offered. Marks and Doug McAdam (1996) refer to the level of opportunity for domestic actors at EU level, or the EU opportunity structure, as an important determinant of the level of domestic input. The concept of the political opportunity structure is a notion originally developed by Herbert Kitschelt (1986) to refer to the level of access to national policy-making for key domestic actors (in his case, protest groups). Key studies by multi-level theorists provide illustrations of increasing opportunities for domestic actors to gain access to the policy process, for example the widespread analysis of the principle of partnership within the 1988 reform of the structural funds (see Chapter 5). Participation of key domestic actors has also been examined through the concept of policy networks of resource-dependent organizations (Rhodes, Bache and George, 1996). Such networks are considered more likely to occur where they are an established feature of the national system, but they also depend on factors such as the particular policy area, the stage of the process and the level of resource dependence. For example, the area of structural funding is expected to have increasing numbers of policy networks, especially at implementation stage. Smyrl (1997, p. 289) emphasizes the different degree to which regions are able to take advantage of the opportunities presented by EU regional policy, which he considers to be determined by the entrepreneurial approach of regional authorities, as well as by the pre-existence of a 'territorial policy community for economic development'. Spanish regions thus have a varying capacity to take advantage of opportunities to participate in the policy process (Bache and Jones, forthcoming).

Despite this emphasis on the increasing participation of subnational actors, theorists are obliged to acknowledge the importance in all countries of the key, moderating influence of central government in reconciling conflicting regional interests (Bachtler, 1997, p. 89). Furthermore, a multi-level governance approach to areas other than cohesion policy could not be expected to come to such firm conclusions. Its use as a tool for analysing EU decision-making is therefore not unproblematic. Multi-level theorists have recognized that, even in the area of cohesion policy, regional mobilization could be considered largely symbolic. It is significant that, in the 1993 reforms of the structural funds, member states were considered to have regained much of the autonomy that they had formerly lost *vis-à-vis* subnational authorities (Hooghe and Keating, 1994). The resilience of state political and bureaucratic elites cannot be underestimated, particularly during the policy initiation and decision-making phases. Multi-level theorists do not assume that increasing regional participation is a straightforward process which directly undermines central state authority. They acknowledge that central states have 'proven adept at retaining their "gatekeeper" status' (Pollack, 1995, p. 363). Redistributive decisions taken at EU level can be regarded as side-payments in larger intergovernmental bargains. However, in view of the potentially increasing involvement of non-central state actors in the subsequent policy process, this book considers that a full analysis of the Spanish case cannot begin and end with a focus on the central state.

Beyond the central state?

The role of central government or the state remains problematic in the literature. Purely state-centric approaches adopt a relatively static view of the policy process, which assumes the central state's ultimate control regardless of key changes in the domestic arena. Most previous studies of Spain fall into this category, as outlined above. However, some works have begun to consider that, even if the Spanish central state is able to retain its autonomy as gatekeeper between the domestic and EU arenas, greater attention must be paid to its aggregation of domestic preferences, and the limits of adherence to EU policy to legitimize its demands in the domestic arena (Closa, 1995). This is considered even more problematic where strong, unambiguous domestic demands exist. In these cases, a 'multi-level' perspective could be viewed as supplementing a more state-centric approach with a range of actors and interactive processes which a statist perspective regards as relatively unimportant. The greater involvement of the Spanish Autonomous Communities in policy-making may be expected to make such an approach increasingly relevant to the Spanish case. The central state thus no longer has the authority to regulate the policy process from above, but is obliged to share control over policy decisions with a range of other domestic actors.

Given that the lobbying process in Spain is at a relatively embryonic stage compared to other more established EU member states, the central state would be expected to have a predominant role in policy-making. However, this book takes a more dynamic view and focuses on key changing elements of the policy process. As illustrated by Tanja Börzel (1997), it is important to capture the dynamic nature of the process; even if central government in Germany monopolized the control of resources during the early days of EC membership, the German Länder have increasingly managed to redress the balance. Views of the actual impact of changes on the roles of central government and other domestic actors differ according to the approach used. A multi-level approach would claim that changes in the policy process, such as increased direct interaction between EU and regional actors, have enabled regional authorities to expand the scope of their competencies. In contrast, the central state could be viewed as retaining ultimate control over policy-making as a result of limited opportunities for input for other domestic actors. In view of the aim of this book to take account of the changing roles of domestic actors, the concept of a political opportunity structure in the domestic arena, which determines the degree of involvement of key domestic groups and their relations with the central state over time, is a useful framework with which to analyse the Spanish case. This framework is explored in the next section.

Towards a framework for analysis: Spain and the EC/EU

The political opportunity structure is used in this book to describe the changing level of opportunity for actors other than the central state to participate in policy-making. The concept was originally developed to describe the 'specific configurations of resources, institutional arrangements and historical precedents for social mobilization...' (Kitschelt,

1986, p. 58), thus highlighting the key areas under analysis, namely the degree of access to policy-making for domestic groups, their capacity to exploit the opportunities for increased involvement, and the extent to which this can be controlled by central government. The framework is used to draw up sets of factors or conditions to test the extent to which non-central state actors can gain access to the policy process, described as the degree to which the opportunity structure is open or closed.

The key conditions identified are considered those which best investigate relations between central government and other domestic actors for the purposes of the analysis in this book. The extent to which central government can retain its autonomy thus depends on conditions influencing the nature of the opportunity structure. The capacity of central government to use political or economic rationales to legitimize policy decisions is a key factor influencing the level of opportunity (condition 1), as well as the size of the government majority (condition 2) and the level of decentralization or the level of competencies of regional authorities (condition 3). Similarly, the extent to which the central state can retain its informational and intellectual roles depends on the level of skills and resources of key domestic actors (condition 4) and on the degree of knowledge of EU policies in the domestic arena (condition 5) which could be closely related to the length of EU membership. The identification of key sets of conditions (see Table 1.1) seeks to determine the nature of the opportunity structure.

The general sets of conditions in Table 1.1 can then be adapted to the particular focus of this book, namely the case of Spain during the EC accession process and during EC/EU membership. During the EC accession negotiations, an overwhelming consensus existed in favour of the political rationale for EC entry. It might thus be hypothesized that this would facilitate a high level of autonomy for central government which could justify policy decisions by referring to Spain's need for

Table 1.1 Sets of conditions expected to influence the domestic opportunity structure

---

1. Rationale behind central government policies: political/symbolic or economic/technical
2. Size of government majority/capacity to enforce policy decisions domestically
3. Level of decentralization/centralization of the state
4. Level of skills and resources of domestic actors
5. Level of knowledge of the EU of domestic actors

---

integration within the European democratic framework. Furthermore, the majority of the ruling party in government in Spain from 1982 to 1986 would be expected to enhance its capacity to withstand domestic pressures, which was likely to be more difficult for the weaker 1979–82 government. Although the regions began to attain increasing levels of competencies during the 1980s, the decentralization process was still at an early stage. Central government's key institutional role was thus not expected to be challenged by regional actors during the accession period. Furthermore, the weakness of civil society in the newly established democracy meant that interest groups would not be likely to gain a significant input to the policy process. This is linked to the fifth condition, namely the low level of awareness about the implications of accession, and the low demand in Spanish society for information about EC entry, which is also expected to close potential opportunities for domestic involvement. These sets of conditions, shown in Table 1.2, are expected to lead to a closed opportunity structure during the accession negotiations.

It can be hypothesized that sets of conditions existing in Spanish society during the EC accession negotiations, which facilitated broadly unopposed, centrally made decisions, would not necessarily continue to be prevalent during EC/EU membership. An opening of the opportunity structure for key domestic groups following accession might be expected to result in a reduced level of autonomy for the central state. For example, economic rationales could be expected to gain in importance following the achievement of the key political objective of Spain's incorporation into the Community. Furthermore, the potential for considerable changes in the nature of relations between central government and other domestic actors existed in view of the loss of majority of the PSOE government in 1993, the advances made towards a decentralized state and the resurgence of group interests in the newly established democracy. An increasing awareness of European policy

Table 1.2 Sets of conditions during Spain's EC accession negotiations expected to encourage a closed domestic opportunity structure

---

1. Political rationale for EC accession which has a capacity to overcome economic or sectoral opposition
2. Strong, majoritarian PSOE government from 1982
3. Process of decentralization still at an early stage
4. Lobbying process yet to be established in a newly consolidated democracy/ low level of resources of domestic actors
5. Low level of demand for information about the EC

Table 1.3 Changed sets of conditions during Spain's EC/EU membership expected to open the domestic opportunity structure

1. Balance in favour of economic over political rationales for policy decisions
2. Loss of PSOE government majority in 1993
3. Process of decentralization at a more advanced stage
4. Development of a more established lobbying process/increased level of resources of domestic actors
5. Increase in demand for information about the EC/EU

among domestic actors during EU membership would also be assumed. Table 1.3 sets out the factors expected to lead to an opening of the political opportunity structure, and to changing roles for central government and other domestic actors.

Marks and McAdam (1996, p. 258) argue that the relative structural access a group has to EU institutions, and the general policy receptivity of the EU, shape the level of constraints and opportunities for any domestic group, described as the EU opportunity structure. This book focuses on changing opportunities at domestic level, although acknowledging in its specific case studies that a more open opportunity structure in the domestic arena does not assume access to policy-making at all stages of the EU policy process and in all policy areas. A higher level of institutionalization in a specific policy area may indicate an evolution towards a more open opportunity structure. For example, Moravcsik (1993a) emphasizes the variability of political mobilization according to issue area, arguing that trade liberalization issues involving significant costs may lead to a tight constraint on government policy as a result of strong producer interests, in contrast to areas such as social policy where central government has greater autonomy in view of relatively weak and less unified domestic interests. These factors are taken into account in the analysis of distinct policy settings in this book, for example in the study of fisheries where sectoral interests would be expected to exert a strong pressure on central government (see Chapter 7).

Distinctions may be drawn between redistributive issues where broad gains and losses are negotiated by central government, for example the Spanish government's negotiation of structural funding at EU level (see Chapter 4), and distributive issues which 'are the stuff of functional politics, of sectoral interests cooperating with national and European administrators' (Wallace, 1996, p. 446). Definition of issues by central governments could be viewed as a key determinant of the access of domestic actors to the policy process. However, Wallace (1996, p. 452) considers that 'it is possible for national governments to hold the gate between domestic and international politics only for a shrinking number of policy areas'. The central state's control over the definition of the national interest is likely to vary across distinct phases of policy-making. It may be capable of retaining a high level of autonomy during policy initiation and decision-making phases of the process when minimal access exists for other domestic actors, but the implementation stage, involving policy-shaping decisions within individual sectors (see Peterson, 1995), generally relies on the participation of a wide range of actors other than central government.

Conclusions

It is hypothesized that the closed opportunity structure at domestic level during the EC accession negotiations (see Table 1.2), enhanced central government's autonomy and limited the involvement of other domestic actors. Even if increasing opportunities exist at EU level for participation, domestic actors have a restricted input while the domestic opportunity structure remains closed.

The opening of the domestic opportunity structure during EC/EU membership (see Table 1.3) is expected to provide greater opportunities for input from a wider range of actors. The focus of this book on the opening of opportunity structures does not indicate an assumption that the role and autonomy of central government is significantly reduced by the changing context. Although changes in the configuration of conditions in the domestic arena may reshape the nature of the bargaining process, the central state may retain, and even be able to enhance, its control of the policy process during EU membership. In fact, a more open political opportunity structure may be encouraged by central government, for example when this strengthens its bargaining position at EU level ('tying hands' strategy outlined by Putnam, 1993), or when it is dependent on the resources of other actors during policy implementation.

In view of the potentially changing policy-making process, this book seeks to reassess approaches previously used for the case of Spain. The roles of central government and other domestic actors are analysed in Chapter 2 on the EC accession negotiations, and in Chapter 3 on EC/EU membership. Sets of conditions determining the nature of the domestic opportunity structure, and its impact on the policy process, form a basis for the analysis. Detailed empirical case studies on cohesion policy and fisheries in Chapters 4–7 then examine the impact of the changing opportunity structure in two distinct policy settings.

2
Relations Between the Spanish Central State and Other Domestic Actors During the EC Accession Negotiations

The focus of the chapter is Spain's negotiations for accession to the EC from 1979 to 1986. In addition to studying the role of the central state at EC level, it examines the input to the negotiating process of other domestic actors in Spain. Most analyses of the accession negotiations rest on the premise of the overwhelming consensus in Spanish society regarding EC entry and the high level of autonomy and initiative retained by central government. This assumption is tested to determine whether an approach lending greater importance to the interaction between the EC and domestic arenas allows a more complete analysis of the accession process.

The main task of the newly elected parliament in 1977 was to draw up Spain's first democratic Constitution since 1931. Although the 1978 Constitution integrated the powers of executive and legislative, and established a firmly democratic framework, the primacy of the central state was still unquestioned in Spanish society. However, the Constitution also led to significant changes in the longer term, namely provisions for the development of a decentralized state of 17 regions or Autonomous Communities, and the restoration of trade unions. Representative trade unions, other than protected elite groups described as a 'thoroughly parasitical bureaucracy' (Giner and Sevilla, 1984, p. 117), had been banned under the Franco dictatorship, while a system of official representation was developed where only large firms and banks enjoyed privileged links with central government. The institutionalization and legitimization of interest groups was thus far less developed than in other European countries, a consequence of the fact that weak domestic groups needed what Juan Linz (1981, p. 367) has described as 'prolonged periods of political stability' in order to create the conditions necessary for the organization of their interests.

The Spanish transition to democracy was managed by reaching a series of agreements between the main political and social forces, for example the Moncloa Pact signed in October 1977 by all major political parties. The consensual style of politics is illustrated by the series of pacts between central government, employers and trade unions, which led to a more corporatist framework in Spanish society. However, the pacts have been described as 'a series of elite bargains among party leaders, with little public participation' (Keating, 1993, p. 317), and did not therefore have a significant impact on the prevailing political system. This historical legacy, described as atypical by one Spanish analyst (Subirats, 1992), forms an essential base for an examination of relations between central government and other domestic actors during the accession period.

EC application

Following his triumph in the Spanish Civil War, General Francisco Franco promoted the isolation of Spain from the international arena to enforce his own nationalist rule. Faced with a weakening Spanish economy, he later sought to re-establish diplomatic relations with the West, illustrated by the signing of a defence treaty with the United States (US) in 1953 and Spain's entry into the United Nations in 1955. Political and economic policy was gradually liberalized under the influence of the technocrat economists from the Catholic lay order, *Opus Dei*, in his administration. Over the following years, the influx into Spain of foreign investment, the increase in number of tourists and the growing migration of Spanish workers to Western Europe all led to greater access to foreign ideas and the end of Spain's isolation.

The Franco regime applied for associate membership of the Community in 1962, but the application was rejected due to the undemocratic nature of the Spanish state.[1] A limited preferential agreement between the EC and Spain, signed in 1970, was the furthest advance that the Community would contemplate. Franco attempted to limit the influence of the EC to economic development until the end of his term, but this restriction was problematic, especially when opposition forces knew that Spain's lack of democratic credentials was the reason for the EC's rejection of its application for associate membership. Although opposition parties were still initially keen to develop links with other parts of the world such as Latin America, the majority viewed incorporation into the European framework as the only way to bury definitively the Francoist legacy and Spain's isolation. 'The idea of Europe would be incomplete without a reference to the presence of the Spaniard' according to King Juan Carlos I following Franco's death in November 1975 (Preston and Smyth, 1984, p. 24). The political importance of Spain's EC entry was fully illustrated by PM Calvo Sotelo's investiture speech on 18 February 1981 when he declared: 'quiero reafirmar aquí el carácter eminentemente político de nuestra opción europea que constituye, ante todo, un objetivo histórico de primera magnitud' (I want to reaffirm here the eminently political character of our European option which constitutes, above all, an historical objective of great importance) (Ministerio de Asuntos Exteriores, 1981, p. 104). As well as the clear objective of EC accession, Calvo Sotelo's government attained Spain's entry into NATO, which was approved by a simple majority in the Spanish parliament in May 1982.

The Spanish Foreign Minister, Marcelino Oreja, under PM Adolfo Suárez in the Unión de Centro Democrático (Union of the Democratic Centre, UCD) government, submitted Spain's application for EC membership on 28 July 1977. On 5 February 1979, formal negotiations were opened following the Commission's Opinion (European Commission, 1978b) supporting Spain's accession in November 1978 and its approval by the Council of Ministers in December 1978. Although the application was made several months earlier than planned because of fears of 'hesitations among sections of industry and commerce about the wisdom of early entry into the EEC' (*The Guardian,* 19 July 1977), Spain's position seemed fairly unproblematic. All political parties were in agreement with central government that 'no economically viable or politically suitable alternative to the European Community existed' (Pollack and Hunter, 1987, p. 138). Not only was Spain economically tied to the Community (in 1976, 46 per cent of Spain's total exports in value terms went to EC countries and 38 per cent of Spain's imports came from the Community) (*European Trends,* no. 54, February 1978, p. 16), but EC entry was vital politically to consolidate the newly formed democratic framework. However, negotiations were never likely to be easy considering that the negotiation of the 1970 preferential agreement had dragged on for eight years. The 1970 accord gave a 60 per cent EC tariff reduction to Spain on industrial goods in exchange, with certain exceptions, for a 25 per cent cut in Spanish industrial tariffs. The negotiation of a more balanced industrial agreement, involving EC concessions on Spanish agricultural exports, was thus expected to be problematic.

Negotiations at interstate level

In April 1978, the Commission (European Commission, 1978a) published its so-called 'fresco' on EC enlargement which stressed the need for a positive answer to both Spain and Portugal. The political decision on enlargement was speedily taken, although the Commission stressed the need for adjustment on both sides. Key member states had shown concern at the time of Spain's application, for example regarding Spanish agriculture (*Europe*, no. 2280, 5–6 September 1977, p. 7), fears shared by France, Germany and Italy. However, in the Council of Ministers on 20 September 1977, national representatives all supported the political objectives of the Spanish application (*Europe*, no. 2291, 21 September 1977, p. 4). This section outlines key elements of the negotiation, focusing on the objectives of the Spanish government, and the demands placed on Spain at EC level.

At domestic level, negotiating EC accession was a centralized process involving a small group of senior civil servants in the Spanish administration. A Ministry for Relations with the EC was initially responsible for the negotiations and the dissemination of information in Spanish society. When Calvo Sotelo took over from Suárez as PM in 1981, he replaced the Ministry with a Secretariat of State for Relations with the EC within the Ministry of Foreign Affairs. Although UCD government officials were critical of a reform which took away its ministerial status,[2] it retained its overall control of the accession process from 1981 to 1986.

Negotiations did not actually begin until after the European Parliament elections in June 1979 and lasted until June 1985. The negotiation period can be divided into three phases: 5 February 1979 – 8 September 1980 and 8 September 1980 – 28 October 1982 when the UCD was in power, and 28 October 1982 – 12 June 1985 when the PSOE government took over (Bassols, 1995, p. 235). Former ambassador in Brussels, and Secretary of State for the EC from 1981 to 1982, Raimundo Bassols, provides the first comprehensive account of the early negotiating period under the UCD. During the first phase, only 12 negotiating sessions were held. The second phase was considerably slowed down by French opposition,[3] and the Spanish delegation sought to avoid allowing technical difficulties to alter fundamental political objectives in the domestic arena. Little progress was made until the third phase on any of the controversial issue areas which urgently needed reform at EC level, namely agriculture, fisheries and the budget. Bassols (1995) highlights the achievements of the 1979–82 negotiating period when the ruling UCD party enjoyed a high degree of autonomy at EC level despite its relatively divided government. However, the slow pace of negotiations meant that agreement had only been reached on six of the less controversial chapters of the 16 to be negotiated in October 1982.

Spain's 'failure to show any flexibility' *vis-à-vis* Commission demands to remove tariffs and other obstacles to selling in the Spanish market was a result of the fact that its industry was uneasy about anything less than a ten-year transition period, and the Spanish government thus feared that early concessions would lead to misgivings about EC membership (*Financial Times* (*FT*), 11 February 1981). Another key illustration of the obligations placed on Spain is the expansion of fishing waters to a 200-mile zone which limited the activity of Spanish fishermen (see Chapter 6). Central government in Spain fully supported its fishermen, but was also obliged to acknowledge the legitimacy of proposals at EC level even when a serious threat to the Spanish sector. The Spanish delegation lacked any bargaining power in its demand for greater access to fishing waters, illustrated by the acknowledgement by Bassols (1995, p. 173) as a member of the negotiating team, that 'nunca me he sentado en una mesa de negociación con menos argumentos en la mano' (I had never sat at a negotiating table with fewer arguments at my disposal). The framework for an annual negotiation of Spanish fishing rights was agreed in 1980, although the Spanish government emphasized the need for a longer-term agreement. Spain's negotiators were accused domestically of making temporary concessions on agriculture to win a better deal on fisheries. Terms agreed during the negotiations caused further difficulties during membership, exacerbated by the achievement of an EC Common Fisheries Policy (CFP) in January 1983, and the Community's reluctance to admit a 17 000-strong Spanish fleet which far exceeded the EC fleet in size (see Chapters 6 and 7).

A key bargaining tool used by the Spanish delegation was to accuse EC negotiators of placing excessive demands on its relatively fragile democracy. It constantly reminded the EC of the dangers of overestimating the stability of the Spanish democratic framework, and of relying on an unquestioning internal consensus whatever the speed of negotiation or the conditions demanded. The pressure exerted by such arguments was limited until the attempted coup by a minority in the Spanish armed forces on 23 February 1981 provided a clear illustration of the fragility of the regime. The coup was followed by a Commission declaration on 24 February which firmly emphasized Spain's place in the EC, and a European Parliament resolution on 13 March stressing the Community's responsibility and urging an acceleration of the negotiations.

France was the key opponent of enlargement throughout the negotiations, although its fears were often shared by other member states such as Italy and Germany. On 5 June 1980, d'Estaing declared the necessity for EC reform before enlargement at a meeting of agricultural representatives, thus threatening a delay in agriculture and budgetary negotiations. Spanish negotiators feared that the French attitude would fuel domestic anti-EC coalitions. The Spanish Secretary of State for Relations with the EC held bilateral talks with key leaders across Europe in November and December 1980 in an effort to speed up the pace of negotiations. The Spanish delegation hoped that François Mitterrand's victory in May 1981 would lead to a more constructive French bargaining position, although the hope was dampened by French opposition in 1981 to texts on customs union and agricultural issues (Bassols, 1995, p. 262).

July 1981 was one of the lowest points in the negotiations according to key officials (Bassols, 1995, p. 263), although acceptance of further debate on EC reform unblocked the deadlock in September. With a view to unblocking talks in other areas, the Spanish government committed itself to the application of Value Added Tax (VAT) on 26 February 1982. However, a further setback occurred when the French delegation demanded an inventory of all problems related to enlargement. The process was only revitalized when a Commission (European Commission, 1982) report in November asked the EC 'to reward Spain and Portugal with a definite date for joining the Communities if they took more drastic steps to cut back key crisis industries such as steel and shipbuilding'. It was also hoped by PSOE officials in Spain that the substantial majority of the PSOE government would give it a stronger position than the former UCD government. The Copenhagen European Council of 3 December 1982 paved the way for the revision of existing rules for certain Mediterranean products within the EC, and reaffirmed the political commitment to enlargement of the EC member states.

Although the EC and Spain agreed on the customs union in 1983, according to Foreign Minister Morán, only 15 per cent of the negotiating task had been completed (*FT*, 27 April 1983). EC proposals in 1983, including rapid access for EC industrial goods to Spanish markets, were viewed as unacceptable by the Spanish delegation. Negotiations seemed once more to be at a standstill. Furthermore, although supporting the enlargement, the United Kingdom (UK) and Germany blocked the associated increase in the agricultural budget. However, progress was made to establish a clear link between EC reform and enlargement under the German Presidency at the Stuttgart Summit, paving the way for further debate at the Athens Summit in December 1983 where German proposals dominated the budgetary negotiations. Spain approved a new agricultural agreement in October which placed high tariff barriers on Spanish fruit and vegetables until full integration. However, the tariffs were regarded as an excessive EC demand in the Spanish domestic arena, and González hinted at dropping Spain's EC application (*International Herald Tribune* (*IHT*), 29–30 October 1983). In November, the tough position of the Spanish government was again revealed when González threatened to cut government purchases of French goods unless Paris adopted a more favourable stance towards Spain (*FT*, 18 November 1983). The approval of larger subsidies for Mediterranean agriculture and the commitment to reform of the Common Agricultural Policy (CAP) persuaded the French delegation to give greater consideration to Spanish demands. According to Bassols (1995, p. 286), 'los agricultores franceses estaban servidos; se podía volver a pensar en España' (the French farmers got their way; they could start thinking about Spain again). González sought to step up Spanish pressure on member states when he wrote a letter to all EC heads of government asking them to declare their position on enlargement prior to the Athens Summit. Spanish officials were optimistic about the progress made, although the press in Spain was critical of any triumphalism (Morán, 1990, p. 166). This criticism was borne out when the clash of national interests at Athens in December prevented any further progress in negotiations.

Fisheries, agriculture and the lowering of trade barriers for industrial goods were still unresolved issues in 1984. The debate of agricultural issues, especially regarding the length of the transition period to integrate goods into European markets, dominated the negotiations. On 21 February 1984, Spain criticized the unreasonable demands made by the EC declaration on agriculture. The Spanish government was prepared to restructure sectors such as olive oil, but considered that other member states, such as Italy, had to adopt similar measures (*Ya*, 26 February 1984, Ministerio de Asuntos Exteriores, 1984, p. 197). Morán called for 'a complete revision of the basic principles on which the negotiations are proceeding' (*FT*, 20 June 1984). It was not until the Brussels Summit in March 1984, and the Fontainebleau Summit during the French Presidency in June 1984, that the foundations for the CAP reform were finally laid and the UK budgetary contribution was determined. In

June 1984, the Commission's focus on French concerns rather than Spanish olive oil and wine markets led to a negative reaction in Spanish sectors (Morán, 1990, pp. 48–9). However, Spain was ultimately forced to accept the deal on agriculture with relatively few EC concessions, its only victory being an increase in the transition period for free access for EC industrial goods into Spain from three to six years (*FT*, 21 June 1984). Spain's attempts to backtrack on these agreements, for example when it hardened its position in July 1984 regarding sensitive products such as olive oil, were rejected by the EC delegation on 23 July. The Spanish government was thus forced to make key concessions in problematic areas in the later years of the accession process. The final accord was dependent on the reform of the regulations for Mediterranean products to satisfy French demands. Additional agreements were made on 29 March 1985 regarding the dismantling of EC tariffs on fruit and vegetable exports over ten years, and the seven-year transition period before the full customs union. The final package formed the basis for Spain and Portugal's integration into the Community on 1 January 1986.

From an economic perspective, despite the final success of the negotiations, Spain accepted a 'punishing treaty of accession' (Harrison, 1992, p. 205). Spain was, in many respects, an unequal partner as it opened its markets to the EC and reduced the external tariff on industrial goods from third countries to the EC average of 5 per cent within seven years. Most Spanish agricultural products were subjected to a waiting period of ten years before being fully integrated into the Community. Despite strong domestic pressures, the Spanish government bowed to EC demands on fisheries, acknowledging the need for restructuring of the sector, while seeking to avoid any further decrease of the size of the Spanish catch in EC waters. The EC immediately took over the management of agreements with third countries and obliged Spain to make concessions such as ending state subsidies on fuel for fishing boats, which led to considerable discontent in the sector (Marks, M., 1997, p. 94) (for full details of Spain's entry terms, see Tovias, 1995, pp. 88–92). Political criticism of the deal in the domestic arena highlighted the relatively tough terms agreed for Spanish agriculture and fisheries, considered as the outcome of the early conclusion of the industry chapter in December 1984. This left the Spanish delegation with little bargaining power in other key areas, although satisfying Spanish industrial groups (Gómez Fuentes, 1986, p. 44).

The key role of the Spanish government in the interstate bargaining framework at EC level was evident throughout the negotiations.

Frequent discussions between González and the German head of state secured German support for Spanish accession, based on its trade surplus with Spain and the strong links between the Socialist parties in the two countries. Similarly, talks between González and Socialist leaders in Athens in October 1983 facilitated an agreement on agricultural markets. The role of key ministers and officials was also evident. Morán (1990) highlighted his personal role in overcoming French opposition to enlargement, for example in the first meeting of Spanish and French ministers in Celle Saint Cloud on 10–11 January 1983. Although intensive interstate bargaining formed a crucial element of the process, this chapter also seeks to take into account the internal coordination of the Spanish position with key interest groups and political parties.

Relations between the central state and other domestic actors

Central government officials claimed that domestic demands were taken into account throughout the negotiations, particularly in vulnerable sectors. This is illustrated by the statement of González when in opposition, in the debate following Calvo Sotelo's investiture speech on 20 February 1981:

> El ingreso en la Comunidad Económica Europea no es sólo un problema del Gobierno; el Gobierno tiene que negociar el ingreso, pero tiene que negociar respetando y defendiendo los intereses de la sociedad…. (Entry into the European Economic Community is not only a problem for the government; the government has to negotiate entry, but it has to negotiate whilst respecting and defending the interests of society…)
>
> (Ministerio de Asuntos Exteriores, 1981, p. 117)

Few studies have focused on non-central government actors during the accession negotiations. Loukas Tsoukalis (1981), for example, discusses the limit to the level of domestic debate in Spain as a result of the consensus in favour of entry. His brief examination of the relatively underdeveloped Spanish civil society and the inexperienced political class addresses the question of the awareness of EC entry at the domestic level. The position of domestic actors such as Spanish political parties, trade unions and pressure groups *vis-à-vis* EC accession have, however, rarely been evaluated. Only a few studies by representatives of these groups provide some insight into their involvement, for example the evaluation of the tensions between the main Spanish business confederation and EC negotiators by Antonio Alonso (1985). A study by Beate Kohler-Koch (1982) of the alignment of political forces in the post-Franco era was written at too early a stage in the negotiations to form a full evaluation of the domestic arena. Berta Álvarez-Miranda Navarro (1995) provides an analytical insight into the rationale behind the Spanish cross-party consensus, but in general, studies refer to the overall pro-European position in Spanish domestic society without evaluating its origins or significance. Although González referred in May 1983 to trade unions and employers as the 'true negotiating forces' through which the government could achieve social and economic reform (Giner and Sevilla, 1984, p. 133), key socio-economic actors, and even the most politically active regional governments, frequently criticized their lack of input to the policy process, further analysed in Chapter 3, during EC/EU membership.

Regional government

The input of the majority of regional governments during the accession negotiations was minimal. This was to be expected in view of the fact that, even though Spain's newly created Autonomous Communities were fast developing a new institutional framework at regional level by the summer of 1983, they still had to wait some time before the competencies they had inherited were officially devolved to them (Newton, 1997, p. 123). However, a minority of the more active regions demanded information on the implications of EC entry and carried out detailed, sectoral studies. The Catalonia parliament approved a motion on 11 November 1980 which called for the setting up of a joint committee to monitor the negotiations. The committee was treated apprehensively initially, but became an acceptable forum for the serious debate of EC issues (Granell, 1982, p. 830).[4] Attempts to have an input to the negotiations were made in other regions at a late stage in the accession process: for example, a Technical Committee for European Economic Community Affairs was established in the Basque Country on 26 June 1984 (Granell, 1984, p. 18).

Socio-economic actors

The level of organization and interests of key socio-economic actors, namely the main trade unions and employers' organizations, are briefly considered prior to an analysis of the nature of consultation during the accession negotiations.

Trade unions

Two main union organizations exist in Spain, the Comisiones Obreras (Workers' Commissions, CCOO), under Communist leadership, and the Unión General de Trabajadores (General Workers' Union, UGT), established at the same time as the PSOE, and traditionally Socialist. Membership of smaller unions declined in the early 1980s, as around 80 per cent of workers who joined a union between 1978 and 1984 opted for either the UGT or CCOO (Pérez-Díaz, 1993, pp. 267–8). However, financial difficulties and legal insecurity after Franco, weak organizational structure and disagreements over key policies limited the input of the two unions to the debate on EC entry. Paul Heywood (1995, p. 242) considers that 'the unequal distribution of resources which characterises the Spanish policy process is reinforced by low, and declining, levels of associational activity'. Although union membership briefly flourished in the post-Franco era, the level of membership fell dramatically between 1978 and 1984: whereas in 1978, the level of affiliation was 57.4 per cent, in 1984 it had decreased to 23 per cent (Pérez-Díaz, 1993, p. 267) (see Chapter 3 for levels of affiliation during EC/EU membership). High levels of membership could not be assured in view of the predominance of small companies in Spain, union reliance on public funding rather than membership figures, and the system of workplace elections where non-members are able to vote (Ross, 1997, p. 119). Although pacts with central government during the transition set a precedent for a consultation process based on a 'neo-corporatist' framework,[5] no regular consultative role existed for the unions apart from infrequent negotiations with central government (Gunther, 1996, p. 52).

Employers

Under Franco, large firms had little need to organize their interests as they were generally offered tariff protection and state subsidies. The organization of Spain's employers thus only began after 1975, also a reflection of the relatively late economic development in Spain. The organization representing employers' interests at national level, the Confederación Española de Organizaciones Empresariales (Spanish Confederation of Employers' Organizations, CEOE), was founded in 1977, partly in reaction to the growing influence of the unions. The CEOE incorporates many important associations within its framework, although they remain relatively autonomous, including the Confederación Española de Pequeñas y Medianas Empresas (Spanish Confederation of Small and Medium-sized Enterprises, CEPYME), which joined in 1980, and the Asociación Española de Banca Privada (Spanish Banking association, AEB). It is divided into sectoral and territorial groups, which leads to conflict of interests as sectoral organizations tend to be more powerful than regional groupings. During the transition, collective bargaining between central government and business associations was commonplace, and the CEOE was one of the main participants in the bargaining process. Although the CEOE supported the right-wing coalition during the 1982 election campaign, its President claimed in 1984 to have established good relations with the Socialist government (*Le Monde*, 12 January 1984). Despite its weaknesses, the CEOE was considered a key channel for communicating business interests to central government.

The impact of both unions and employers during the accession negotiations was uneven as their participation was not institutionalized. The development of 'civil society' was still only in its preliminary stages, although the most powerful domestic actors sought to increase their input to the negotiating process. The lack of a pluralist tradition and the low level of associational activity are evident from a study of the main unions and, although the employers' confederation represented a growing number of employers, it had yet to establish access points to the policy process. This resulted in a lack of awareness of negotiations at EC level in domestic society.

Domestic awareness of negotiations

The 1970 agreement between Spain and the EC was hardly known in the domestic arena despite the considerable benefits to Spain.[6] At the start of the accession negotiations, a similarly limited knowledge of EC issues existed in Spanish society. This led the Ministry for Relations with the EC to organize a series of information days from 2 October to 20 December 1978. The objective was to inform regional and sectoral actors of the implications of EC entry, to ensure their participation in the process and to gauge the opinions of a wide range of actors (Ministerio para las Relaciones con las Comunidades Europeas, 1978). The Chambers of Commerce,[7] which had a proactive role at local and regional levels during the early stages of the accession process, played a key part in the organization of around 500 *ad hoc* meetings with regional authorities, business and trade unions. Meetings with agricultural and business representatives took account of their particular concerns regarding EC entry, the final report noting the 'reacciones pasionales y, a veces, de espíritu nacionalista, ante la aparición de problemas específicos, sectoriales…' (the passionate and sometimes

nationalist reactions to the emergence of specific sectoral problems...)
(Ministerio para las Relaciones con las Comunidades Europeas, 1978,
p. 8). Regional concerns focused on the potential increase in economic
inequalities, and the likelihood of greater privileges being given to
some regions to the detriment of others, while agricultural representatives feared losing out to industrial interests as a result of their limited
influence on central government. In March 1982, the Secretariat produced a internal action plan which set out its strategies for continuing
the dialogue with sectoral representatives (Secretaría de Estado para las
Relaciones con las Comunidades Europeas, 1982).

Although individual companies were relatively ignorant about the
negotiations, the CEOE was generally regarded to be better informed.
One analyst considered that the Spanish business community was
more closely involved in negotiations than its counterpart in Greece,
and that Spain was better prepared than either Greece or Portugal in
terms of background work and technical studies (Tsoukalis, 1981,
pp. 126–7). The Minister for Relations with the EC, Calvo Sotelo,
affirmed that meetings with the Head of the CEOE, Carlos Ferrer Salat,
were held whenever requested during the early years of the negotiations, the aim being to reassure the Confederation about the implications of EC entry.[8] However, he also acknowledged the often tense
relations resulting from the CEOE's claim that he was not adequately
defending their interests (Calvo Sotelo, 1990, p. 163). Members of the
opposition even suggested that the UCD government was avoiding
putting EC entry to public analysis (Morán, 1980, p. 336). However, it
was reported that the Secretariat of State for Relations with the EC promoted or participated in 2593 colloquia, conferences and round tables
on EC entry, and organized 175 trade union and business working
groups, 210 sectoral meetings and four journalists' seminars between
5 February 1979 and 28 October 1982 (Bassols, 1995, p. 237). A, perhaps predictable, discrepancy thus emerges between the claims of UCD
government officials and other domestic actors regarding the level of
information about EC accession during the early years.

The opinions of UCD and PSOE politicians and officials also differ
markedly, each claiming that adequate measures were taken to inform
Spanish society during their term in office. Former UCD government
officials described the negotiation as external rather than internal
in the post-1982 period,[9] illustrated by complaints in the agricultural
sector of the minimal consultation with Spanish negotiators (*FT*,
27 March 1985). Members of the main opposition party claimed
that they frequently had to read the press to find out about ongoing

negotiations, particularly regarding the economic costs of concessions made to reach an agreement[10] although, according to PSOE officials, information was widely disseminated from 1982 to 1985, and criticism was considered to be largely politically inspired.[11] The PSOE government claimed that, from January 1983 to August 1984, the Secretariat of State for Relations with the EC held more than 300 meetings with representatives of Autonomous Communities, professional sectors, Chambers of Commerce and trade unions, the number having reached 450 by February 1985, which represented a total of more than 2000 hours of work.[12] Furthermore, the Secretariat organized and participated in more than 462 public information events and meetings between January 1983 and July 1985 (Consejo Superior de Cámaras de Comercio, 1985, p. 5).

Despite the information campaign described, just before the Accession Treaty was signed, eight out of ten Spaniards interviewed considered themselves badly informed about EC membership, and more than 60 per cent of small and medium-sized enterprises (SMEs), and 41 per cent of bigger firms, complained of inadequate information about EC entry conditions according to a Citibank España survey of 508 firms (Gómez Fuentes, 1986, pp. 17–18). The two main unions claimed that they had been marginalized throughout the accession process although, according to government officials, they had shown little interest in EC issues when informed of the negotiations.[13] In its official opinion on EC accession, the UGT stressed that 'ni nuestro sindicato ni ningún otro, ha sido consultado previamente de forma global sobre los distintos aspectos de la negociación...' (neither our union nor any other has been previously fully consulted on the various aspects of the negotiation...) (UGT, n/d, p. 6). Similarly, the CCOO was critical of meetings with the Secretariat of State for the EC, which were described as consisting of a posteriori information on the bargaining position without any evaluation of the likely socio-economic implications. CCOO officials referred to the sporadic nature of meetings, the importance of which was reduced by the limited nature of information made available (CCOO, 1985a). The exception was the area of social affairs, where talks with the Secretariat were often held prior to negotiations.

Key sectoral actors and business organizations seemed less marginalized from the process, although the president of a key business association, the Círculo de Empresarios (Business Circle) claimed in December 1984 that neither business organizations nor individual sectors had been kept informed of the progress of negotiations (*Diario 16,*

26 December 1984). The Coordinating Committee of the Chambers of Commerce held regular meetings from October 1983 with the administration to discuss contact with regional actors throughout Spain (Ministerio de Asuntos Exteriores, 1983, p. 743). Another illustration of the developing relations between the administration and key associations is CEPYME's plan to inform SMEs about the EC in 1981 (CEPYME, 1981), which was drawn up in close collaboration with the Secretariat of State for Relations with the EC.

Regional authorities were generally better informed than other domestic actors about the EC. A technical working group with the Secretary of State for the EC was set up by Catalonia to lobby for its regional interests and demand explanations for negotiating positions (Recio Figueiras, n/d, p. 19). It presented a document (*libro blanco*) listing its demands to the Secretariat of State on 17 June 1982 (Ministerio de Asuntos Exteriores, 1983, p. 454). Conferences were also organized to discuss the likely effects of EC integration with other representatives of the Autonomies, for example those held by the Ministry of Territorial Administration in 1984 (*Ya*, 11 June 1984) and, in Andalusia, a European programme was established in December 1983 to evaluate the accession negotiations. Despite central government's reticence, regional authorities also made direct contact with EC institutions, for example the Presidents of the regional governments of Catalonia and Andalusia headed a delegation to the Commission in June 1983 (Granell, 1984, p. 17). However, at an early stage in the decentralization process, the majority of regions remained largely sidelined from the process, although the more active authorities monitored more carefully the implications for their region in the later stages of the negotiations.

In the first parliamentary debate on EC entry in June 1979, some opposition members not only advocated greater parliamentary involvement via an institutionalized evaluation committee, but proposed establishing permanent consultation mechanisms with socio-economic actors (Congress, no. 21, 27 June 1979, pp. 1039–110). The Minister for Relations with the EC responded by highlighting the efficient functioning of existing consultation mechanisms, even if not formalized. Although the creation of a forum for consultation with socio-economic actors was advocated in the Constitution, namely the Economic and Social Council, the Spanish administration had no intention of establishing it during the negotiations (Congress, no. 21, 27 June 1979, pp. 1093–4) (it was eventually established in 1991, as described in Chapter 3). Opposition MPs were concerned about the lack of parliamentary scrutiny of negotiating positions at EC level, accusing the PSOE of using the excuse that making information publicly available could serve the interests of other EC member states. One opposition member considered that 'un Gobierno que goza de una amplia mayoría parlamentaria…rehúya las posibilidades que esta Cámara le ofrece…' (a government which enjoys a large parliamentary majority…rejects the possibilities which this Chamber offers…) (Congress, no. 98, 29 February 1984, p. 4617). When the Accession Treaty was signed, key ministries were accused of not having met representatives from affected sectors for many years. For example, the Ministry of Agriculture, Fisheries and Food was criticized for only consulting national farming organizations at a very late stage in the process (Armero, 1989, p. 168). One commentator noted that 'parece una gran incongruencia que quienes iban a tener que competir con Europa no fueran escuchados a la hora de negociar' (it seems highly incongruent that those who were going to have to compete with Europe were not listened to when it came to negotiating) (Armero, 1989, p. 168). It is probable that the consensus in favour of EC entry in Spain, described in the next section, made central government less obliged to consult other domestic actors throughout the process.

Internal consensus in favour of EC entry

Even before negotiations began, one press article asserted that 'politically, the case for applying to join the EEC goes unchallenged among Spanish businessmen, union leaders, Government officials and all political parties' (*Daily Telegraph*, 2 May 1977), and the basic consensus was not eroded throughout the negotiations. Tsoukalis (1981, p. 121) describes the picture in Spain at the time of the EC application as 'dull' as everyone seemed to agree about the desirability of accession. Limited discussion of economic implications occurred in key sectors, while political integration was accepted seemingly unquestioningly by the Spanish public. The loss of sovereignty which membership would entail was hardly debated in the Congress prior to the ratification of the Accession Treaty, and the overall unanimity on its ratification, along with the generally positive press coverage, underlined Spanish enthusiasm for its incorporation into the European framework (Congress, no. 221, 25 June 1985, pp. 10177–217). The portrayal of Spain's EC accession as a vital historical goal by central government encouraged an almost instinctive acceptance of the urgent need for incorporation into the European framework, which tended to inhibit the involvement of non-central state actors in the process. Foreign Minister Pérez-Llorca referred in 1981 to EC entry being supported by the political will of the Spanish people and the overwhelming majority of political parties and unions as well as central government (Ministerio de Asuntos Exteriores, 1981, p. 130).

Although a more critical ethos in society was gradually built up after Franco, it did not succeed in encouraging widespread debate of EC issues, especially at the outset of negotiations. The lack of Spanish tradition in the analysis of international affairs may have made Spain overly optimistic and unrealistic about the implications of EC entry (Calvo Sotelo, 1990, p. 125). An opinion poll carried out by the Public Opinion Institute (attached to the PM's office) in October 1979 showed that 67 per cent of Spaniards were in favour of entry and only 7 per cent were opposed (26 per cent did not respond), although it was reported that support for Spanish entry was, perhaps predictably, 'still instinctive rather than rational' (*FT*, 4 October 1979). The significance of EC membership for the Spanish public is also demonstrated by *Eurobarometer* polls: in 1984, 73 per cent of Spanish interviewees felt Community affairs to be important or very important (*Eurobarometer*, no. 22, 1984, p. 97).[14] The Spanish and international press played a key role in encouraging support for Spain's accession, generally unanimously backing EC entry and, in some cases, criticizing the lack of progress when negotiations came to a halt, for example on 23 March 1985 when the French delegation blocked any further advance (Gómez Fuentes, 1986, p. 45).

In the parliamentary debate on EC accession on 27 June 1979, the Minister for Relations with the EC argued that even vulnerable sectors such as fisheries would ultimately benefit from accession (Congress, no. 21, 27 June 1979, p. 1048). Government officials sought to place the issue of EC entry above party considerations (Morán, 1990, p. 45), thus maximizing parliamentary consensus on the issue. Some differences in focus existed, illustrated by the Communist Party's hope for long-term economic and social change including improved rights for workers, compared with the PSOE's focus on economic modernization. However, both the Socialists and Communists gave full support to government policy towards the EC from a very early stage in the process (*The Guardian*, 28 July 1977). The limited discussion of EC entry in the Spanish parliament was partly a reflection of the broad consensus. Its input was generally regarded as minimal by government officials, and the former chair of the parliamentary Foreign Affairs Committee from 1982 to 1986 acknowledged that political parties were 'only effective by being ineffective' given that no voice of opposition to EC membership was raised in the Committee.[15]

A similar consensus existed among trade unions. The UGT declared that it had expressed for a long time 'una posición claramente favorable a la adhesión de España a las Comunidades Europeas' (a clearly favourable attitude towards Spain's accession to the European Communities) (UGT, n/d, p. 1), illustrated by its support for the modernization of the Spanish economy and the adaptation of the labour market to the European model. Unions accepted the overall necessity of EC membership, forced to acknowledge that they had no alternative to offer to central government's medium-term economic policy. Widespread debate about the implications of EC entry was unlikely given the workers' preoccupation with more immediate needs such as high unemployment, the level of income, and the low level of politicization of the unions (Kohler-Koch, 1982, pp. 52–9). Spanish unions also voiced their overall support for EC entry via pan-European organizations at EC level such as the European Confederation of Trade Unions (ETUC) in Brussels, which regularly pressurized the Commission to speed up negotiations, and the Economic and Social Committee,[16] which retained a favourable position regarding EC entry throughout the accession process.

Despite some reservations regarding conditions which threatened to weaken the position of Spain *vis-à-vis* her European partners, the CEOE considered EC membership as a clear priority for Spain. Similarly, the Chambers of Commerce collaborated closely with central government officials throughout the negotiations. A majority view in favour of EC entry was evident in successful exporting industries such as the Barcelona-based chemicals industry; around thirty Catalan companies had already successfully set up subsidiaries over the French border. The positive attitude of larger firms is illustrated by a survey carried out in 1980 where out of 1500 larger Spanish firms, 68 per cent said they were prepared for EC entry in 1980, and 83 per cent predicted that they would be by 1985 (Fundación para la Investigación Económica y Social y Asociación para el Progreso de la Dirección, 1980, p. 3). Although less optimistic about EC entry, firms attached to the state industrial holding company, Instituto Nacional de Industria (National Institute of Industry, state holding company, INI), supported the application for EC entry.

This brief analysis of the views of key domestic actors illustrates the overwhelming consensus in favour of EC entry. Although this enhanced the central state's strongly pro-European position, the

Spanish delegation, fearing that this might reduce their bargaining power at EC level, also drew attention to the serious concerns over the implications of EC accession expressed in specific sectors.

Internal opposition to EC entry terms

A press article in 1978 announced that 'the political fanfare is over and the hard economic bargaining is on the horizon' (*The Times*, 20 March 1978), although it was several years before any serious debate of EC entry began in Spanish society. In the early stages of negotiations, despite some sectoral resistance, voices of dissent did not threaten the domestic consensus because of the lack of alternatives and often minimal awareness of the full implications of accession. However, although the Economic and Social Committee considered that the EC was far more aware of the difficulties than Spain itself and described the Spanish as being 'unwaveringly optimistic' compared with the more sombre assessment in Brussels (*IHT*, 20 November 1978), Spanish public opinion developed a greater critical capacity as negotiations continued (Morán, 1984, p. 53). Increasing reservations about the implications of EC entry were fuelled by the publication of in-depth sectoral studies. In particular, Spanish industry feared that it might be weaker and less competitive in the short term because of its inflexible labour laws, its weak managerial structure and the poor relations between management and the trade unions (*FT*, 6 February 1979). In January 1984, in the parliamentary assembly of the Council of Europe, González highlighted the Spanish public's waning enthusiasm as negotiations proceeded (Armero, 1989, pp. 163–4).

Although expressing the CEOE's strong support for the overall objective of EC entry, its Director General of International Relations accused central government in 1981 of sacrificing sectoral interests to obtain a political success (Calvo Sotelo, 1990, p. 166). The Confederation monitored carefully the negotiations, although its input was mostly reduced to criticism of terms of entry which had already been negotiated. The Spanish government's agreement to introduce VAT from the time of accession in early 1982 was particularly criticized as an unjust concession demanded by the EC; as leader, Ferrer declared in Brussels in 1983 that the CEOE would not apply VAT without adequate transition periods for industrial products. The declaration led to considerable tension with the Minister for Relations with the EC (Alonso, 1985, p. 144). In view of the likely rise in prices, the question of VAT was a sensitive issue in the domestic arena, which ensured strong public support for the CEOE's tough position. The CEOE also rejected the Commission's proposal for a transition period in industry of one year before a 50 per cent reduction in tariffs, stressing the need for a ten-year transition period (*Le Monde*, 12 January 1984). This blocked the talks on customs union in 1984 until the EC made concessions on agriculture (Morán, 1990, p. 394). The CEOE slogan was 'adhesión si, pero no a cualquier precio' (accession yes, but not at any price), a phrase originally used by Calvo Sotelo when Spain's application was made in 1979. Bassols (1995, p. 236) described the CEOE's opposition as 'una fisura en el bloque español, un signo de desconfianza hacia el negociador...' (a break in the Spanish consensus, a sign of a lack of confidence in the negotiator).

The President of the Chambers of Commerce, José María Figueras, was less critical of EC entry in 1984 than the CEOE, considering that it would ultimately have less impact on SMEs than on large companies (*El Nuevo Lúnes*, 4 June 1984). However, small, often inefficient firms were accustomed to a highly protected market and felt particularly threatened by EC accession (Pollack and Hunter, 1987, p. 145). They were represented by CEPYME within the CEOE, although its input to central government's negotiating position was limited, as illustrated by its dissatisfaction with the agreed EC entry terms. A low level of organization within sectors frequently inhibited their involvement in the policy process. For example, the citrus fruit industry's lobbying capacity was described as 'stunted', thus leaving 'more sophisticated and concerted sectors, though not necessarily more deserving, at the head of the queue in the government's dealings with Brussels' (*FT*, 10 May 1979). Demands were sometimes weakened by divergent interests within sectors. For example, the fears expressed by the car manufacturer, Seat, of the threat to its domestic market were not shared by Ford, which was more export-oriented (*The Times*, 31 March 1977). Similarly, the variation between farming types reduced the influence of agricultural lobbies; although the tomato and banana-growing industries in the Canaries would benefit from the fall in tariffs following membership, accession threatened to cause serious problems for small and relatively inefficient dairy farmers in Galicia and Cantabria, where a large anti-EC lobby resisted any change.

Although the fragmentary nature of lobbying in both agricultural and industrial sectors strengthened central government's capacity to win over opposition to EC entry, certain sectors, such as steel, succeeded in exerting considerable pressure on the government. Steel became a very tough area of negotiation as a result of the strongly opposed interests of producers in Spain and the EC, and the lack of willingness of the Spanish industry to make concessions (*European Trends*, no. 59, May 1979, pp. 23–33). The sector was particularly vulnerable as severe financial difficulties demanded efforts to increase its exports to the European market while EC demand was falling. The Spanish delegation sought to negotiate longer transition periods and limits to tariff barriers for the industrial sector, while still insisting on early accession (*European Trends*, no. 72, August 1982, p. 5). This position was criticized by EC negotiators, who were unwilling to make major concessions to placate sectoral interests. Awareness at EC level of the politically sensitive nature of restructuring in view of the inevitable job losses made the negotiation of entry terms for steel producers problematic.

Despite domestic opposition, particularly within politically sensitive regions, central government was generally able to enforce unpopular decisions in the domestic arena. An example of the restructuring carried out was the modernization of olive oil production, involving the disappearance of over 12 per cent of the existing two million hectares, and a total of 16.4 billion pesetas in credits and subsidies (*FT*, 15 October 1981). Previous plans had been viewed with reserve by the relatively powerful agricultural workers' union in Andalusia, but the PSOE government stressed that fear of an increase in unemployment had to be weighed against the need for adaptation, justifying tough policies by convincing regional constituencies that they would be compensated once inside the EC. The PSOE government also set aside 200 billion pesetas for the industrial sector between 1981 and 1983 to subsidize the necessary investment for restructuring (*The Economist*, 17 April 1982, p. 67). The government later insisted that plans to slim down loss-making sectors had to go ahead (*The Economist*, 17 March 1984, p. 54).

Harsh criticism was voiced of the more conciliatory approach adopted by Spain at EC level in the final negotiations between March and June 1985. Despite enthusiastic responses from industrial lobbies such as Confemetal representing the metal industries when the negotiations were concluded (*Le Monde*, 13 June 1985), the mood at the time of the agreement was described as an 'anti-climax' (*Daily Telegraph*, 31 December 1985). A sizeable farm lobby against EC entry terms had developed at a relatively late stage in the negotiations, as illustrated by the protests when the Spanish government was asked in 1983 to cut off aid to olive growers and to begin phasing out subsidies over a ten-year transition period in order to pacify French and Italian farmers. Even sectors which had largely supported EC membership throughout the negotiations were critical of the entry terms. The citrus fruit industry claimed that the sector would not enjoy the same conditions as exporters in Morocco for a further six years (*El País*, 30 March 1985). The Confederación Nacional de Agricultores y Ganaderos (National Farming and Livestock Confederation, CNAG), including many of the bigger, more prosperous farmers, and the Coordinadora de Organizaciones de Agricultores y Ganaderos (Coordinated Farming and Livestock Organizations, COAG) representing smaller farmers were both highly critical and urged the government to help out the worst hit sectors. While the prospects for Spanish Mediterranean agriculture, essentially citrus fruits and vegetables, were relatively positive, sectors in Northern Spain, such as dairy farming, cattle rearing and cereals, were severely hit by entry terms (*The Times*, 10 June 1985).

The two main unions were also critical of entry terms, particularly the CCOO. The resolution adopted by the CCOO Executive Committee in 1985, although in favour of EC entry, criticized the electoral and party-led interests of central government, the lack of debate in Spanish society, and the Treaty itself, which did not reflect national interests (CCOO, 1985b). The union considered that more pressure could have been placed by the Spanish government to gain concessions in the worst hit sectors (*El País*, 29 March 1985). The CCOO Secretary-General highlighted the harmful effects of the immediate application of VAT, the lack of priority given to employment issues and Spanish workers' rights, and the negative effects on sensitive sectors. In June 1985, the two main unions protested against the lack of social measures accompanying the modernization of Spanish society.

Regional opposition to EC entry developed in the final stages, although the majority of regional authorities had generally been in favour during negotiations. In June 1985, the President of the Canaries resigned after parliamentary opposition groups rejected the terms of Spain's EC entry by 30 votes to 27. In a struggle between economic lobbies on the islands, the importers won over the producers of cash crops, the preference thus being to opt out of the customs union (*The Times*, 16 July 1985). Although free-port status and other fiscal privileges were maintained (*IHT*, 24 June 1985), conditions enjoyed by third countries in the fruit and vegetable sector would not be attained until two years after accession (Congress, no. 195, 27 March 1985, p. 8917). Basque terrorists resorted to killings on the day of the signing of the treaty in Madrid as a protest against entry. One region which maintained its full support for EC entry was Catalonia; its leader, Jordi Pujol, claimed that this was a sign of its strong European credentials compared with more hesitant, isolationist tendencies in other parts of Spain.

Although parliamentary ratification of the Accession Treaty was largely a foregone conclusion, opposition parties in Spain already referred to a phase of renegotiation within the Community (*FT*, 29 October 1985). Some opposition MPs also criticized González for using Europe to enhance his own image domestically and internationally. Key sectors, such as the agriculture sector in Galicia, considered that final negotiations were rushed in view of the imminence of general elections and the linkage with NATO membership; other sectors agreed and highlighted their lack of preparation for EC entry. This analysis provides evidence of widespread opposition to EC entry terms, even if the overall political rationale in favour of accession was not seriously doubted. Criticism was only fully articulated when the negotiations drew to their conclusion in 1985, which led to a more intense interaction between the EC and domestic arenas in the final stages.

Conclusions

At the EC level, Spain set forward its tough bargaining terms and demanded recognition of its right as a middle-ranking power 'to be treated as an equal by the Community' (Preston, 1997, p. 85). At the domestic level, central government had to maintain the balance in favour of EC membership throughout the negotiations (*El País*, 22 March 1985). This set the scene for a long and complicated accession process in which central government played a key role at domestic and EC levels. The influence of domestic actors on the negotiations depended not only on their power, information resources and visibility, but also on the extent to which the political opportunity structure allowed them access to the policy-making process. Chapter 1 set out key factors which were expected to lead to a closed opportunity structure during the accession process. Evidence from the analysis in this chapter affirms the predominant role of central government in the process as a result of the following sets of conditions:

1. *Political rationale for EC accession which had a capacity to overcome economic or sectoral opposition.* The overall political consensus in favour of EC accession was very important in dispelling major opposition to entry. It gave central government a broad-based level of support,

enabling it to remain in control of the negotiations. Disputed entry terms were accepted, if reluctantly, because of the overall imperative of EC entry for which there were no real alternatives.

2. *Strong, majoritarian PSOE government.* The task of holding the balance in favour of membership, despite the existence of anti-EC lobbies in some key sectors, was far easier for a strong central government backed by an ample majority in parliament. This was the case for the Socialist government which took power in 1982. González was able to carry through electorally unpopular economic policies which the former UCD government had been less able to do. In February 1985, Secretary of State for the EC Manuel Marín denied that a strong government needed to make concessions at EC level to satisfy electoral objectives, considering that its strength lay in the conviction that public opinion would support the adoption of a firm position (interview in *Ya*, 17 February 1985, Ministerio de Asuntos Exteriores, 1985, p. 231). This is one illustration of the confidence of the PSOE government in the support of its domestic constituency, which considerably enhanced its level of autonomy at EC level.

3. *Process of decentralization still at an early stage.* The moves towards EC integration were occurring in parallel with the process of decentralization in Spain so that, in key EC policy areas, the distribution of competencies between central and regional authorities was still being defined. This made regional involvement in EC negotiations a key issue; only some of the regions had the right to receive information on the drawing up of international treaties and agreements in areas of specific interest written down in their recently created statutes. Regional competencies had developed considerably since 1978 when 89 per cent of all spending was controlled by central government (Gunther, 1996, p. 53), but the level of transfer of competencies was still limited when negotiations were concluded in 1985.

4. *Lobbying process yet to be established in a newly consolidated democracy.* Lobbies were only just beginning to establish themselves in the new democratic framework, despite the 'hurried ferment of interest group formation' noted in the years of the consolidation of the democracy (Giner and Sevilla, 1984, p. 134). The Spanish polity had recently emerged from the era of protected, elite groups under Franco, and civil society needed to establish itself to create the conditions necessary for the organization and legitimation of interests. The lobbying process in Spain was therefore noticeable for its fragmented nature during the accession negotiations, when even

the strongest domestic groups only had sporadic and restricted influence over policy decisions.

5. *Low level of demand for information on the EC.* A general lack of information about the implications of EC entry existed in Spanish society which, in some cases, meant that criticism only emerged late in the process when domestic actors became more aware of the length of transition periods and the detail of safeguard clauses. Only a minority of better-informed regions sought to obtain an input to the negotiating process, and trade unions had a limited knowledge of negotiations at EC level.

During the talks on accession, tough economic decisions solidified the PSOE's status as the only political force able to deal with EC issues, thus contributing to its 'electoral hegemony' (Marks, 1997, p. 76). Otto Holman (1996, p. 92) highlights the key importance of the incorporation into the Community for the Spanish government when he describes the progressive subordination of its domestic policies to the PSOE's European project. The need to build and sustain an internal coalition in favour of EC accession was minimized by the overwhelming consensus generally existing in Spain, although discrepancies between domestic expectations and EC obligations had to be explained in sectors set to lose heavily from EC entry. Constituent support was important in view of the national elections in 1986. However, despite interparty criticism, even the main opposition parties could not oppose the fundamental objective of attaining EC entry. The PSOE government thus generally enhanced its level of autonomy in the formulation of European policy. González had unquestioned control over government, the party and the electorate, which meant he was able, unlike the UCD who had resorted to financial palliatives, to carry through electorally unpopular economic policies. Even former UCD government officials acknowledged the use of EC entry as a strategy to carry out essential domestic restructuring:

La adhesión nos marca el camino del progreso, sin coste político alguno … ya que la transformación legislativa y la modernización se nos imponen desde fuera …

(Accession sets out the path towards progress, without any political cost … given that legislative changes and modernization are imposed on us from outside …)

(Bassols, 1995, p. 170)

EC accession acted as a strong force against established vested interests opposed to liberalization in Spanish society. It is thus that 'interests that create intractable obstacles to international agreements in the short run … are likely to be the object of restructuring efforts in the long run' (Evans, 1993, p. 400). For example, the Agriculture Minister, Carlos Romero, stressed that one-third of the agriculture sector would be lost without EC entry (*El País*, 20 April 1985), arguing that the benefits would become evident in the medium term even if the transition period was difficult. González assured his constituents that 'the EC will not impose further demands beyond our social and economic means' (*Europe 86*, no. 253, January–February 1986, p. 48). However, despite the overall domestic consensus, the PSOE's objectives were strongly attacked from outside the party, and underlying tensions were even caused within the party by the increasingly neoliberalist direction of policy (Holman, 1996, p. 84).

Spanish central government had to adjust its policies considerably to reconcile its domestic policies to long-term EC aims. Therefore, 'each part of the government's domestic, social, and economic policy was presented and legitimized by reference to the necessity of adjusting Spanish socio-economic and political structures in the light of future membership of the EEC…' (Holman, 1996, p. 80). For example, the interests of the fisheries sector had to be compromised in return for the expected benefits of EC membership. Michael Marks (1997, p. 94) concludes that 'in the end, the Socialist government changed from protecting the narrow interests of Spain's huge fishing fleet to adopting the Community line that it was best to limit the size of the Spanish fleet in favor of strengthening the Common Fisheries Policy of the EC.' The aim was to prove to its counterparts in the negotiating arena that its policies would also largely benefit the EC as a whole.

Couching membership negotiations in political terms was an effective government ploy to overcome opposition in certain sectors, although the EC tried to emphasize the economic realities of entry. French opposition to Spanish produce was thus seen as 'an attempt to keep Spain in backward isolation' rather than sectoral opposition to the threat to their markets (*Europe 85*, no. 5, May 1985, p. 15). A study of the UK domestic negotiating arena leading up to EC accession showed how interest groups concerned with material benefits had less influence as the negotiations became more politicized (Lieber, 1970). In the case of Spain, the balance between economic and political rationales was reversed, as negotiations were politicized at the outset, and economic concerns only became more pronounced later. The political imperatives for EC entry were able to counteract narrow economic interests. Friman (1993, pp. 393–4) refers to the shaping of perceptions of domestic actors by stressing the broader issues at stake, thereby increasing the costs of opposition, at least morally. It is thus that 'domestic factors are manipulated by elites in order to create support for their chosen policy initiatives' (Marks, M., 1997, p. 6).

In 1980, according to PM Calvo Sotelo, 'los ámbitos empresariales y la opinión pública…se encontraban cada vez más desengañados ante el hecho de que los intereses económicos de la Comunidad pesasen ahora más que el interes político…' (business circles and public opinion…became increasingly disillusioned with the fact that Community economic interests now had greater weight than political interest…) (Bassols, 1995, pp. 241–2). González later used the growing tide of disillusion nationally to increase pressure on key member states. The Secretary of State for the EC described EC agricultural demands in 1984 as going beyond what could reasonably be expected of Spain in sensitive sectors such as the olive-growing industry in Andalusia (*Ya*, 26 February 1984, Ministerio de Asuntos Exteriores, 1984, pp. 194–8). The transition ban on fishing in EC waters for ten years, proposed for the Spanish fishing sector in 1984, was also regarded as unacceptable by the Spanish government. It anticipated firm opposition when it presented such terms for endorsement to its parliament, particularly as many fishermen were in politically sensitive regions such as the Basque Country (Harrison, 1992, p. 207). However, many opposition politicians considered that central government was freed from even minimal parliamentary control over its running of external affairs by the EC context (Herrero de Miñón, 1986, pp. 146–7).

Control over resources and agenda-setting gave Spanish negotiators the power to build up coalitions of support domestically, and to reconcile sensitive sectors to intransigent EC demands. However, a study of the accession negotiations as a single, unopposed, rational choice by the Spanish government at EC level without any reference to other key actors in the domestic arena would be incomplete. An example of the impact of other actors on the negotiating position at EC level occurred when a ten-year integration period for Spanish fruit and vegetables was decided on 20 June 1984 and, in the light of increased opposition from the sector, the Spanish government declared in July that it was seeking a general seven-year programme, with the exception of citrus crops (*Keesings Contemporary Archives*, no. 3, May 1985, p. 33590). However, central government was not significantly constrained by opposition to entry terms in the domestic arena, which ultimately gave it full control over the negotiations. Furthermore, the majoritarian PSOE government was able to justify tough measures agreed at EC level to key sectoral actors. This was even the case when demands clashed with those of the electorate, with the danger that 'the long-term benefits that economic restructuring was expected to have might not materialize in time to vindicate the governments' actions in the eyes of voters and economic interest groups alike' (Marks, M., 1997, p. 12). In the case of the steel producers, domestic demands were used to increase central government's bargaining power at EC level, and thus obtain the optimal deal for the sector. Although the Spanish delegation argued that it was at the mercy of key sectoral interests, the extent to which the EC took this negotiating ploy seriously is doubtful in view of the consensus in favour of membership commonly known to exist. The 'tying hands' strategy to increase the bargaining advantage, as described in Chapter 1, was thus of limited utility in Spain's accession negotiations.

Although debate in the domestic arena was limited, an analysis of domestic political considerations helps to explain how national preferences were aggregated, and clarifies the strategies adopted by central government to achieve its international goals. A greater input of key domestic groups was inhibited during the 1979–86 period by sets of conditions which allowed central government to monopolize the interface between the EC and domestic arenas. The evidence examined in this chapter supports the predominant assumption in the literature that central government's strategies to retain a consensus in favour of EC entry in the domestic arena were facilitated by its high level of autonomy. The costs of non-agreement were high in view of Spain's political necessity for EC accession, and it was ultimately the central state which remained the exclusive channel for the representation of domestic interests throughout the negotiating process.

3
Changing Relations Between the Spanish Central State and Other Domestic Actors During EC/EU Membership

The role played by the Spanish central state during the negotiations for Spain's EC accession and the limited participation of other domestic actors in the process were presented in the previous chapter. The nature of the political opportunity structure during EC/EU membership, as a result of the changing sets of conditions outlined in Chapter 1, may be expected to lead to a higher level of participation of non-central state actors in the policy-making process after accession. This chapter takes account of this potential for greater participation, aiming to reconsider the existing, relatively static interpretations of Spain's EC/EU membership.

The institutional arrangements and key actors involved in the national policy-making process are examined in the first section, prior to analysing the mechanisms developed for the formulation and coordination of EU policy during Spain's membership. An initial focus on the pre-existing national framework allows a consideration of how it mediates the process of adjustment to EC/EU membership. Conclusions are then drawn on the extent to which the political opportunity structure has changed, and its potential impact on the roles of central government and other domestic actors in the policy-making process.

Institutional framework

As outlined in Chapter 2, the framework for policy-making in Spain is a relatively recent development following the end of the Franco era in 1975. The centralist control of both political and economic structures in Spain was a key element of the Francoist dictatorship, thus enhancing the role of central government whilst inhibiting the development of independent organizational life. This section highlights significant features and key developments in the nature of the policy-making process more generally, focusing on the roles of central government, parliament, regional government and key socio-economic actors.

Central government

In Spain, the domination of the policy-making process by the executive is particularly marked. Its role is enhanced in the 1978 Constitution, as illustrated by the privileged position of government bills, the vast majority of which are initiated by the executive. The primacy of the Spanish central state has led to analogies with the institutional structure in France (Lequesne, 1993), in contrast to a more dispersed executive in other member states such as Germany (Bulmer, 1986). Political circumstances have enhanced the role of central government, for example highly disciplined Spanish political parties (see section on parliament), and the single-party majoritarian PSOE government from 1982 to 1993. The Constitution accords particular importance to the strength of the president of the government, described here as the Prime Minister (PM), who is chosen following the King's consultation with representatives of the main political groups and elected by means of a vote of investiture in the parliament.

The PM enjoys considerable autonomy in shaping the political agenda in the Spanish policy-making process. It is the PM's programme that is voted on, a personalization which indicates the importance of the position in Spain (Heywood, 1991, p. 99; 1995, p. 90); this emphasis continues during José María Aznar's term of office in the late 1990s, described as the 'sobredimensionamiento de la figura del jefe del Gobierno en el ordenamiento constitucional' (exalted status of the figure of head of government in the constitutional order) (*El País*, 8 March 1998). According to Michael Newton (1997, p. 77), the PM 'becomes almost synonymous with the government'. Article 98.2 of the Constitution outlines his powers as the direction and coordination of central government's activities, and supreme control over all ministries including the appointment and dismissal of ministers. The Constitution also refers to the existence of one or more deputy PMs without indicating their specific duties, which have largely depended on each leader's objectives. The PM is responsible for the management of the party, and also has an expert team of advisers which keeps him regularly informed of policy developments. His control of the policy process depends on many contingent factors such as the unity and homogeneity of the party, the extent of the party's parliamentary majority, and the level of popular support he commands (Bar, 1988, p. 112). In addition to these endogenous factors, exogenous challenges also determine the level of control of the policy process (Heywood, 1991, p. 100; 1995, p. 91). For example, Suárez faced considerable political challenges during his 1976–81 term of office, namely establishing the new Constitution, economic recession and demands for regional autonomy, whereas González had a far more solid basis for political success in 1982, using the prospect of economic recovery and EC accession as a foundation for his policies (Heywood, 1991, pp. 105–6; 1995, pp. 95–6).

The top political category of the government is the cabinet (Consejo de Ministros), described by Newton (1997, p. 81) as 'the highest political and executive body in the land'. The cabinet is headed by the PM and includes the Deputy PM(s) and the ministers. The agenda is prepared by the General Committee of Secretaries of State and Under-Secretaries which allocates the budgets to the various ministries and plays a key part in the decision-making process, only passing on the most controversial issues to the cabinet for discussion. The key roles of the cabinet are to formulate and approve national policy, to discuss and present draft bills to parliament, and to propose regulations for the implementation of law. Five cabinet committees have been established, which act in an advisory capacity and improve policy coordination between departments; the Committee for Economic Affairs is the most frequently convened. Ministers form a key element of the core executive as well as managing public administration departments, indicating an overlap between administrative and political positions. They enjoy considerable autonomy in the running of their ministry, although they are ultimately responsible to cabinet, and to the parliament, where they can be called upon to explain their policy decisions at any time. Figure 3.1 shows the structure of a typical ministry in Spain.

The positions of Secretary of State and General Secretary were introduced by the 1983 Law on Central Government Structure and are filled by political appointees, whereas the majority of positions below this level are, in theory, restricted to career civil servants. The PSOE sought to clarify political and administrative roles in 1984 when an effort was made to establish specific guidelines for all positions (Keating, 1993, p. 336). No other radical reforms of the administration occurred until 1997 when two new laws updated that of 1983. Changing political circumstances have led to alterations in the structure and role of ministries. For example, in May 1996, the new PP government merged the Ministries of Culture, and Social Affairs, with existing ministries and

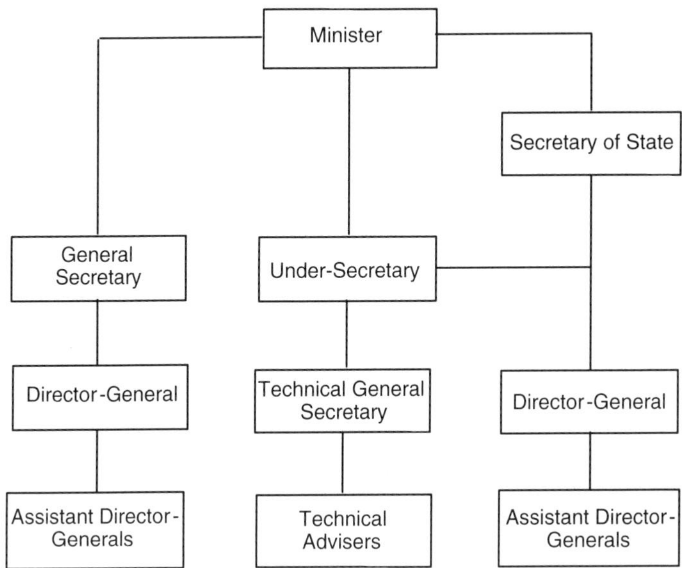

Figure 3.1 Structure of a typical ministry in Spain.

(*Source*: Newton, 1997, p. 94.)

Notes:

- The Secretary of State, despite considerable power within the ministry, is not involved in legislative functions, but can stand in for the Minister, for example in parliamentary hearings. Not all ministries have this position, although they are increasing in number. The Secretary of State may attend the Council of Ministers if invited, but is not a formal member of the Cabinet.
- The Under-Secretary is responsible for the administration of the ministry, for communication between its various divisions and for drawing up legislative documents. The position has an important role in the weekly General Committee of Secretaries of State and Under-Secretaries meetings.
- The General Secretary, which does not exist in all ministries, officially has the same rank as the Under-Secretary, but does not enjoy the same prestige (Newton, 1997, p. 96).
- The Technical General Secretary often enjoys direct contact with the Minister, despite ranking below the Under-Secretary, and heads an important team of advisers to the ministry. Some commentators consider that this position has declined in status, given the importance of the minister's own team of advisers (Ross, 1997, p. 38).
- The Director-Generals and their Assistants are responsible for the day-to-day running of departments.

established a 'Ministry of Enterprise'. Restructuring is more an indication of the priorities of the new PM and central government and their power to shape the institutional structure than of substantial changes in policy-making. The monopoly of the PSOE government over the policy-making process was criticized by one analyst who concluded that 'the government, and the premier in particular, have not always

resisted the temptation (offered by an initially unassailable parliamentary majority) to act in ways that have been allegedly authoritarian'
(Newton, 1997, p. 89). However, Holman (1996) highlights the less
assured power base of the PSOE in the 1990s, namely the end of its parliamentary majority in 1993, the growing internal divisions within its
organization, and the increasing conflict with domestic groups over
tough economic decisions. These factors could be expected to have a
considerable impact on central government's relations with parliament, although the strong role of the executive in Spain, and pacts
with regionalist parties, have enabled central government to retain its
key position in the policy process.

Parliament

The Spanish parliament or Cortes Generales is divided into two houses,
the Congreso de los Diputados (Congress or Lower House) which has
precedence in most matters, and the Senado (Senate or Upper House).
According to Article 66 of the Constitution, the role of the Cortes is to
'exercise the legislative power of the state, to approve the state budgets,
to control the actions of the government and to exercise the other
powers vested in them by the Constitution'. However, the emphasis on
consensus and negotiation during the transition resulted in a weak parliament whose main role was to facilitate pacts between the different
political parties. The defeat of the government using a formal vote of
censure is extremely unlikely, and the cabinet only needs the support
(ordinary majority) of the Congress. The Senate is described as the
chamber of territorial representation (see section on regional government in EC/EU policy-making) but, as for the Congress, the vast majority of representatives are elected from the provinces; its effectiveness is
questionable when it is given only two months, or in urgent cases
20 days, to review bills passed to it by the Congress (Heywood, 1995,
p. 100).

Although a more active role was possible for the parliament in the
post-Franco period in the early 1980s, parliamentary debate was not
enhanced by the majoritarian PSOE government. The strength of
González's position as PSOE leader was reinforced by the low levels of
party membership, and the fact that few cabinet members were simul-
taneously members of the party's executive committee. Furthermore,
the role of the parliamentary Socialist group was weakened by the
highly centralized nature of the party. This resulted in the parliament having a 'subordinate position in which its role amounts to little
more than that of a privileged observer of the direct and intense

relationships that exist between the government and the opposition. Accordingly, it tends to limit itself to supporting dutifully whatever the government does or proposes to do' (Capo Giol et al., 1990, pp. 116–17). All members of the Spanish parliament are generally bound by a strict party discipline, especially on matters requiring voting. Little space is left for divergent views or independent initiatives when the party spokespersons tightly control both procedure and outcomes. The decline in parliamentary influence is exacerbated by the rare occasions for spontaneous debate, the few opportunities to question the PM and the focus of the electoral system on parties rather than individuals (Newton, 1997, pp. 71–2).

Legislation can be initiated by parliamentary groups and, if central government presents no objections to the bill within 30 days, it is submitted to the Congress followed by the appropriate committee for debate. However, from 1982, 90 per cent of all legislation debated was proposed by the government, the majority of which was speedily approved in parliament with minimal debate and minor amendments (Alda Fernández and López Nieto, 1993, p. 257). Few limits to the power of the executive exist when a passive parliament generally follows the government's line, rarely setting up investigative commissions and not even serving as a forum for public debate. Domestic groups prioritize dialogue with central government officials and generally regard parliamentary debate as being of minor importance for their interests. The lack of an effective opposition party reinforced the strength of central government, and even the lack of majoritarian government after 1993, while making parliament a more significant arena (Heywood, 1998, p. 115), did not significantly change the executive–legislative balance.

Regional government

The Constitution establishes that regions may have a degree of limited self-rule; Article 148 defines areas where powers would be assumed by the Autonomous Community, and Article 149 lists those powers reserved for central government. The speed of devolution depended on the route to autonomy used, the so-called 'rapid route' used by Catalonia, the Basque Country and Galicia permitting higher levels of regional competency sooner than the slower route,[1] although it was intended that all regions would eventually be able to attain the same level of autonomy. The devolution process began in Catalonia and the Basque Country, whose Statutes of Autonomy were ratified in parliament in 1979, and power was transferred to all regions by 1983.

The rapid development in Spain of a semi-federal structure ensured expanding regional competencies in an increasing number of areas formerly controlled by central government.

Each region has a legislative assembly elected by universal suffrage, a government headed by a president and a high court of justice. The Statutes of Autonomy determine the regional government's capacity to draw up, approve and administer laws, and its relations with central government, while it is left to each regional executive to decide on the structure of public administration. From the outset, regional governments have been given considerable freedom in drawing up their own budgets, although the state generally retains responsibility for taxation[2] (see Chapter 4 for the system of regional financing). The Autonomy agreements of 28 February 1992 advanced the open-ended process of devolution, seeking to harmonize the level of decentralization between the regions, and establish intergovernmental cooperation between central and regional authorities. The dependence of central government on regionalist parties for a majority in parliament from 1993 resulted in an enhanced bargaining power for key regions such as Catalonia and the Basque Country (see section on the framework for EC/EU policy-making).

Socio-economic actors

Despite the considerable development of key domestic groups in Spain, trade unions and employers continued to criticize the lack of consultation with central government officials. Few existing studies of the consultation process between central government and other domestic groups in Spain provide more than a straightforward description of the key channels used for dialogue (see Molins and Morata, 1994). Relations between trade unions, employers and central government are considered here with a view to highlighting the attempts of socio-economic actors to obtain a greater input to the policy process.

Trade unions

The declining influence of the union movement can be noted in most EU member states, including Spain, in the 1980s and 1990s, partly as a result of structural changes in European economies which have inhibited union activity. The level of affiliation was still only around 10–15 per cent of the Spanish working population in 1994 according to most estimates. However, between 1989 and 1993, the UGT recorded an increase of over 50 per cent in their membership, partly explained by its growing distance from the increasingly unpopular PSOE government, and its more militant policies in favour of workers (Newton, 1997, p. 234). The CCOO also reported rising membership, although the number of members declined in regions with high unemployment (Newton, 1997, p. 239).

A more fragmented movement has emerged in the 1990s due to the rise in importance of smaller unions representing particular sectors, and the greater autonomy of regional federations in the decentralized structure of the two main unions. A further cause of weakness has been the disunity between the UGT and CCOO. The CCOO has often advocated militant methods to win concessions from central government, while the UGT has mostly adopted a more moderate line, focusing on negotiation with both individual employers and central government to highlight its demands. In general, the UGT's strategy has been more successful than the CCOO's militancy, but both unions combined forces in the late 1980s, reflected in the united action agreement of February 1988, which was facilitated by the election of a new, more flexible CCOO leader, Antonio Gutiérrez. Faced with the PSOE government's increasing cuts in social spending in the late 1980s, three major strikes were called between 1988 and 1994 by the two unions, the UGT having formally severed its links with the PSOE in 1988. Even though the unions sought to maximize their influence on government policy, particularly on issues such as wage bargaining and labour market reforms, widespread opposition to economic policies in the 1990s seemed to have little impact (Heywood, 1995, p. 253). This is illustrated by the statement of the former Economy Minister Miguel Boyer to the UGT leader Nicolás Redondo that 'the norm in democracies is that the government takes decisions and afterwards informs the social agents' (Petras, 1993, p. 120). Tripartite negotiation with employers and central government became increasingly problematic in the 1990s, and it is significant that neither the Competitiveness Pact (1990) nor the Social Contract for Progress (1991) was ultimately signed. Despite moves towards cooperation with social partners by the new PP government, such as the pact signed in 1997, relations were reported to have worsened in 1998 (*El País*, 8 March 1998); union influence is thus still limited. Increased dialogue with central government officials remains a key focus in view of the lack of success of public protest, as well as joint UGT/CCOO strategies to enhance their influence on policy decisions.

Another channel used to gain access to the policy process has been the Economic and Social Council, belatedly established by the Law 21/1991 of 17 June, as originally set out in the 1978 Spanish Constitution (see Chapter 2). The Council is a consultative organ on economic and social issues, providing trade unions, business and other representatives with a forum in which recommendations can be given to central government on draft laws submitted to them by ministries. However, the forum has little impact on the policy process given that the cabinet is not obliged to implement recommendations, which are made in the absence of central government representatives. Furthermore, because of the large number of members, it is difficult to reach consensus on the range of issues which fall within its remit (Soláns Latre, 1995, pp. 93–4). Evidence from interviews would suggest that trade unions will have little confidence in the Council until its structure and status are reformed.[3]

Employers

The CEOE is a loose alliance of organizations which, in the 1990s, incorporates around 184 employers' federations representing nearly one million employers (Newton, 1997, p. 258). The majority of business organizations have affiliated to the Confederation, accounting for 75 per cent of all employment (Keating, 1993, p. 340).[4] Conflict of interest between sectoral and territorial groups is common, especially in important sectors such as metals and construction, although regionally based groups, for example in Madrid and Catalonia, have also become more established (Keating, 1993, p. 340).[5] The size and broad-based membership of the CEOE should make it a privileged discussion partner of central government in economic questions, but it lacks negotiating authority (Heywood, 1995, p. 255). Few policy areas exist where the CEOE has a substantial input, although it has sought to expand its areas of intervention. Ironically, its attempt to reduce labour involvement in policy-making ultimately restricted further its own input to policy formulation (Martínez Lucio, 1991, p. 47). Despite its monopoly of business interests, it has still not developed the capacity to represent the demands of diverse sectoral and business groups. As well as the loose nature of its organizational structure, the high level of foreign ownership works against organized employers' interests. Spanish industry lacks 'leader' companies to play a key role and strengthen the CEOE's influence, and competition between employers has further inhibited the development of an influential organization. Other bodies such as the Chambers of Commerce constitute an important form of representation for smaller employers at local level, while larger, multinational firms frequently negotiate directly with central government. Newton (1997, p. 259) considers that 'the supremacy of the CEOE-CEPYME was clearly signalled when it secured the totality of employer representation on the Economic and Social Council'. However, the Council's lobbying power was limited, not least because of the obligation to reach a common position with the unions with whom its interests often conflicted.

Despite the limitations of the CEOE, its attempts to improve links with both central and regional governments as well as with the unions may lead to greater access to the policy process. The Confederation's relations with the party in power have been important in determining its influence. In the latter half of the 1980s, under the leadership of José María Cuevas, it placed greater emphasis on deregulation, wage restraint and liberalism than previously, and was less committed to achieving pacts with central government and unions. Access to the policy process under the Socialist government was more difficult, and relations with the unions also became increasingly strained.[6] In the early 1990s, attempts at political dialogue with the unions and central government were renewed, but the CEOE was often marginalized from debates. Although its support for the PP varied according to its policy line, close links with the party were expected to increase the CEOE's potential for influencing government policy from 1996. However, during the election campaign in 1995–6, Aznar highlighted the distinction between the Confederation's demands and his party's policy (Ross, 1997, p. 117).

Other than the lobbying mechanisms established by the CEOE, Spanish employers lack an effective system of interest mediation, thus making their participation in the formulation of Spanish government policy problematic. Interest groups tend to be small and weak, and have limited capacity to negotiate on behalf of their members. This is partly the result of the relatively new democratic framework established in Spain, and also of public reliance on the state to deal with domestic problems, as is consistently shown in opinion polls (Ross, 1997, p. 131). Consequently, pressure is largely channelled through state-controlled organizations. Some economic sectors, such as the banking sector, exert a greater influence. Its control of considerable commercial interests has ensured its impact on government policy, although a succession of mergers, while increasing their commercial power, has not enhanced their collective political influence. Main banks often work independently rather than presenting a unified policy position (Ross, 1997, p. 115), and the increasing presence of foreign banks in Spain has limited their autonomy. Nonetheless, they remain one of the most powerful Spanish lobbies. By contrast, the lobbying strategy of other economic sectors is considerably underdeveloped, as illustrated by the limited influence of the agricultural sector, with the exception of certain well organized sectors dependent on exports such as fruit and vegetables, and wine. In view of the generally weak representation of business interests, the CEOE has acted as the most important point of reference for employers despite its limited access to the policy process, thereby contributing to the forging of an employers' identity at national level (Martínez-Lucio, 1991, pp. 53–4).

In conclusion, the policy-making process in Spain is characterized by a strong executive and a relatively weak legislature. A pluralist framework is only gradually developing in comparison with the more established lobbies found in other European countries. Little evidence exists for the development of access points to the policy process for key domestic actors such as trade unions and the employers' confederation, although regional authorities have been able to increase their competencies and influence to a greater extent as the decentralization process has advanced.

Framework for EC/EU policy-making

Spain's incorporation into the European framework led to new opportunities for access to the bargaining process for a wider range of actors. Studies of domestic actors such as business organizations, trade unions or key political parties do not tend to focus on their involvement in EU policy (see Gillespie, 1989, 1990; Share, 1989; Martínez Lucio, 1991), and even the inclusion of a European context in studies of key groups such as political parties tends to be confined to an analysis of interstate negotiation at EU level rather than the domestic consultation process (for example Gillespie, 1996, on the PSOE). This is less true of the Spanish regions who are the focus of numerous studies analysing the implications of institutional change at regional, national and EU level on their involvement in EU policy. This section explores the role of key actors in the EU policy-making process with a view to drawing conclusions on their changing relations during EC/EU membership.

Central government

From an analysis of the impact on national administrations of the need to accept organizational modernization and reform on accession to the Community, Vincent Wright (1996) concludes that, depending on the prevailing domestic political climate, a change in the balance of power is likely. The process of Europeanization can be considered as 'an incremental process reorienting the direction and shape of politics to the degree that EC political and economic dynamics become part of the organizational logic of national politics and policy-making' (Ladrech, 1994, p. 69). The Spanish government adapted rapidly to the new demands, its first EC Presidency in 1989 being widely regarded as proof that Spain, as a relatively new member, had developed the necessary administrative framework for European policy-making. The impact of some EU policy areas on the Spanish administration has been notable, for example cohesion policy (see Chapters 4 and 5) and environmental policy, which was largely a new area prior to accession. Pressure from the Commission may have contributed to the government's allocation of responsibility for the environment to the Secretary of State for Water and Environmental Policies in 1991 and, following the initial impetus, the policy area gained ministerial status in 1993, and a separate Ministry for the policy area was created by Aznar's government in 1996. It should be noted, however, that a recent study indicates that the overall impact of the EU on the institutional set-up in Spain may be far more limited than that in specific policy areas (Molina, 2000).

The Secretariat of State for Relations with the EC within the Ministry of Foreign Affairs, responsible for coordinating the Spanish position during the accession period (see Chapter 2), continued to be responsible for coordinating EU policy during EC/EU membership (Law 1458/1985 of 28 August, replaced by Law 758/1996 of 5 May) (Secretariat of State for the EC, now the Secretariat of State for Foreign Policy and the EU, hereafter SSEU). SSEU officials are recruited from different ministries, which facilitates coordination because of their direct experience of departments and networks of contacts. The formal convocation of coordination meetings is within the framework of the Interministerial Committee for EU Affairs chaired by the SSEU (Law 1567/1985 of 2 September, replaced by Law 2367/1996 of 18 November), although many other informal meetings are held with ministerial representatives (for a study of the many horizontal and vertical coordination measures, see Molina, 2000).

The Interministerial Committee seeks to achieve a consensus on issues causing conflict between ministries in working groups. However, it has less power than the government's cabinet committees, and can only make recommendations. Ministry representatives are usually officials of lower rank than Director-General, which does not enhance the Committee's standing (Dastis, 1995, p. 333). When agreement is not achieved on this level, or when the issue is considered highly important politically, the debate is transferred to the government's cabinet Committee for Economic Affairs (Law 1568/1985 of 2 September) or ultimately to the cabinet. The final decision becomes an instruction communicated by the SSEU to the Permanent Representation in Brussels. The Spanish Permanent Representation (SPR) was set up in 1986 (Law 260/1986 of 17 January) to ensure the defence of Spain's interests in Brussels, and to inform the domestic arena about developments at EU level. The SPR officially sends its initial draft position to Madrid for approval, but often votes in Council meetings without formal written instructions from central government. It thus enjoys a certain degree of autonomy in its formulation of the Spanish position, which is enhanced by the EU expertise built up by key officials in Brussels. The horizontal vision enjoyed by the Spanish Permanent and Deputy Permanent Representatives, and their close contact with senior officials in Madrid, has ensured their key role in the policy process. The PM is informed of all politically sensitive EU issues, and plays a key coordinating role in the preparation of the European Councils. High-level policy decisions would thus seem to be the domain of a very small team of experienced officials which has remained fairly constant from Spain's EC accession negotiations.[7] Figure 3.2 sets out the official structure for EU policy-making, although this is likely to vary according to the policy area and the particular issue in question.

Problems of policy coordination, such as the contradictions between instructions from the SSEU and influential ministries such as Agriculture, were commonplace even during the early years of membership (Hayes-Renshaw et al., 1989, p. 131). The Interministerial Committee has frequently struggled to define Spain's position on issues on the COREPER and EU Council of Ministers agendas (Molins and Morata, 1994, p. 118). Aggregation of internal interests became more problematic as ministries increasingly tended to establish direct contact with their interlocutors in Brussels, although the SSEU was mostly kept informed of the issues discussed. Zapico Goñi (1995, p. 55) considers that the SSEU's Interministerial Committee is merely a forum for information exchange, and argues that a permanent coordination unit within the SSEU would lead to a more horizontal, strategic defence of Spanish interests. It has been suggested that the SSEU would enjoy a greater degree of authority if directly attached to the Presidency of the government (Moderne, 1987, p. 154; Zapico Goñi, 1995, p. 55), although one advantage of its position within the Ministry of Foreign Affairs was less likelihood of conflict with regional governments over division of competencies (Dastis, 1995, p. 331). Coordination within the central administration may be made more problematic by the lack of specialized units within ministries to deal with EU matters (usually the responsibility of Technical General Secretaries) (Salas and Betancor, 1991),

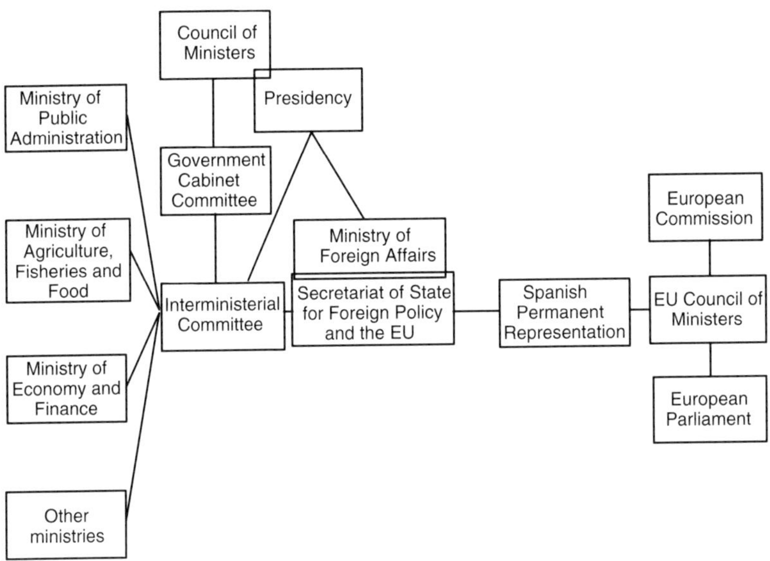

Figure 3.2   Official structure for EU policy-making in Spain.

and the lack of a committee focused on EU issues in the cabinet (Molina, 2000).

Although the SSEU generally has minimal contact with domestic groups, ministries active in EU policy maintain close relations with key domestic actors during the drafting of directives and formulation of the ministry's position. This indicates a 'compartmentalization' of government where ministries develop their own relations with sectoral actors, as has occurred in member states such as Germany (Bulmer, 1986, pp. 38–9). Access to the policy-making process is far more problematic during the policy initiation and decision-making phases; for example, national positions formulated by officials in Brussels and Madrid have not necessarily been approved domestically (Molins and Morata, 1994, p. 129). Where relations between central government and other domestic actors have developed, they remain *ad hoc* and informal rather than institutionalized. In many cases, central government has had the opportunity to strengthen its decision-making functions and increase its monopoly over the policy process during EU membership. The role of the PM in formulating the Spanish bargaining position is particularly important. González made a key contribution at the EC/EU level where he often enjoyed greater autonomy than in the domestic arena. This indicates the continued centralization of the policy process, involving a higher number of ministries and a less developed role for the SSEU, but more rarely including the involvement of other domestic actors in the formulation of central government's position. Parliamentary debate of the Spanish bargaining position prior to negotiations in Brussels could potentially act to lessen the high level of autonomy of central government, but limitations to the role of the parliament have remained during EC/EU membership.

Parliament

The PM reports on each European Council Summit in parliamentary plenaries, and resolutions and recommendations resulting from the debate should then be taken into account in the formulation of the Spanish position. In reality, briefings made by González to parliament on Spain's achievements at EU level were largely accepted without debate. The lack of parliamentary participation in EU policy is not unique to Spain; in all EU member states, central governments remain responsible for transferring information to parliaments, and hence largely control the extent of their involvement. However, in the case of Spain, the existence of a majoritarian government for most of the 1980s, the generally high degree of consensus on EU policy and the weak nature of opposition parties, at least until 1993 meant that the parliament was particularly unlikely to exert a high degree of influence on government policy.

Although the parliament does not have a direct role in defining Spain's position on EU policy, a Joint Committee for the EU (Comisión Mixta Congreso-Senado para la Unión Europea) (Law 47/1985 of 27 December) was created in 1986 to monitor European policy, as has occurred in varying forms in all EU member states. The Committee initially focused on examining the enactment of regulations and directives into Spanish law. Twice a month, the Secretary of State for the EU answers questions in the Joint Committee for the EU as well as the Congress Budget Committee, although little interest is taken by the parliament or public in this opportunity to monitor the implementation of Community policy (Molins and Morata, 1994, p. 118). The objective of the Committee is to formalize the systematic and permanent transfer of information from government to parliament, merely aiming, according to one Spanish parliamentary official (Delgado-Iribarren, 1997, p. 15), to avoid the duplication of information in the Congress, Senate and the various committees.

The acknowledgement of the inadequacy of the guidelines established for the monitoring of EU policy led to the reform of July 1988 (Law 18/1988 of 1 July), which allowed the Committee to expand its competencies. In the reform, it was recommended that it should be informed by central government of all agreements and decisions in the Council of Ministers affecting Spanish membership, and of its objectives at EU level. The reform also allowed it to write reports on key issues, and provided for the development of relations with Spanish MEPs and other national parliaments. The 1988 reform led to a higher level of activity, especially following the creation in 1990 of three sub-committees on the effects of EC accession, EMU and political union, which encouraged greater parliamentary debate. Furthermore, the competencies of the Committee have increased during the third legislature, leading to some increase in its standing.[8] In 1993, the opposition PP proposed involving it more closely in the preparation of the IGC. The creation of a Subcommittee for the Monitoring of the IGC in the 29 October 1996 session of the Joint Committee led to a unanimously approved report on the IGC in its session of 29 May 1997 following 13 Committee sessions.[9] In 1994, it was established that the Committee should be informed by the Ministry of Foreign Affairs about proposals made by the Commission relevant to Spanish interests, along with an evaluation of their likely effects (Law 8/1994 of 19 May). More generally, information would also be transferred on the activities of the EU institutions to allow the Committee to intervene at an earlier stage in the process. However, the fact of not being able to question EU policy until 'after the event' led to a growing demand for greater accountability. The May 1994 reform included the Committee's capacity to request discussion on the floor of the House of a specific legislative proposal; this led to the passing of a resolution on 14 November 1994 setting out the terms of reference for central government's negotiation of the reform of the market for wine production, which gave rise to a full debate with the Agriculture and Fisheries Minister on 27 April 1995. Increasing requests for ministers to explain their policies before the negotiation of important legislative proposals are a key illustration of the Committee's attempts to adopt a more active role in European policy.

However, despite some positive developments, the actual impact of the Committee on European policy remains minimal. It is not a legislative committee. Its initial task was to examine the 15 legislative decrees issued by central government to adapt Spanish legislation after accession, but their opinions, according to Closa (1996, p. 141), 'did not have any political relevance nor were they discussed in plenary session'. No significant bilateral relations have developed with either EU or national institutions as a result of the 1988 reform, and the *ad hoc* subcommittees set up on EMU and political union have had little effect; the document on political union, after only two hearings with ministers, was issued after the Maastricht Summit (Closa, 1996, p. 143). An official in the Spanish Parliament questioned the function of the Committee after the 1988 reform:

> Cuál era entonces la función de esa Comisión? Limitarse a ser un buzón de recepción de documentación gubernamental y, todo lo más, celebrar comparecencias sin que todo ello se tradujese en acuerdos o tomas de posición sobre los asuntos tratados?
> (What therefore was the function of this Committee? Limited to being a postbox for government documentation and, what is more, holding hearings without these developing into agreements or positions on the issues debated?)
>
> (Delgado-Iribarren, 1997, p. 15)

Despite some increase in the Committee's standing, subsequent reforms have also seemingly failed to give it any importance in the policy process. Although the committee on the IGC in 1996–7 had considerably more hearings, its conclusions largely reflected central government's position. In parallel with other EU member states, the links between national parliaments and the EU have thus been described as having 'un carácter indirecto y bastante débil' (an indirect and fairly weak character) (Sánchez de Dios, 1995, p. 105). The Committee has generally sought to reach an overwhelming consensus on government policy *vis-à-vis* the EU and avoid interparty conflict (Martín Martínez, 1995, p. 466). The minimal level of discussion of its conclusions on EU policy is an indication of its limited role, although some members justify the greater degree of consensus in comparison with other committees as being required to strengthen central government's position at EU level and, therefore, as a key objective of the proceedings.[10]

The level of efficiency of the Committee seems to be far less than in other committees such as Foreign Affairs and Agriculture, which have a higher political standing and a greater capacity to hold informed debate on specific issues. Analysts have illustrated this with statistical data which show that, in 1996, taking into account the reduced activity due to national elections, only eight sessions of the Committee were held with a total duration of 18 hours, compared to the Economy, Trade and Finance Committee, which met 12 times for a total of 45 hours (Delgado-Iribarren, 1997, p. 17). In practice, the huge increase in paperwork received by members on all subject areas as a result of the 1994 reform has not necessarily enhanced the level of political debate and, for so long as the information received from central government still arrives after the Spanish position is determined,[11] its role will remain largely symbolic. Central government argues that the rapidity with which decisions must be taken makes parliamentary backing for positions on EU legislation impossible (Sánchez de Dios, 1995, p. 108). Therefore, although an increase in the exchange of information between government and parliament has occurred, the number of questions and hearings having doubled between 1989 and 1993 (Closa, 1995, p. 141), the Committee continues to have little input to the EU policy process.

Spain's incorporation into the Community would thus seem to have distanced the parliament from the decision-making process. Despite the greater powers for acquiring information in the 1994 reform, the evaluation of the information in reports produced by the committees lacked any significant input. A Committee member denied that its non-legislative nature reduced its importance, and highlighted the limited remit of all parliamentary committees which can only approve or reject EU treaties.[12] However, in practice, the lesser political standing of the Committee tends to mean that it is less prioritized by the bureau of each House responsible for passing on legislative proposals from government to committees. Even if the Committee's debates occasionally have a greater input, for example on the question of regional participation (see section on regional government), it has not formed an essential part of the EU policy-making process up to now; the key problem according to commentator Magdalena María Martín Martínez (1995, p. 461) is the 'escaso o nulo valor concedido por el Gobierno a la actividad que la Comisión desarrollaba' (little or no value given by the government to the activity carried out by the Committee). Without legal modifications, which are unlikely, the Committee will continue to receive a posteriori information on EU issues. According to the Speaker of the Congress in a speech in 1997

> parece aconsejable dotar a nuestra Comisión Mixta de mayor agilidad y entidad. Posiblemente haya llegado también el momento de plantearse la posibilidad de desdoblar la actual Comisión Mixta en dos comisiones nuevas, una en el Congreso y otra en el Senado.
> (Enhancing the energy and capacity of our Joint Committee seems advisable. The moment has possibly also come to consider the

potential for dividing the current Joint Committee into two new committees, one in the Congress and the other in the Senate.)

(Trillo-Figueroa, 1997, p. 9)

The fact that the President and Speaker of the Lower House acknowledges that a fundamental reform of the Joint Committee is necessary illustrates its lack of input. Although the majority of national parliaments have a limited role in EU policy, the level of parliamentary control in Spain seems to be less developed than in other member states. One parliamentary representative claimed that key domestic groups 'were not specifically interested in their national parliament's position, but only in what is being actually negotiated behind closed doors in Brussels'.[13] The minimal interest of key sectoral actors and the Autonomous Communities in parliamentary debate of EU issues indicates its lack of implication in the process.

Regional government

In the debate on Spain's EC accession in June 1985 (Congress, no. 221, 25 June 1985, pp. 10177–217), Foreign Minister Morán acknowledged the necessity for increased cooperation between central government and the regions. Despite progress at EU level in attaining greater regional participation, most notably in the Maastricht Treaty,[14] obstacles remained at national level. According to the Spanish Constitution, although the government is able to delegate power to the Autonomous Communities via Article 150.2, international relations are the exclusive competency of the central state (Article 149.1.3). However, higher levels of regional competency in key policy areas have led regional governments to demand greater subnational input to European policy during membership.

Regional participation in EU policy can be divided into three main periods according to the progress made: 1985–7; 1988–92; 1992 to the present (Ministerio para las Administraciones Públicas, 1995, p. 137). During 1985–7, the series of draft accords drawn up only identified the key problems to be addressed in the second phase. In December 1988, a meeting was held to inform the Autonomous Communities of the priorities for the Spanish Presidency in the first half of 1989. At this meeting, the need for a formal institutional mechanism to manage relations between central and regional governments was recognized. On 15 February 1989, the Spanish parliament approved a motion which recommended establishing a more formal dialogue and, in a meeting on 16 March 1989, a series of issues were prioritized for the following months. It was not until the 5 April 1989 session of the Joint

Committee for the EC that the Minister of Public Administration acknowledged that attempts to reach an overall accord were being abandoned due to the lack of a common regional agreement. A more progressive approach was then adopted based on gradual and often partial agreements within policy areas rather than a more global vision (Burgorgue-Larsen, 1995, p. 132). Although regular meetings between regional and central government representatives on specific policy areas had existed since 1983, sectoral meetings (*conferencias sectoriales*) were now formalized, and a forum was established for the discussion of horizontal issues related to the EC, the Conferencia para asuntos relacionados con las Comunidades Europeas (hereafter *Conferencia*). The plenary meeting of this committee is attended by the Minister of Public Administration, the Secretaries of State for the EC and for Territorial Administration, and representatives from each of the Autonomous Communities. The global outlook of the forum gives it an added importance as compared to the technical focus of sectoral meetings, its main functions being to provide information on European Council meetings and EU policy developments, to work towards an agreement on the method of regional participation in EU affairs, and to monitor the activity of the sectoral meetings.

Two agreements were signed by central and regional authorities on 29 November 1990, first on the position of the regions in cases of violation of EC rules involving regional competencies brought to the Court of Justice by the Commission (according to Article 169 of the EC Treaty), and second on the procedure to follow regarding Commission rulings on state aids.[15] Although these were small advances, as a result of the first agreement a dialogue has developed between the Secretary of State for the EC and the Autonomous Communities, and meetings held by the Commission to discuss violation of EC rules have included regional representatives. The forum also set up a permanent working group responsible for the preparation of plenary meetings, the Coordinating Committee for EC affairs, and agreed to establish the position of coordinator in each region (Ministerio para las Administraciones Públicas, 1995, pp. 150–1).

It was during the post-1992 period that further progress was made. On 28 February 1992, agreements on the Autonomies were signed by the two main political parties which proposed that the *Conferencia* should be institutionalized. This occurred on 29 October 1992.[16] The only significant change was the decision to hold regular, formal meetings, for example prior to each European Council. A further small step forward was taken on 14 June 1994, when an agreement was signed establishing that areas other than purely Community issues would now also be discussed, for example relevant issues debated in the Council of Europe. It also set out an internal code of conduct which was approved unanimously.[17]

The first important agreement to be signed, after almost two years of negotiation, was that of 30 November 1994. It set out the framework for the internal participation of the Autonomous Communities in EU affairs.[18] Significantly, the accord obliged central government to take into account the common viewpoint of the regions in policy areas within exclusive regional competencies when formulating its initial negotiating strategy. In the case of shared competencies, the views of central and regional government would be coordinated. Central administration would be obliged to keep regional authorities informed of the negotiations in areas within the exclusive competency of the state. Cesáreo Gutiérrez Espada (1994, pp. 225–7) has identified two elements which threaten the coherence of the 30 November 1994 agreement: the fact that it is not legally binding and is therefore dependent on the political will of the participants, and the difficulty of achieving a common regional agreement, particularly considering the independent position adopted by the Basque Country.

The biggest threat to attempts at enhanced regional collaboration is the tendency of more active regions to develop individual mechanisms for representing their specific interests. Central government only has to be informed of the various arguments put forward by the regions if no common position is possible and bilateral agreements between central and regional governments are still prevalent (for example those with Catalonia and the Basque Country). This was a key issue for the Länder in the German framework set up in 1979 (Bustos Gisbert, 1995, p. 160), and is especially the case for the Basque Country; it did not sign the 29 October 1992 and 14 June 1994 agreements until 30 November 1995 in response to the establishment of the Bilateral Committee for cooperation between the central and Basque administrations on EU issues.[19] The Basque position has generally been the most extreme whereas Catalonia, although articulating individual demands, has been keener to adopt multilateral solutions. An intermediate group has included regions, such as Andalusia and Galicia, which are generally active, but less vocal in their demands. Finally, some regions have shown little interest in EC/EU issues and have not articulated specific demands for greater participation (Ministerio para las Administraciones Públicas, 1995, pp. 130–1). Colino (2000) highlights the greater interregional collaboration as well as moves towards constitutional homogeneity towards the end of the 1990s. However, divisions between the Autonomous Communities, illustrated by factors such as the different political allegiances according to the ruling party in each region (whether PP, PSOE or regionalist), should not be underestimated. The formulation of a regional position, including the opinions of the 'historic Autonomies',[20] would be facilitated by higher levels of coordination, for example in the form of a permanent meeting (Burgorgue-Larsen, 1995, pp. 138–9). Amendment of the 1978 Constitution to transform the Senate into a genuinely territorial chamber has been proposed as a way of establishing a firmer basis for articulating joint regional demands (for example Calonge Velázquez, 1995, p. 13). A Committee for the Autonomies was established within the Senate in 1994, but indications are that plans for reform have been shelved (*El País*, 16 November 1999). Central government fears that stronger regions such as the Basque Country would perceive reform of the Senate as the first step towards greater regional autonomy go some way to explaining the lack of progress. Constitutional reform remains a politically sensitive issue.

A number of criticisms have been made of the implications of the 30 November 1994 agreement in practice, such as the lack of transparency of the institutional mechanisms developed, as well as the need for greater coordination of meetings. Sectoral meetings had been largely ineffective in the past both because of the wide range of topics covered, and the large number of participants (López Castillo, 1993, p. 147). This problem remains. Relevant information is often received by regional authorities at too late a stage for their interests to be defended adequately, especially if the Spanish position is adjusted during the negotiations themselves. In practice, taking into account regional interests is difficult in view of the time constraints and the lack of subnational representation in EU institutions. Although the Coordinating Committee of the *Conferencia* set up a working group to evaluate the 30 November agreement and mechanisms for regular monitoring of sectoral meetings were planned, little evaluation of the functioning of the agreement has occurred. In practice, the general norms established have not been adapted to the needs of each policy area. A few of the meetings, for example in the area of the environment and agriculture, have been more effective and have given greater priority to EU issues, although they are still largely reduced to a posteriori evaluation of issues which have been negotiated in the EU arena.[21] Furthermore, any agreement adopted requires the approval of central administration, limiting the degree of regional influence. Political factors brought to the fore by the March 1996 elections reduced the level of activity of the *Conferencia* in the mid-1990s.[22] However, the elaboration of a common position on regional participation in EU policy for the IGC, which was passed in the plenary of the *Conferencia* of 21 April 1997, was a sign of renewed activity, even if its position was substantially modified by the Spanish government before it was presented at EU level.[23]

In a meeting between central government and regional representatives on 22 July 1996, the plan set out in the pact between the new government and the Catalan party Convergència i Unió (Catalan Nationalist Party, CiU) to have a representative for the Autonomies in the SPR in Brussels was approved. This development is, to some extent, an indirect result of the PP government coalition with regional parties after the 1996 elections. Further concessions may be less likely following the absolute majority obtained by the PP in the elections on 12 March 2000. The representative has established relations with regional offices in Brussels and distributes information to the Autonomies, forming part of the Spanish delegation in meetings debating issues within regional competencies. At the same 22 July 1996 meeting, a motion was passed to create a legal basis for the regulation of the *Conferencia*, which was approved in the Spanish parliament in March 1997. However, an Andalusia government official considered that only a law which regulated regional participation as a whole could make a significant difference. Such a law was proposed by Andalusia at the 22 July 1996 meeting, but did not receive the backing of other regional representatives.[24]

Although the SSEU is responsible for relations with the Autonomous Communities, regional authorities seek to make direct contact with officials in Brussels wherever possible. Regions such as Andalusia have backed the demands of Catalonia and the Basque Country for direct participation in Council of Minister meetings. In December 1993, González stressed that the responsibility for foreign policy remained with central government, and that regional representation, potentially resulting in a doubling of the number of participants at Council of Ministers meetings, was not feasible (*El País*, 19 December 1993). Opposition to regional representation at this level was echoed by the PP Foreign Minister Abel Matutes in the Spanish parliament on 28 February 1998, when he highlighted the PP government's need to represent the overall national interest and arbitrate between conflicting regional demands (*El País*, 5 March 1998). However, the Joint Committee for the EU voted unanimously in favour of Spanish regional representation in the Council of Ministers in their session of 4 March 1998, a move welcomed by regional authorities. Furthermore, on 21 September 1999, the Autonomous Communities reached agreement on the presence of a representative within the Spanish delegation in the Council of Ministers to defend the Autonomies' interests in areas within their competency. Although the acceptance of regions such as Catalonia was dependent on recognizing the need for a bilateral approach in areas of specific interest to one region, this was a clear demonstration of a move towards a more multilateral framework. However, central government was not willing to accept their proposal for regional representation.

Central government has been increasingly obliged to take regional interests into account in the formulation of European policy during membership. The level of political autonomy of the region would seem to be a significant factor in encouraging the assertiveness of subnational actors. An example is the Spanish Constitutional Court's ruling 165/1994 of 26 May[25] on the appeal presented by the Basque regional government. The ruling that relations between EU and Basque public institutions would not be regarded as within the area of international relations exclusively controlled by the central state, as outlined in Article 149.1.3, was viewed as an important advance. Moves towards a greater regional input to the EU policy-making process are significant compared with the lower levels of participation of the parliament and socio-economic actors in policy-making, although advances are the outcome of a long and laborious process.

Socio-economic actors

The input of socio-economic actors, at least in the early years of Spain's EC membership, was limited by the low level of demand for increased participation. However, during EC/EU membership, the demand for information and greater consultation increased, and trade unions and employers gradually began to adapt their administrative structure and lobbying mechanisms to the new European context.

Trade unions

The two main unions both have departments responsible for EU affairs, the EU department in the CCOO having been set up at a relatively late stage in 1990, while the UGT's EU section, within the International Relations department, was established at the outset in 1976. Both unions have become increasingly aware of the implications of the EU level for national policy, as illustrated by increasing reference to European issues in their documentation. The UGT/CCOO document 'Union Initiative for Progress' of November 1991 is written in the context of Spain's relatively weak position in the EU (Newton, 1997, p. 247), and the two unions made a joint statement on Spain's European Presidency in 1995 (UGT/CCOO, 1995). Although generally adopting a pro-European position, the unions also expressed their criticism of moves to fulfil EU economic obligations through neoliberal policies with high social costs.

Although the unions were somewhat slow to react during the first years of EC membership and focused their efforts on the national level, their declining national influence may well have encouraged efforts to recuperate this power at EU level (del Campo, 2000). They have thus increasingly realized the importance of representation at EU level. The UGT has its own office in Brussels, and both the UGT and CCOO are members of ETUC. The UGT has also become a member of the European Syndicals Committee whose objective is to provide a forum for sectoral interests at EU level (Newton, 1997, p. 234). In conjunction with ETUC, both unions have actively campaigned for greater priority to be given to social issues, and for a more democratic European executive. One illustration is the joint UGT/CCOO statement published in *El País* in March 1996 on the ETUC's proposals on employment and social affairs for the IGC (*El País*, 28 March 1996). The unions have also aimed to enhance their influence via the Economic and Social Committee at EU level, although its impact on policy as a purely consultative body is limited.[26]

The unions' involvement in policy formulation is often reduced to sending their evaluation and recommendations to the relevant ministry at national level, as well as to officials at EU level, in the absence of formal consultative measures. Central government was criticized by the unions in the 1990s for only going through the motions of consensus, while using the EU to justify the ratification of unpopular measures domestically. Mechanisms to increase union influence include the development of more established personal links with ministers and officials. For example, relations with the SSEU were enhanced when Westendorp was Secretary of State for the EU. Information was made available to the unions more readily than previously, thus facilitating their awareness of, and participation in, the policy process.[27] The Economic and Social Council at national level is seen as a useful forum for obtaining information on EU policy, but union officials generally consider that dialogue with central government has not been facilitated by its establishment.[28] Although a moderate increase in information and greater transparency of EU policy formation has developed during EU membership, union influence remains limited by the reluctance of central

government to encourage their input to the Spanish bargaining position. Dialogue with government officials is thus still described by
union representatives as a 'diálogo forzado' (a forced dialogue).[29]

Employers

The CEOE has widely supported EU membership and further European
integration. It has not always fully endorsed central government's bargaining position, but has largely shared its priorities, particularly with
regard to its promotion of free-market deregulating policies. Business
organizations have been hesitant about their actual involvement in the
EU arena, giving the CEOE a key role in influencing EU policy development. The Confederation has aimed to establish itself as a significant
lobbying force, belonging to the major international economic and
employers' institutions. It joined the Union of Industrial and
Employers' Confederations of Europe (UNICE) as soon as Spain became
an EC member. However, its bargaining strategies at the EU level
remain underdeveloped, and it cannot regard itself as the sole representative of employers. Few regional and sectoral actors rely on the
Confederation for representation in Brussels, thus minimizing its influence in EU affairs. The Chambers of Commerce tend to represent
smaller employers (the vast majority of Spanish businesses) at local
level which the nationally based CEOE neglects. Furthermore, the lack
of Spanish multinationals weakens the Confederation's lobbying
power, and larger companies and the more important industrial sectors
tend to lobby independently in Brussels rather than rely on intermediary
channels.

No tradition exists in Spain of close relations between public administration and private interests, nor have they developed in the area of
European policy. Morata (1996, p. 150) notes that 'participation of the
private sector in the decision-making process is seen as an obstacle in
the achievement of the so-called "public interest"'. However, the
increasing establishment of direct contacts between the EU level,
national ministries and interest groups may transform this situation,
for example the reliance of key ministries on technical expertise provided by sectoral representatives. This is also reflected at subnational
level where administrations increasingly encourage the involvement of
regionally based interest groups. New access points to the EU policy-
making process have been established in both the EU and domestic
arenas, as illustrated in Figure 3.3. Key actors can bypass central
government by contacting EU officials directly, thus indicating a new
political opportunity structure. However, the lobbying procedure is still

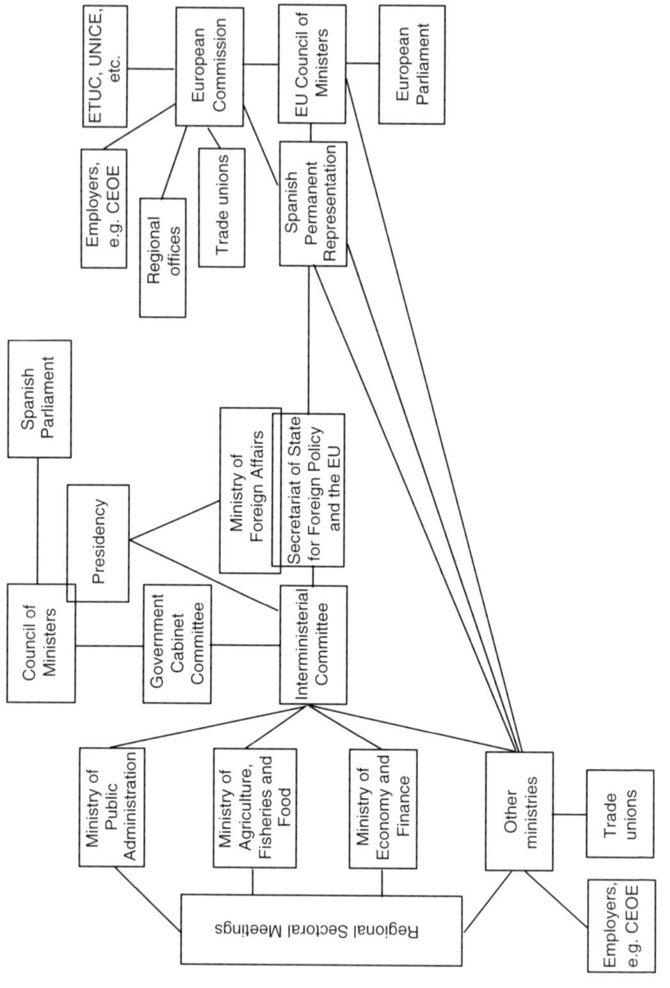

Figure 3.3   Development of the structure for EU policy-making in Spain.

much less developed than in many other European countries. Spanish domestic groups generally have a far more reactive than active strategy, linked to structural weaknesses inhibiting the development of stronger lobbies. For example, the large number of small Spanish companies (over 90 per cent in 1995 had less than nine employees) are generally less well informed about European policy, although greater knowledge of Community procedures as a result of increased representation and networking in Brussels is improving their capacity to participate compared to the early years of EC membership. Despite the early establishment of a CEOE representation in Brussels, some sectors have been slower to realize the advantages of a base at EU level, for example agricultural lobby groups. The fragmentation of the national agricultural lobby has led to its informal approach to European policy, with relatively few contacts at national and EU levels. For example, the union COAG does not have a permanent delegation at EU level.

The incorporation into the European framework has transformed the economic and political circumstances in Spain, demanding considerable adaptation by existing lobbies. However, adjustment to the new context by trade unions and employers has only been very gradual and, in contrast to the progress made by regional authorities, their access points to the policy process in both the EU and domestic arenas have largely resulted in little substantive input to government policy.

Conclusions

A preliminary evaluation of the changing policy process during Spain's EC/EU membership seems to indicate the continued strength and autonomy of central government which has been able to control access to the policy process for key domestic actors. According to Heywood:

> In contrast to the high degree of institutional co-ordination characteristic of policy communities, in which a professional public administration acts to marshal and regulate competitive interests within a bureaucratic market place, the policy process in Spain appears to favour dominant elites, notably the party of government, which is able to utilise the resources of the state to control access to the policy arena.
>
> (Heywood, 1995, p. 241)

In view of the fact that no clear evidence exists for a decline in its capacity to control Spain's EU policy, central government has thus retained its legitimate monopoly over the formulation of Spain's bargaining position at EU level. One Spanish official in Brussels concluded that European policy is ultimately determined by a small, relatively constant and highly talented elite of EU experts or 'veterans', the outcome being that 'European policy is not negotiated domestically'.[30]

While acknowledging the key role retained by central government, this analysis also takes into account the changing nature of the political opportunity structure in Spain during EC/EU membership. Chapter 1 outlined the expected changes in the sets of conditions which could reduce the autonomy of central government and provide greater access to the EU bargaining process for domestic actors. Evidence from the analysis in this chapter affirms the prevalence of these conditions:

1. *Balance in favour of economic over political rationale for membership.* The overwhelming political consensus in favour of incorporation into a European democratic framework during the accession negotiations allowed central government to determine the national bargaining position with minimal consultation of domestic groups. In view of the more economically oriented critique of EU policies which has developed during membership, the bargaining position of central government is no longer passively accepted by its domestic constituency. This was particularly the case where tough economic policies had to be implemented in line with long-term EU objectives, described by Holman (1996, p. 211) as ' "top-down" internalization of austerity'. One illustration is the rising tensions between central government and unions caused by the high social costs of policies aimed at meeting EU macro-economic targets.
2. *Loss of PSOE government majority.* During the first years of membership, the majoritarian PSOE government enjoyed a large margin of manoeuvre, which enhanced the predominance of the executive in the EU policy-making process. Its loss of majority in the 1993 elections meant that its high degree of autonomy could no longer be assumed. Although it has retained its central position in the policy process, imposing EU policies in the domestic arena may require building up favourable coalitions, particularly within sensitive sectors in key regions. The strong role of the central state in actively shaping domestic demands thus became less assured during membership when the PSOE's 'electoral hegemony' (Marks, M., 1997, p. 76) ceased to exist.
3. *Process of decentralization at a more advanced stage.* A more developed institutional structure has increased the regions' capacity to

participate in European policy. Considerable progress towards developing mechanisms for subnational participation in EU policy created a new framework for consultation in the domestic arena as the decentralization process advanced. This has strengthened the argument that central government cannot represent Spain if a particular aspect of the policy area is within regional competencies, as illustrated by a statement from a Basque spokeswoman, who claimed that it was logical for a regional representative to accompany the Industry Minister at EU level when discussing the issue of the steel industry in the Basque Country (*El País*, 11 April 1994). The approval of Spanish regional representation at Council of Ministers level in the Joint Committee for the EU in March 1998, and the interregional agreement on the issue in September 1999, represents an important initial step towards a greater regional presence in the EU arena, although without central government approval.

4. *Development of a more established lobbying process.* Key domestic actors were increasingly organizing their interests more effectively and developing lobbying strategies at national and EU levels. The growing number of Spanish associations and interest groups with representations in Brussels illustrates a greater awareness of the importance of seeking to influence the EU agenda. Although institutionalized dialogue between unions, employers and central government was still peripheral to the bargaining process, a more regular consultative role was developing for key domestic actors compared with the infrequent debate of EC issues during the accession negotiations, indicating some opening of the opportunity structure.

5. *Increase in level of knowledge about the EC/EU.* The level of awareness in the domestic arena of the implications of EU policy, and of potential access points to the bargaining process at national and EU levels, has increased during EC/EU membership. For example, central government transfers increasing amounts of information on EU legislation at an earlier stage to the parliament and to subnational authorities, and the presence of ministers is requested more regularly to answer parliamentary questions on key policy decisions. The actual impact of domestic groups on the bargaining process may still be questioned, but their greater awareness of the policy process during EC/EU membership is clear.

Domestic lobbying activity is rarely aimed at central coordinating institutions, namely the SSEU in Madrid and the SPR in Brussels, but at specific DGs within national ministries, which then have the task of channelling demands directly to the EU level. Particularly influential ministries reluctantly cede any power to the SSEU, and the task of making sectoral priorities compatible with a national bargaining position is thus often beyond the remit of the Interministerial Committee. Although some analysts have highlighted more effective coordination of EU policy (for example, Zapico Goñi, 1995), evidence suggests that a less centralized policy process with less dependence on the SSEU is a logical evolution, even if coordination mechanisms in key ministries have not always been established. Growing autonomy of ministries may facilitate access to the policy process for key domestic actors in specific policy areas. Furthermore, domestic groups can increasingly obtain direct contact with EU officials, thus bypassing established mechanisms for consultation in the domestic arena. However, interest group representation remained less developed in Spain than in many other EU member states. Potentially important channels of influence provided by the changing opportunity structure were still underexploited, for example via the SPR, the Chambers of Commerce, or regional offices in Brussels (Bescós, Ferraz 1995, p. 28). Furthermore, the level of access to the policy process in the domestic arena continued to be controlled by central government structures, thus tending to marginalize domestic influence, particularly of the parliament and key socioeconomic actors.

Despite evidence of the opening of the domestic opportunity structure, the actual impact on the policy-making process and on the level of autonomy of central government may, in some cases, be marginal. The far stronger institutional mechanisms established for regional participation were only effective in a few cases, the majority of sectoral meetings being reduced to a posteriori discussion of issues previously negotiated in the EU arena. In fact, many of the regions considered that their institutional position had been weakened by the transfer of competencies to the EU level, leading Morata (1996, p. 153) to conclude that 'the integration process has had a negative impact on both the horizontal and the vertical division of powers'. Central government is only obliged to consider the regional position if a common agreement is reached between the Autonomies which, given the heterogeneity of interests, is itself a formidable challenge.

However, although EU membership has tended to facilitate the control of central government structures over the policy process in key areas, some redressing of the balance has occurred in Spain in areas within regional competency (see Börzel, 1997 for the case of Germany). Evidence from the analysis in this chapter would seem to indicate that institutional mechanisms established have encouraged a move towards greater coordination of regional interests; the regions have managed to agree on sensitive areas such as their representation in EU Council of Ministers meetings. A higher level of interregional cooperation has thus helped to advance their cause. Kitschelt (1986, pp. 66–7) considers that the opening of the opportunity structure to domestic actors may not necessarily lead to a substantive impact on policy formulation, but may have the potential to transform the opportunity structure further by legitimizing new channels of influence in the longer term. This is illustrated in this chapter by the gradual progress made towards establishing a new institutional framework to enhance regional input. Even if sectoral meetings currently remain 'an internal coordination instrument that does not diminish the exclusiveness of state representation *vis-à-vis* the Community' (García, 1995, p. 128), they have the potential to become more significant in the long term.

The changing domestic context does not necessarily reduce central government's autonomy. In fact, domestic pressures could be an asset rather than a liability if demands result in a smaller 'win-set' which can gain a better deal at EU level. The position of central government as the locus of political power in EU policy-making is not therefore necessarily displaced. As argued by Dehousse (1996), it is less a question of a loss of central state autonomy, which can be enhanced by integration into the EU at key stages of the process, than of its adaptation to a new context. Central government in Spain has thus had to adapt to an opening of the political opportunity structure to a range of other actors, even if it has retained its high level of autonomy and initiative.

Despite the changing domestic context, the history-making decisions described by Peterson (1995) continue to be coordinated by a relatively small elite of high-ranking central government officials, which allows little access for other domestic actors to decisions on key strategic issues. An analysis of the institutional framework established in Spain for EU policy-making clearly indicates the resilience of central government as a strong national gatekeeper between the EU and domestic negotiating arenas. According to one analyst of the policy-making process in both Spain and Portugal, 'la mayor parte de las relaciones de cada uno de los dos Estados con la CE es vehículada a través de sus gobiernos' (the majority of relationships between each of the two states and the EC is channelled through their governments) (Colomer,

1995, p. 236). The focus in Chapters 4–7 on specific issue areas, where networks of sectoral and regional actors would be expected to have greater expertise, resources and access to the process, will further analyse the implications of a changing opportunity structure on the policy process in Spain.

4
The Role of the Spanish Central State in the Negotiation of Cohesion Policy

The development of EU cohesion policy has been a priority for Spain throughout its membership of the Community. Chapter 4 analyses the key role the Spanish government played in setting the agenda, and negotiating the optimal level of funding. A substantial body of literature on cohesion policy focuses on the increasing role played by regional governments, arguing that central government is less in control of the policy-making process in view of enhanced subnational input. The multi-level governance approach has frequently been used for the analysis of regional policy, where theorists seek to illustrate the potential threat to the monopoly of central government over European policy-making represented by increased regional mobilization, as illustrated in Chapter 1. Chapter 4 tests this assumption by focusing on the resilience of state political and bureaucratic elites, particularly during the policy initiation and decision-making phases, which has led to the 'retention of almost exclusive powers of negotiation by the states in the phase of policy formulation with the Commission' (Nanetti, 1996, p. 87). This chapter considers the development of cohesion policy, the role played by the Spanish government in negotiations, and the interaction between the EC and domestic arenas, with a view to gaining a better understanding of the role played by the central state at key stages in the policy process. Chapter 5 will then consider the role of actors other than the central state in the area of cohesion policy.

Development of cohesion policy at EC level

The SEA, which came into effect in 1987, made promotion of economic and social cohesion in the Community a key requirement for the first time. Article 2 of the Treaty of Rome merely referred to the objective of 'a harmonious development of economic activities' via the establishment of a common market and the approximation of the economic policies of member states. The key aim of Article 130a of the SEA was to promote the development of the Community by 'reducing disparities between the various regions and the backwardness of the least-favoured regions'. Article 130b specifies the means of achieving these objectives, namely the implementation of common policies and of the internal market, supported by three structural funds, the European Regional Development Fund (ERDF), the European Social Fund (ESF) and the European Agricultural Guidance and Guarantee Fund, Guidance Section (EAGGF).

The SEA coincided with the enlargement of the EC to include Spain and Portugal on 1 January 1986. The accession of the two Iberian countries led to a widening of regional disparities in the Community, namely a doubling of the population of the least-favoured regions (those with a per capita Gross Domestic Product (GDP) of less than 50 per cent of the EC average) (European Commission, 1989b, p. 9). The funds coordinate multi-annual programmes for the promotion of economic development in the less developed areas of the EU. The objective of achieving the internal market by 1993 required the convergence of member states' economic policies, and a reduction in major regional disparities. By signing the SEA in 1986, the member states thus laid the foundation for a major advance in the development of the Community's structural policies. At the London European Summit on 5 and 6 December 1986, the President of the Commission, Jacques Delors, gave a detailed report on the state of the EC's finances, and concluded that a thorough revision would be necessary. In February 1987, he presented the Delors 'package' to the European Parliament, calling for a settling of the budget, and a doubling of the structural funds over the following five years. Cohesion policy thus became one of the key priorities in the Community, strongly promoted by the Spanish government from the time of its EC accession, and linked to the development of its domestic regional policy.

Development of regional policy at domestic level

The process of decentralization of powers to the Autonomous Communities (see Chapter 3) remained problematic during EC/EU membership due to the varying level of competencies between regions and the shared responsibilities between national and subnational levels. The issue of regional financing was also controversial given the high level of disparity between the regional economies. Article 2 of the 1978 Spanish Constitution refers to the aim of achieving solidarity between Autonomous Communities. The Fondo de Compensación Interterritorial (Interterritorial Compensation Fund, FCI)[1] was created to fulfil the objective of reducing regional disparities by providing grants for capital investment according to relative levels of income, migration and unemployment rates. Since 1986, its budget has been limited to 30 per cent of the state's total public investment (Heywood, 1995, p. 152). The FCI was reformed in 1990 in an attempt to prevent the financing being channelled to services in the more developed regions (Newton, 1997, p. 128). Central government also provides aid to the regions via the Regional Incentives Programme, administered by the Ministry of Economy and Finance, as well as via specific projects in areas such as public transport.

Article 156 of the Constitution recognized the right of the regions to financial autonomy, and the 1985 Organic Law on Financing of Autonomous Regions established the key variables determining transfer of resources. This laid the basis for the first instruments of a full regional policy. The Consejo de Política Fiscal y Financiera (Council for Fiscal and Financial Policy), consisting of Economy Ministers at central and regional levels, and the Minister of Public Administration, was a consultative forum created for the coordination of key economic policies. The Council reached an agreement in November 1986 on public sector spending for the 1986–91 period, followed by another set of accords for 1992–6 agreed on 7 October 1993. One of the most important elements of the 1993 agreement was the access of all Autonomous Communities, apart from the Basque Country and Navarre which have a special statute (see Chapter 3), to 15 per cent of personal income tax generated at regional level. Many regions were opposed to the concession, and considered the agreement largely a result of strong Catalan pressure, which was particularly influential given the PSOE's dependence on Catalan support in parliament from 1993.[2] Despite this concession, and the right of the regions to count their own resources as part of their total revenue (Article 157.1 of the Constitution), central government transfers continue to provide the majority of the funding. For example, in Andalusia, regional resources only amounted to 8.2 per cent of their total funding in 1995 (Newton, 1997, p. 127). However, regional governments have been granted a high level of freedom to draw up their own budgets and, in 1995, the budget for Andalusia alone was 1 905 488.2 million pesetas (Newton, 1997, p. 124). The increase in regional power over the budget is illustrated by the fact that, while central government was in control of 84.5 per cent of public expenditure in 1979, this had fallen to 65.5 per cent by 1990 (Heywood, 1995, p. 154). In 1996, the regions were responsible for 25 per cent of total public expenditure, and for approximately one-third of public investment (Morata, 1996, p. 136).

According to Article 8 of the Law 7/1984 establishing the FCI, all Autonomous Communities had to elaborate their own programme of regional development, thus laying the groundwork for their involvement in EC regional policy. EC accession prompted the reintroduction of the concept of regional planning to Spain, which might not have developed very far without the external stimulus of the Community (Lázaro, 1988, p. 6). Central government endeavoured to coordinate the actions of the FCI, ERDF and other financing mechanisms in an effort to create an efficient, global system of regional funding. Initial regional plans were, to a great extent, inspired by EC norms, and formed the basis for those presented to the Commission during the first year of membership. The working methods of the FCI have increasingly been brought into line with those of the ERDF. For example, areas funded by the FCI in 1990 and 1991 coincided exactly with Objective One areas funded by the ERDF (Lázaro, 1991b, p. 305). The structural funds have thus had a considerable influence on the system of regional funding in Spain, although it was already adapting to the increased level of competencies at subnational level.

Role of the Spanish government in interstate negotiations

Following its EC accession, Spain considered that its position as a net contributor during the first year should be amended. One of its key objectives was the inclusion of a firm commitment to economic and social cohesion policy within the SEA which required the Commission to implement major budgetary reform. The proportion of EC redistributive funds had been increased: for example the new 1986 budget, agreed on 10 July, took the financing of enlargement into account, and included 175 million ECU of ERDF funding for Spain. However, the funding arrangements did not satisfy the Spanish government which, during discussions of the 1987 draft budget on 22 July, insisted that non-obligatory spending be increased (Brewin and McAllister, 1987, p. 364). Spain vigorously argued its case in negotiations over the Community's resources, demanding financial compensation for economic adjustments caused by the Single Market.

The first 'victory': the 1988 Brussels Summit

Towards the end of 1987, strong pressures were put on Spain by other member states to accept the 1988 budget, but Spain would not remove its veto unless its demands on funding were accepted. The Copenhagen Summit of December 1987 sought to reach agreement on the package, but ended in major disagreements between member states which were only resolved at the emergency summit called by the German Presidency in Brussels in February 1988. At Copenhagen, González was critical of the lack of political will of the richer member states, particularly as they approved an increase in agricultural spending while refusing a similar rise in the structural funds. Spain's main demand during the negotiations was the doubling of funding, and it threatened to obstruct the package deal if there was any reduction in the amount of money originally proposed by the Commission. Its position was not energetically supported by the other poorer countries, who were satisfied with an increase in funding only for their most underdeveloped regions which, unlike Spain, covered the majority of their national territory. Germany, the largest member state contributor, eventually agreed to Spanish demands over a six-year period when it was decided that the EC budget would gain a new source of finance in the form of a contribution based on member states' GDP. Likewise, despite strong objections initially, the UK was eventually convinced by the compensations received in the form of agricultural payments. The structural funds increased from approximately seven billion ECU in 1987 to 14 billion in 1993. Spain had established itself as a tough negotiator during its first years of membership, and the successful outcome at Brussels owed much to its uncompromising, often isolated position.

Spanish strategies at the 1991 Intergovernmental Conference

The Commission supported the Spanish arguments for budgetary increases in the structural funds, as illustrated by the communication on cohesion by Delors at the Luxembourg Summit in June 1991, which skilfully justified regional redistribution. However, he warned the Spanish delegation that excessive demands would jeopardize the IGC negotiations. His cabinet was critical of Spain's subordination of all other aspects of the negotiations to gaining higher levels of financing, and Commission officials were also irritated by Spanish criticism of the functioning of the structural funds, which they feared would reopen a complicated dossier (Ross, 1995, p. 153). The Commission would have preferred to delay greater financial commitments until after Maastricht, seeking to pacify Spain by promising that the structural funds would be doubled in the Delors II package. However, the Spanish minister responded that 'Spain would not let Maastricht get by without treaty insurance on cohesion' (Ross, 1995, p. 182), thus showing its determination to hold up the IGC rather than wait for future concessions which were less likely given the demands of Central and Eastern Europe. The Spanish government placed further emphasis on cohesion policy in 1991, as not only was Spain a more experienced player at the EU negotiating table, but it was also concerned about a decline in net receipts from the Community in 1990. Two-thirds of Community funds came from VAT, thus penalizing the high-spending, low-saving Spanish economy which was also dependent on its tourist industry. The Spanish delegation considered that it had been discriminated against in both regional and agricultural funding since its EC entry (*El País*, 17 March 1991), and that only the receipt of larger amounts of funding would prevent it becoming a net contributor. For example, González stressed in the Maastricht negotiations that, although Spain's per capita income was 22 per cent below the EC average, it obtained proportionately less overall income from EC funds than the other three less advanced countries (*The Guardian*, 3 December 1991). However, proposals for ambitious resource transfers were particularly resisted by net contributors to the Community, who were themselves facing recession. Furthermore, even Ireland, who backed the demand for an equalizing budgetary fund, was willing to delay debating the issue until later negotiations. According to one EC diplomat, 'there was no applause from the other beneficiaries' (*FT*, 18 June 1991), which often left Spain arguing for the inclusion of cohesion on the EC agenda from an isolated position.

The issue of social and economic cohesion remained an obstacle throughout the Luxembourg Presidency. Spain strongly criticized the contrast between repeated EC commitments to redistribution, and the lack of reference to cohesion in the IGC negotiations. A Spanish working group, including officials from the Ministry of Economy and Finance, the Bank of Spain and the Secretariat of State for the EC, sought to maximize Spanish input to negotiations at EC level. Documents outlining the Spanish position were presented to the Commission in March and May 1991. The March 1991 document, clearly negative about existing Community efforts, stressed the need to reinforce the concept of cohesion in general while, two months later, more specific recommendations were put forward (Spanish delegation, 1991a,b). The three major proposals were: an increase in the share of

Community funding to structural programmes; the setting up of a fairer system of resources where member state contributions are measured by their relative prosperity; and the establishment of a fund for interstate compensation, or an equalizing budgetary fund, based on the FCI at national level. The proposals generally faced firm opposition in the Community, the Northern member states accusing Spain of jeopardizing the Treaty talks to obtain solutions to financial problems which were outside the IGC's brief (*FT*, 18 June 1991). The interstate compensation fund was regarded as unrealistic by the Commission and, despite the backing of Portugal, Ireland and Greece, the proposal was rejected during the Luxembourg Presidency. However, Spain continued to argue for fiscal transfers to make EMU viable for poorer states. The Spanish Secretary of State for Economy, Pedro Pérez, declared that such transfers would not be open-ended, but 'only until the playing field is more or less level' (*FT*, 18 June 1991).

When the Netherlands took over the Presidency in 1991, their draft treaty on political union largely ignored Spanish demands on cohesion which they described as intransigent, isolated and unacceptable to the majority of member states (*El País*, 15 November 1991). It was not until the penultimate ministerial meeting in November that, in response to Spanish pressure, the issue was debated, using the Luxembourg draft treaty as a basis. Spain's position remained unchanged, but the Commission sought to influence the Irish and Portuguese who were considered 'softer' negotiators (Ross, 1995, p. 188). The Spanish delegation did not directly threaten to veto the Maastricht agreement, but the Economy Minister, Carlos Solchaga, made clear that the national parliament would not necessarily ratify the EU Treaty if it was dissatisfied with the negotiations (*El País*, 15 November 1991).

Little advance was made on the cohesion issue on the first day of the Maastricht Summit. The Commission's support for Spanish proposals was crucial, as it not only broke Spain's isolation, but also encouraged the other poorer countries to be more vigorous in their demands (*El País*, 26 November 1991). A meeting was held to discuss cohesion in which Spanish and German diplomats, and the Head of Delors' cabinet, Pascal Lamy, participated.[3] The Spanish delegation demanded legal guarantees on the issue within the Treaty and, by the morning of the second day of the Summit, the Dutch Presidency had proposed the inclusion of a 'cohesion fund' in a protocol as well as an agreement on relative prosperity. Although the majority of member states considered a non-binding declaration sufficient, the Dutch Presidency proposed a legally binding protocol as a compromise between the two positions.

Initially, German officials would only consider an environmental fund and dismissed a compromise proposal, put forward by Belgium and Italy, which proposed addressing Spanish concerns in a protocol. However, talks between Helmut Kohl and Felipe González on the eve of the summit enabled a compromise to be reached. This commitment, along with the agreement to base budgetary contributions on the relative prosperity of member states, led one Spanish spokesman to declare that Spain had 'won everything we set out to achieve at Maastricht' (*The Independent*, 11 December 1991). González, although recognizing that EMU remained a formidable challenge, said that it was 'now almost inconceivable that by 1996 Spain was not in the group of countries that begins the process towards a sole currency' (*FT*, 12 December 1991). The review of the EU's finances in 1992 was closely monitored by Spain, to ensure that a firm legal commitment to cohesion was retained.

The second 'victory': the 1992 Edinburgh Summit

Just as the 1988 Brussels European Council was the 'essential financial counterpart' of the SEA, the Edinburgh Summit performed this role for the Maastricht Treaty (Duff et al., 1994, p. 135). Delors presented the Commission's proposals (the so-called Delors II package) to the European Parliament on 12 February 1992, and an agreement was reached in Edinburgh in December 1992. Michael Shackleton (1993, p. 11) describes the fact that the budgetary negotiations were concluded in a marginally shorter time than in February 1988 as surprising in view of the lack of an urgent need to raise the amount of Community resources. However, Spain's threat of a veto of the European Free Trade Association (EFTA) enlargement unless it obtained the full Delors II package, designed to double the receipts of the poorer countries by 1997, ensured that priority was given to budgetary issues. The Spanish government thus had a key role in setting the agenda for the negotiation of cohesion at the Edinburgh Summit.

The Portuguese Presidency in the first half of 1992 sought agreement on general guidelines rather than specific figures, in an atmosphere which was generally negative following the Danish 'no' in their EU referendum (*FT*, 26 June 1992). This left the main decisions for the UK Presidency which Spain feared would be far less receptive to Southern member state demands. Although Spain was the strongest advocate of the doubling of structural funds, Portugal also backed tough Spanish statements in pre-Summit meetings (*El País*, 20 June 1992). The UK and Dutch delegations firmly opposed any raising of the ceiling before

1997, and other member states were unsympathetic towards the amount of funding demanded by Spain, even suggesting that the Cohesion Fund could be delayed until 1999. Delors tried to bridge the North/South divide by conceding that his plan to raise EC spending by one-third could be spread over another two years, and would affect key policy areas such as research and development (*FT*, 26 June 1992). However, the Commission was more critical of specific Spanish proposals, such as its demand in January 1992 for 487 500 million pesetas, of which 300 000 would be received by Spain (*El País*, 24 January 1992). Kohl was described as the most vocal in his refusal to pledge more aid, arguing, with support from the UK and France, that a substantial increase in funding could undermine the support for Maastricht in the richer countries (*IHT*, 29 June, 1992). The final Lisbon communiqué declared that the budget from 1993 was set for either five or seven years, and that it would lead to an 'appropriate' increase in support. González accused the UK and Germany of reneging on prior commitments. However, a private Commission note, sent to offices after the Summit, considered a doubling of the financial effort by 1997 in the poorer member states likely, thus indicating a move in Spain's direction despite the lack of progress made at Lisbon (*The Times*, 29 June 1992).

Spain's bargaining power was strengthened at Edinburgh by the need for its support for the acceptance of both the Danish exemptions from Maastricht and enlargement. The UK plan was presented to a meeting of EC Foreign and Finance ministers in Brussels in November. It was immediately criticized by the less developed countries, particularly Spain, as the plan was to freeze EC spending for the following three years, and to limit growth to 1.2 per cent of GDP until 1996–7, and 1.25 per cent in 1998–9 (*FT*, 30 November 1992). France was more sympathetic to Spanish demands, as it needed Spain's support for its renegotiation of farm subsidies with the US, but the UK sought to prevent Spain from strengthening the previously isolated French position. It warned of the market risks of a Summit failure during its tour of capitals prior to the Edinburgh Summit. The UK highlighted reductions on VAT from 55 to 50 per cent, which Spain had obtained immediately rather than over five years, as a significant victory in an attempt to pacify the Spanish delegation. Furthermore, it stressed that the difference between the amounts of funding it proposed, and those put forward by the Commission, was only 2.5 billion ECU a year. Diplomatic sources claimed González was 'bordering on outright anger' because of the UK and Danish delays on Maastricht ratification, even before the UK had tabled the compromise EC financing plan (*The Independent*, 1 December 1992). González described the proposal on the budget as 'insufficient', and the spending package as 'minimal' (*FT*, 2 December 1992). However, the Spanish delegation agreed to compromise on certain of its demands, including the approval of a less generous budgetary deal than that originally demanded, which enabled informal talks to begin on enlargement before a financial agreement was reached (*El País*, 10 December 1992).

The establishment of a multi-annual financial framework was eventually agreed at Edinburgh, involving an increase from 18.6 to 30 billion ECU in the budget by 1999. The main increase was in the structural funds, with the newly created Cohesion Fund (see Chapter 5) making up the 2.6 billion ECU balance.[4] The budget froze the ceiling on resources at 1.2 per cent of GDP for two years, with a phased increase to 1.27 per cent by 1999. The Spanish delegation was generally satisfied, although the agreement fell short of the original Spanish proposal of 1.37 per cent. The importance of interstate relations in reaching a final agreement is underlined by Kohl's claim that he had made a 'substantial verbal contribution' to convince González that a compromise on financial arrangements was possible (*FT*, 14 December 1992). The Spanish delegation had been a key player throughout the negotiations; according to the Foreign Minister Francisco Fernández Ordóñez in his briefing to the Joint Committee for the EC on 13 October 1988, 'lo que se haya hecho en cohesión se ha hecho con el impulso de España' (what has been achieved in cohesion has been the result of Spanish initiative) (Ministerio de Asuntos Exteriores, 1988, p. 386). Although cohesion policy was on the EC agenda prior to Spain's accession, 'it took Spain to pitch it at the level it deserved' according to a former adviser to González.[5] The fact that it was fully taken into account in the areas of research and development, the Single Market, the EFTA enlargement and environmental policy was viewed by key Spanish government officials as largely the outcome of Spain's initiative. Its tough position was retained in 1994 during enlargement negotiations, when it insisted on an increase in cohesion funding using the contributions of the new members, Austria, Sweden and Finland, of between 2000 and 4000 million ECU (*El País*, 15 February 1994). The Spanish government was not prepared to facilitate the entry of other countries into the Community by changing the rules in key areas such as cohesion policy, arguing that their position was entirely logical in view of the tough EC accession terms which had been imposed on Spain.[6]

An analysis of negotiations at EC/EU level clearly depicts an inter-state bargaining framework to which domestic actors had minimal access. Considerable evidence exists for the key role of the Spanish government in the negotiation of cohesion policy, its skilful bargaining tactics being widely recognized by both the Commission and other EU member states. The Spanish delegation thus enjoyed a high level of autonomy *vis-à-vis* other domestic actors. The next section examines more closely the role of the central state in the domestic arena during the negotiations.

Interaction between the domestic and EU arenas

Marks (1992, p. 194) argues that the clearest way of explaining the growth in structural funds is to consider the funding as a side payment to the poorer countries in return for the assent to the Single Market, thus amounting to 'a combined optimal solution'. His analysis high-lights the fact that countries such as Spain lack a cushion of affluence against any downturn in the economy, and could suffer from a 'nega-tive political fallout' if the Spanish population's high expectations of the EC are not fulfilled (Marks, 1992, p. 203). The tough position on funding adopted by the Spanish government at EC/EU level was, to a certain extent, a response to the need to present a successful out-come to parliament and public opinion in the domestic arena. In the press conference following the Brussels Summit on 12 February 1988 (Ministerio de Asuntos Exteriores, 1988, p. 127), González highlighted the politically sensitive process of explaining the outcome of the sum-mit to the public in each member state by the head of government, thus underlining the importance of the domestic ratification process. In the 1988 press conference, González stressed that Spain's gains at EC/EU level were not for senior government officials, but for Spanish citizens (Ministerio de Asuntos Exteriores, 1988, p. 129). The high visi-bility of the structural funds, representing the direct gains from Spain's incorporation into the European framework, made their presentation in the domestic arena particularly important for retaining an internal consensus in favour of membership.

Definitions of cohesion

Cohesion was defined by the Spanish delegation in its March 1991 document to the IGC as a 'necessary political balance between effi-ciency, stability and equity', and not merely as compensation for EMU (Nicoll and Salmon, 1994, p. 274). This took into account the varying effort required by economies at different stages of development to implement EU policies. The Spanish Presidency's statement to the European Parliament in January 1989 declared that the SEA not only set out specific measures to strengthen cohesion, but included 'an effective and parallel presence of that objective in developing the various policies and the internal market' (European Commission, 1989a, p. 88). Cohesion policy is thus viewed as part of the progress towards European integration, rather than a quantitative concept detached from key developments. The EC's obligation to the Spanish domestic arena in return for the tough conditions imposed for accession was highlighted, for example by incorporating the concept of cohesion in the reform of the CAP.[7] In a speech in 1988 in Brussels, González declared:

> Si unos hacen un ejercicio duro, pero necesario, de convergencia de políticas económicas…otros deberán, lógicamente, corresponder con una aproximación semejante por la vía de la solidaridad, mediante la aceptación de decisiones que impliquen un grado mayor de cohesión económica y social.
> (If some countries go through a tough, but necessary, exercise in order to converge their economic policies…others should, logically, respond with a similar effort of solidarity by accepting decisions which imply a higher level of social and economic cohesion.)[8]

González was aware of the likely resistance of key EU member states to the development of cohesion policy, but sought to maximize support for his demands at EU level by presenting Spain's objectives as part of a political, pro-integrationist discourse, rather than highlighting the gains at domestic level (Closa, 1995, p. 304). González thus called for an increase in structural funding as a key element of his Europeanist vision. For example, in September 1987 in Bonn, González rejected the notion of a mere free trade zone[9] and, in October 1987 in Florence, he described the close relationship between the internal market and cohesion in an integrated Europe.[10] The protocol obtained at Maastricht was considered by González as the minimal solution to avoid a damaging political climbdown domestically. He had stressed from an early stage that Spain's fulfilment of EC obligations would be compensated for by the Community's 'indispensable solidaridad política y económica' (indispensable political and economic solidarity).[11]

Domestic responses to negotiations at EU level

The Spanish government's tough negotiating position on cohesion policy was generally supported by all political parties, including influential regional parties such as the CiU and the Partido Nacionalista Vasco (Basque Nationalist Party, PNV). Likewise, central government received the full backing of the CEOE in its negotiation of cohesion funding, whose only major fear was regarding its distribution to less developed regions and to SMEs (Youngs, 1996, p. 201). Key domestic actors were concerned to maximize Spain's net benefits from Community membership; criticism that Spain had become a net contributor during the first year of EC membership was voiced by the CEOE and opposition parties (*El País*, 9 January 1987). González sought to gain the approval of key actors, such as the main trade unions, by highlighting the economic benefits obtained in negotiations in Brussels to counter their increasing criticism of governmental reforms (see Chapter 5 for a fuller discussion of the input of domestic actors). However, relations between central government and the unions had generally deteriorated in the 1990s, and were exacerbated by Spain's attempts to meet the EMU convergence criteria during a time of growing economic crisis.

As illustrated in Chapter 3, the sets of conditions which enhanced central government autonomy during the negotiations for EC accession (see Chapter 2) were changing during membership. The increased lobbying capacity of domestic actors, and the greater vulnerability of political leaders to their demands, meant that a new context for policy-making was developing. Richard Youngs (1996) draws a clear distinction between the 1986–90 and the post-1990 periods in his analysis of the domestic political context in Spain; key changes included a hardening of public opinion *vis-à-vis* the EU, and a greater consideration of the extent to which Spain's EU membership benefited national interests. This is illustrated by the harsh criticism of the Izquierda Unida (United Left, IU)[12] of the ratification of the Maastricht Treaty without prior EC commitments to economic and social cohesion, and the opposition parties' initial rejection of the draft text on Maastricht in the Joint Committee for the EC (*El País*, 19 November 1991).[13] Key actors in the domestic arena increasingly demanded more information on EC/EU policy decisions, as illustrated by the criticism of the lack of information from central government in the Joint Committee for the EC of 13 October 1988 (Ministerio de Asuntos Exteriores, 1988, p. 395); according to opposition parties, this had encouraged a break in the Spanish consensus on Europe (*El País*, 20 November 1991). In its defence, the PSOE government referred to the lack of amendments made by the opposition to the text on political union in the Joint Committee for the EC over a four-month period, also arguing that it could not be bound to a parliamentary resolution when it had to retain a high degree of flexibility and autonomy during negotiations in the EC/EU arena (*El País*, 21 November 1991). Obtaining increasing levels of European funding to present to the domestic arena had thus become more urgent in view of the less assured consensus on European policy. Business and trade union representatives, and opposition parties, urged the blocking of advances in other policy areas if Spain did not obtain its demands, and parliamentary debate, particularly during pre-election periods, frequently criticized the PSOE government's negotiating position in Brussels. In November 1991, González declared in the Spanish parliament that he would exercise his veto if no satisfactory agreement on cohesion policy was obtained, and the chief Spanish negotiator at Maastricht in 1991 acknowledged that uppermost in his mind was the probability that a weak agreement on cohesion would not get through the national parliament (*El Mundo*, 7 December 1991).

Despite the growing criticism, central government ultimately relied on full parliamentary backing for its bargaining positions. For example, Spanish Commissioner Abel Matutes referred in December 1992 to the similar understanding of the Cohesion Fund of the PSOE and PP (*El País*, 11 December 1992). Nonetheless, the increasingly critical stance put pressure on the Spanish delegation at EC/EU level, and increased the public awareness of the issues at stake. In the July 1992 plenary following the Lisbon Summit, the main parliamentary groups highlighted the lack of achievement following the commitment to cohesion policy made at Maastricht. Central government's triumphalist propaganda was strongly criticized by the opposition, while government officials drew attention to the difficult circumstances in which the negotiation had occurred (Congress, no. 204, 1 July 1992, pp. 10014–50). Opposition parties emphasized the disillusionment in the domestic arena, and the lack of consensus on European policy among the main political parties and trade unions. They were particularly critical of the lack of dialogue between central government and other domestic groups (Congress, no. 204, 1 July 1992, pp. 10014–50).

While González highlighted the firm defence of Spanish interests at Edinburgh (Congress, no. 238, 15 December 1992, p. 12040), the leader of the PP pointed to the Spanish government's 'begging stance' within the EU (as *pedigüeños*) while they were prone to high spending in the domestic arena (*El País*, 13 December 1992). Other key points of criticism were the minimal nature of the funding (the fact that the Cohesion Fund actually represented less than 0.5 per cent of the overall national budget), and the neglect of Spanish sectoral interests while concentrating on EU funding; this was described as 'un punto débil para influir en la evolución de la Comunidad y en la protección de nuestros más inmediatos intereses' (a weak way in which to influence the development of the Community and protect our most immediate interests) (Congreso, no. 238, 15 December 1992, p. 12025). The PP highlighted the insufficient EC commitment to the Cohesion Fund which it considered to be a declaration of intentions rather than a firm guarantee (*El País*, 15 December 1991), and the IU stressed the need to address the problem of growing inequalities instead of relating cohesion funding purely to the EMU convergence criteria (Congress, no. 238, 15 December 1992, p. 12030). Outside the parliamentary arena, both the CCOO and the UGT criticized the considerable reduction in funding from the level agreed at Maastricht. Although much of this criticism could be viewed as part of a politically motivated, premature election campaign, the uncompromising position of González on Spain's financial demands was influenced by the need to present a good deal to his domestic constituency to consolidate their support prior to national elections.

Morán claimed that an overall consensus on European policy still existed in Spain in 1992, arguing that 'el caso español se caracteriza todavía por una menor maduración crítica respecto al proceso europeo…' (the Spanish case is still characterized by a less mature critical outlook with respect to the European process) (*Diario 16*, 24 May 1992). However, the demand for more participation in European policy was coupled with greater awareness of EU obligations at a time of economic recession. A united position was even difficult to achieve within central administration once the concerted effort to attain a coordinated policy on EC accession was over. For example, the Ministry of Economy and Finance argued for an increase in ERDF funding, while the Social Affairs Ministry was concerned that this increase was not to the detriment of the ESF, thus leading to internal wrangling over Spanish priorities (*El País*, 24 January 1992).

Conclusions

Despite the presentation in the domestic arena of the negotiation at Brussels in 1988 and Edinburgh in 1992 as major victories for Spain, the Spanish government wanted to avoid being labelled as a *demandeur* of increasing amounts of funding at EU level. González affirmed that the defence of Spain's interests in the area of cohesion policy had been demanded by all political groups, but that it was not 'un elemento decisorio de la solución de nuestros problemas respecto de nuestra aproximación a los índices de prosperidad de la Comunidad Europea' (a decisive element for the solution of our problems in meeting the European Community's indicators of prosperity) (Congress, no. 204, 1 July 1992, p. 10049). By reconciling its key role as a pro-integrationist player at EU level with its strong defence of national interests, the Spanish government sought to deflect potential criticism from other member states. On 26 November 1992, the Secretary of State for the EU declared in the Joint Committee for the EU that the government would ultimately opt for further European integration rather than concrete benefits for Spain (Ministerio de Asuntos Exteriores, 1992, p. 771), indicating that European unity should not be endangered by Spain's tough negotiating tactics. The Spanish government also wanted to avoid raising overly high expectations in the domestic arena regarding transfers of funding from the EU, particularly as it had been accused in the plenary following the Lisbon Summit of using Europe and Maastricht as scapegoats for the failure of its national economic policies (Congress, no. 204, 1 July 1992, p. 10042). A delicate balance between domestic and EU objectives thus had to be achieved whereby central government could succeed in consolidating its bargaining power and standing in both arenas.

Evidence from the analysis in this chapter points to a clear interstate bargaining framework where central government enjoys a high level of autonomy even when domestic pressures for an optimal deal on EU funding have increased. The negotiation of funding and distribution of resources were purely central state-run operations, even where interstate bargains potentially conflicted with the domestic groups it was representing. The input of the domestic arena was reduced to criticism of policy decisions following the bargaining process at EU level. One official referred to the key role of González and the importance of his personal convictions regardless of pressure from the recipients of funding at regional level, especially in the first years of EC membership.[14] Negotiations at intergovernmental level among national executives thus enhanced the central state's autonomy *vis-à-vis* other domestic actors. The closed nature of the EU opportunity structure during the decision-making phase meant that even strong, unambiguous demands, increasingly articulated as a result of the opening of the opportunity structure in the domestic arena, had little impact on the central state's bargaining position at EU level.

Pollack (1995, p. 363) concludes that member states have 'proven adept at retaining their "gatekeeper" status'. At national level, cohesion policy was used to illustrate the visible benefits of EU membership, and to distract attention from domestic economic problems. At EU level, domestic constraints helped to justify Spain's intransigent negotiating position to its counterparts. However, the growing awareness of European issues increasingly obliged member states to act as aggregators of domestic interests to consolidate their power, and construct coalitions in favour of EU membership. This was even the case in an area where backing for central government's negotiating position was unproblematic. An examination of the negotiation of cohesion policy at EU level indicates that regional mobilization has little impact on the policy initiation and decision-making stages of the process. However, a closer examination of subsequent stages of the policy process might be expected to yield more evidence of an increase in subnational involvement. The potential impact of this is the focus of Chapter 5.

5
The Input of Other Domestic Actors to Cohesion Policy

The role of the Spanish central state in the area of cohesion policy is evident from the analysis of negotiations at EC/EU level in Chapter 4. This chapter seeks to broaden the study of the policy area to consider the role of domestic actors other than central government. In view of the potential for an increase in regional mobilization in the EU context, and the importance of the subnational level in the area of cohesion policy, the Spanish regions are a valid focus of enquiry in this chapter. However, the input of other domestic groups, such as key socio-economic actors, is also analysed, and compared with the advances made by regional authorities. Despite key limitations, institutional mechanisms established by the regions to enhance their involvement in the EU policy-making process were shown to represent a significant advance in Chapter 3. This provides a framework for an evaluation of their access to policy-making in a specific issue area in this chapter.

A survey by the Commission (European Commission, 1996e, p. 61) in EU member states concluded that the highest level of enthusiasm for greater regional input to EU policy-making existed in Southern Europe, for example some 83 per cent of those surveyed in Spain. However, the nature of the opportunity structures at EU and domestic levels did not enhance subnational involvement at all stages of the policy process. Many analysts have highlighted the essentially centralized nature of the cohesion policy process, resulting in the central state's retention of its control at key points of the negotiation. For example, Morata and Xavier Muñoz (1996, p. 196) adopt a sceptical attitude regarding an increase in regional participation in the case of Spain, on account of 'the dominant role played by national authorities in fixing priorities and managing Euro-funds'. However, as established in

Chapter 1, other analysts consider that the multi-level governance framework is far more appropriate for an examination of areas such as cohesion policy. For example, Hooghe (1995) emphasizes the development of partnership between the EU, central and regional administrative levels, which has resulted in an acceleration of subnational mobilization since the mid-1980s, particularly during the implementation phase of structural funding. The divergent conclusions of key analysts on the role of the central state and other domestic actors in the implementation of cohesion policy are evaluated following the analysis of the specific case of Spain in this chapter.

The chapter pays particular attention to the case of Andalusia as the beneficiary of the highest level of Objective One funding, and to the ERDF as the largest source of funding in the region. The ERDF was created in 1975 and aimed to 'redress the principal regional imbalances in the Community through participating in the development and structural adjustment of regions whose development is lagging behind and in the conversion of declining industrial regions' (Article 130c).

Reform of the structural funds

As well as a substantial increase in the amount of funding (see Chapter 4), the operational rules of the structural funds underwent a fundamental reform in 1988. In Article 130d of the SEA, the Commission was asked to present a proposal for a reform of the structural funds to the Council and, in February 1987, it outlined the major developments it advocated in the document 'The Single Act: A new frontier for Europe' (the so-called 'Delors I' package) (European Commission, 1987a). In June 1988, the Council of Ministers approved the legal base for the reform, and implementing legislation for the ERDF was passed on 19 December 1988, coming into force on 1 January 1989.[1]

The 1988 reform could be regarded as the first attempt to impose uniform procedures for regional policy on all member states. It sought to make structural actions more consistent with member states' economic policies, and to improve the administration of the funds through multi-annual budgetary planning, greater simplification and flexibility, and more efficient monitoring of operations. The reform also referred to the additionality of EC resources which should not replace national funding. The 1988 reform established the Community aspects of the policy area, thus enhancing the power of the Commission by, for example, allowing it to use 15 per cent of ERDF resources for its own initiatives without Council of Ministers approval (Lázaro, 1991a, pp. 80–1). The key innovation in 1988, relevant to the focus of this chapter, was the introduction of the concept of partnership, which can be viewed as the basis of the reform as it determines the implementation of the other principles (European Commission, 1989c, p. 14). According to the framework regulation, the principle is 'established through close consultations between the Commission, the Member State concerned and the competent authorities designated by the latter at national, regional, local or other level, with each party acting as a partner in pursuit of a common goal'. The reform was intended to shift the balance of power between actors at different levels of administration in relation to the planning, implementation and monitoring of the structural funds. A speech made by Delors to a meeting of Objective Two regions in July 1991 expressed the view that 'Nous voulons favoriser ce partenariat pour une raison simple: nous croyons qu'aujourd'hui, penser le développement c'est plus une affaire des agents locaux qu'une affaire de l'échelon central' (We want to promote this partnership for one simple reason: we believe that development today is more an issue for local agents rather than for actors at central level).[2] According to the principle of partnership, regional authorities are given a key collaborative role in the implementation of programmes. The principle reflects the concept of subsidiarity, according to which initiatives should only be taken at EU level where the objectives of the proposed action cannot be adequately achieved nationally. Firstly, the Commission intended that regional authorities should be fully involved in the drawing up of Regional Development Plans (RDPs), where maximum consultation with the competent authorities designated by the member state was recommended for their preparation, although the final plan would be presented by central administration. Secondly, the adoption of programmes through negotiation of the Community Support Framework (CSF) with the Commission should include representatives of all the regions in its meetings. Thirdly, the objective was to encourage subnational actors to participate fully in the implementation stage, involving the drawing up of operational programmes (OPs) and the monitoring and assessment of projects. Separate regional multi-annual plans were intended to encourage a greater role for regional monitoring committees.

The six revised regulations for the structural funds for the period 1994–9, adopted by the Council of Ministers on 20 July 1993, maintained or strengthened the major principles adopted in the 1988 reform. Article 4 of the amended framework regulation[3] advocates the participation of socio-economic actors as well as regional and local authorities, although 'in full compliance with the respective institutional, legal and financial powers of each of the partners' (European Commission, 1996a, p. 17). The seventh annual report on the structural funds in 1995 (European Commission, 1996b, p. 229) recognized that participation depended on member states' institutional structure, highlighting the fact that 'the effective operation of the regional partnership in the context of the Structural Funds is influenced of course by this institutional and political diversity'. A further factor which led to inadequate implementation of the partnership concept was its lack of clear definition which permitted a variety of interpretations (Smith, 1995, p. 133). In practice, central government could use its interpretation to limit the input of other actors to the process, which was still the case in the 1999 reform despite an attempt at a more explicit definition (Bache, 1998, p. 141).

Analysts considered that national policy-makers became increasingly concerned about the influence of the Commission during the 1989–93 period, and thus attempted to reinforce their position in the 1993 reforms (see Wishlade, 1996, p. 55). In 1993, member state priorities and national statistical data were emphasized in the designation of areas eligible for funding, thus shifting the focus towards the national level. Even if Marks (1996, pp. 395–6) argues that the 1993 reform enhanced the role of the Commission as arbiter at the centre of the policy process in view of increased competition between member states, and between regional authorities, a move towards greater control of the process by member states was evident. It is significant that, in many respects, this was further strengthened in the 1999 reform. For example, the reduction in Community initiatives from 13 to four indicated a reduced Commission role, as well as less Commission involvement in partnership activities.

Institutional framework

The level of access to policy-making for key actors is determined by the nature of the institutional framework at domestic and EU levels, and the degree of willingness of EU and central government actors to accept greater domestic participation. This framework is examined here prior to a detailed analysis of the policy process.

European Union

The EU's regional policies and cohesion are the responsibility of Directorate-General (DG) XVI of the Commission. It deals exclusively with regional issues and has full responsibility for relations between the Commission and the General Affairs Council (Smith, 1995, p. 454). Furthermore, it is responsible for managing the largest amounts of funding, namely for Objective One and Two areas. The DG has thus been described as 'the informal leader of cohesion policy' (Hooghe, 1996b, p. 90). The political importance of DG XVI was enhanced by the firm support of Delors throughout his Presidency, the high priority given to the DG by Commissioner Bruce Millan, and the appointment of a close colleague of Delors, the Spanish socialist Eneko Landaburu, as Director-General in 1986 (Smith, 1995, p. 456). During the reorganization of its structure in 1994, DG XVI acquired responsibility for the Cohesion Fund, and for relations with the Committee of the Regions from the Secretariat General, which further boosted its budget and range of competencies.

DG XVI is extensively involved in the negotiation of the allocation of funding, the priorities of the programmes, and the implementation of policy. In 1997, the DG, consisting of approximately 200 A-grade civil servants, was divided into seven directorates which are shown in Figure 5.1. A large number of experts seconded from their member states are based in the DG (30 per cent of the A-level Commission staff

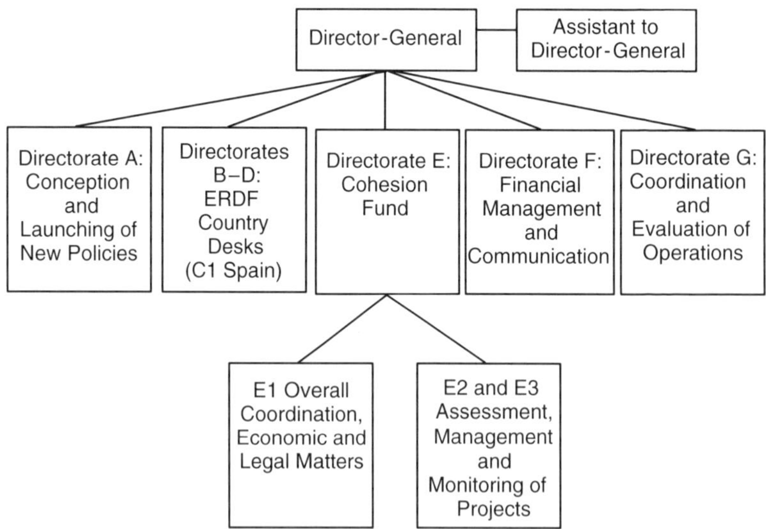

Figure 5.1 Structure of Directorate-General XVI (Cohesion and Regional Policies), European Commission.

in early 1993) which, as well as potentially enhancing member state influence on policy, also leads to a high level of in-house expertise (Hooghe, 1996b, p. 108). The implementation unit responsible for Spain has around the same number of administrators as other countries such as Ireland, despite the higher level of funding received. The low number of EU officials responsible for Spain increases the likelihood of greater responsibility being given to Spanish central and regional governments for the administration of projects. This development is more probable than an expansion of the division at EU level according to one DG XVI official.[4] Enhanced national and regional input is also likely in view of the increasing priority given by the Commission to strengthening its policy conceptualization at the expense of project administration carried out by traditional desk officers (Hooghe, 1996b, p. 104).

The European Commission is a significant autonomous actor in the promotion of greater regional participation. Its powerful agenda underlying the 1988 reform was hardly altered in the Council of Ministers. Hooghe (1996b, pp. 99–100) describes how 'the insular drafting, the backing of Jacques Delors, the timing, and the careful selection of the negotiation team suggest that the Commission had not been acting on behalf of the states', thus highlighting its 'monopoly of initiative on the institutional design'. However, operationalizing the concept of partnership was problematic, exacerbated by competing interests within the Commission which did not always allow a clear-cut policy on subnational participation (see Hooghe, 1996b, pp. 93–5). The changing opportunity structure at EU level thus depended, to some extent, on the balance of power within the Commission's administration.

Other EU institutions have sought to enhance regional input to the policy process, although their influence has been relatively limited. The European Parliament has frequently called for a strengthening of the partnership principle. Although the influence of its proposals on the policy process remains limited,[5] it frequently acts as an effective mediator between EU institutions and regional authorities, thus creating the possibility of bypassing central government structures, even if the central state still retains its key role in the funding process. The Committee of the Regions[6] is regularly consulted on economic and social cohesion. It demanded greater regional participation in the Cohesion Fund in its plenary session of 5 April 1994 (*El País*, 6 April 1994), and its own-initiative opinion of 20 July 1995 (Committee of the Regions, 1995) called for greater regional and local participation in the structural funds. In 1997, the Committee (Committee of the Regions,

1997) advocated the Commission's reinforcement of the partnership principle at the programming stage. However, despite a Commission communication in April 1995 on a potentially stronger consultative role for the Committee of the Regions, its influence is restricted to a limited advisory role (European Commission, 1996a, p. 35).

Central government

The Ministry of Economy and Finance has the most involvement in European policy along with the Ministry of Foreign Affairs, largely because it is the general coordinating agency for all EU structural funds and initiatives. Within the ministry, the structural funds are coordinated by the DG for Analysis and Budgetary Programming, as shown in Figure 5.2. The sub-DG for Administration of the ERDF is responsible for the implementation of funding and constitutes a permanent Secretariat for the preparation of documentation in conjunction with regional authorities, including the organization of monitoring committees (Instituto de Desarrollo Regional, 1997a, pp. 614–15). It is significant that the Secretariat of State for Foreign Policy and the EU only has a secondary role in the funding process, and that the Ministry of Economy and Finance frequently has direct contact with the Permanent Representation in Brussels on cohesion policy issues.[7]

The centralized funding process initially established by Madrid, where central government is responsible for the proposal of programmes and requests for payment to the Commission, the authorization of any modification of projects, the administration of ERDF receipts and the transfer of funding to the appropriate authority, has not changed substantially during EC/EU membership. The number of officials responsible for EU funding at central level is still very small, and interviewees in Brussels highlighted the lack of resources for more global thinking on regional policy, given the huge administrative and technical workload, and the non-involvement of the Ministry of Public Administration in the EU funding process.[8] The participation of regional authorities, especially for the implementation of projects, was therefore needed in view of the limited resources at central level.

Ministry of Economy and Finance officials consider that the transfer of all information and resources should be via central government, and that the development of multilateral relations between the Commission and regional actors would not enhance the functioning of the system.[9] According to a Ministry official, 'the state is finally responsible and central control and co-ordination are essential'.[10] Central

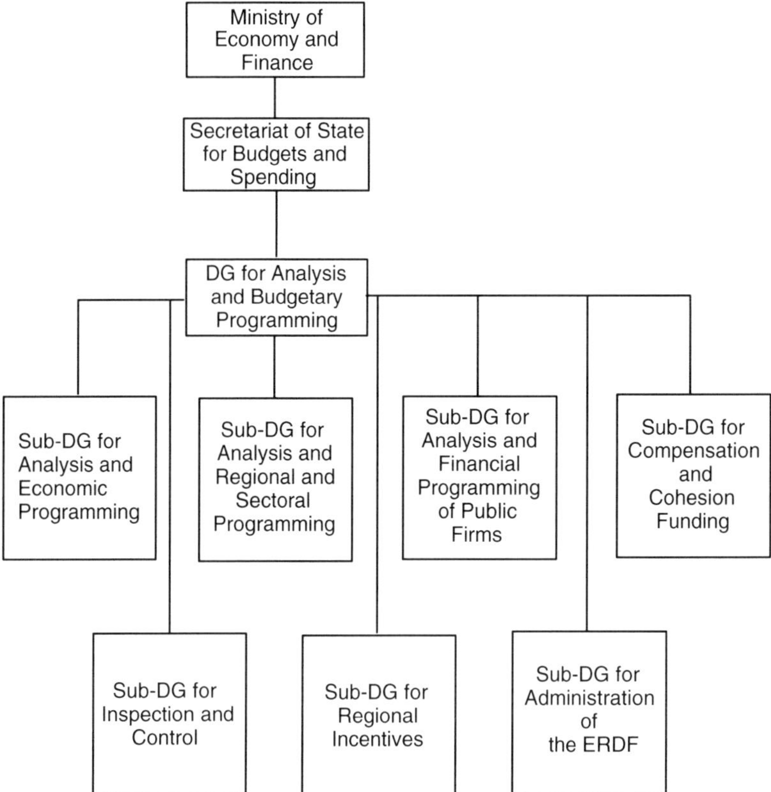

Figure 5.2   Organization of structural funding at central level.

government officials consider that the regions have generally seemed satisfied with the negotiation of funding by the Spanish government at EU level (see Chapter 4), suggesting that this acceptance has increased rather than diminished as regional authorities have acknowledged the importance of a coordinated, national approach.[11] However, continued tensions over the distribution of resources and responsibilities are inevitable, even if resistance to greater regional input in central administration has declined during EC/EU membership.

Regional government

Raffaella Nanetti (1996) describes the new industrial model where the region becomes an active participant in the development process, gains a proactive role in policy formulation and is increasingly recognized as the appropriate level for development planning. The process of learning the complex funding procedures has been important in increasing regional capacity to participate in the process. Growing demands for information, and a greater subnational input, can no longer be resisted by member states in policy areas within regional competencies. The learning process at regional level could thus be ultimately more important for enhancing subnational involvement than reform at EU level (Ordovas Blasco, 1989, p. 94). Regional governments are increasingly taking the opportunity to lobby the EU institutions directly rather than relying on central government to lobby on their behalf.

In the case of Andalusia, only one person in the regional administration was responsible for ERDF funding when Spain joined the Community.[12] In 1987, a Comité Técnico de Coordinación para asuntos relacionados con las Comunidades Europeas (Technical Committee for Coordination of European Community Affairs) was created to coordinate European policy, including the structural funds. The regional government attempted to enhance the standing of the Committee in 1988 by attaching its Secretariat to the regional Presidency, but the capacity of the institutional structure established for the EU funding process remained limited. The new structure of the Committee was partly in response to the greater opportunities for regional participation in the 1988 reform of the structural funds. Further significant institutional changes were not made until 1996, when the new PP government created the DG for European Funding within the Ministry of Economy and Finance, as shown in Figure 5.3. The DG groups together the three structural funds for the first time, and is responsible for the evaluation of all structural funding and the management of the ERDF. The management of ESF and EAGGF funding is carried out in the Ministries of Employment and Social Affairs, and Agriculture respectively.

Regional participation from 1986 to 1988

Regional authorities were described as the absentees in EC regional policy by one analyst in 1984, in view of the fact that central government was responsible both for sending the regional plans to the Commission, and for monitoring their implementation (Granell, 1984, pp. 38–9). The Commission was concerned about the marginalization of regional authorities and had already proposed their greater involvement in 1981, for example through the elaboration of regional plans, and the direct receipt of funding for projects which were within their

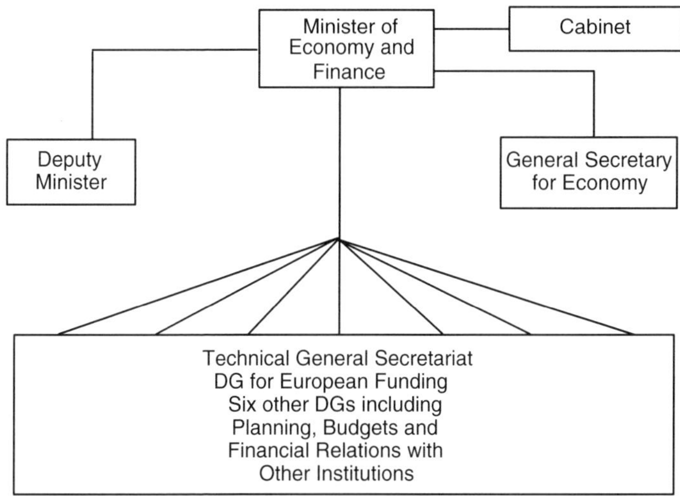

Figure 5.3   Organization of structural funding at regional level.

area of responsibility (Granell, 1984, p. 39). Although a more effective relationship between the Commission and regional authorities had been recommended in the 1984 ERDF reform, advisory bodies such as the Committee for Regional Policy still only consisted of national and Commission representatives. Central government enjoyed a high degree of autonomy until 1988; as Hooghe (1996a, p. 2) describes, 'essentially the European Commission wrote a cheque and the individual state executives cashed it'. The result was that funding became the instrument of national rather than European policy-making, whereby 'governments tended to regard ERDF commitments as a welcome but unexpected windfall which could most usefully be employed to mitigate the national budgetary implications of regional policy incentives'. The fixed national quotas enabled governments to filter project applications and thus enhance their predominant role in the funding process (Scott, 1995, pp. 17–18).

Spain presented its first regional plan to the EC in July 1985, under the coordination of the Ministry of Economy and Finance, in order to be able to take full advantage of EC resources from the beginning of its membership. The capacity of new member states to obtain and manage EC funding in their first year had been limited during previous enlargements, and Spain thus applied for funding for national projects which already existed, and where EC transfers could merely substitute national funding. According to EC guidelines on the formulation of regional plans, the law establishing the 1985 budget set 31 January 1985 as the deadline for the approval of a common methodology. The list of eligible regions and development plans were presented by central government to the Commission for its approval, although the Autonomous Communities had contributed to the formulation of the sections dedicated to their region (Lázaro, 1986, p. 150). However, all EC funding went to the national budget during the first year, which was regarded as important for the reduction of its deficit of 4.5 per cent of GDP in 1986. This led to tensions between central government and regional authorities, illustrated by the criticism of the government openly expressed in Valencia and Catalonia (Hildenbrand, 1987, p. 138). The system was considered provisional until the revision of the financial system of the Autonomous Communities was completed, and it was agreed that a definitive plan would be presented during 1986 which would aim to cover the 1986–90 period.

The agreement on financing of the Autonomous Communities on 7 November 1986 created an automatic mechanism which allowed the participation of regions with territories eligible for EC funding. The level of financing was up to a maximum of 30 per cent of the resources received from the FCI. While all the projects were the responsibility of central administration in 1986, the management of ERDF funding was already changing from 1987, when projects within regional competencies were presented and approved at subnational level (Lázaro, 1988, pp. 13–14). However, the absence of guidelines for the distribution of funding during the early years gave central government a significant weight in the policy process (Conejos i Sancho, 1993, p. 327). Central administration continued to initiate and coordinate the funding of projects, largely because of its wider experience and more established contacts with the Commission. Furthermore, only a minority of the more active regions, such as Catalonia and the Basque Country, demanded greater involvement and direct contact with the Commission. Regions such as Andalusia focused on maximizing the amount of resources received, and were little concerned, at least initially, about gaining an input to the policy process.[13]

Development of regional participation since 1988

From 1988, greater knowledge and experience of the funding process, coupled with reform of the structural funds, enhanced the prospects for regional participation throughout the EU. Spanish regions sought to develop their status as interlocutors of the Commission in the implementation of regional policy, particularly in the operationalization of programmes. The collaborative effort between central and regional authorities was intensified, especially in the formulation of RDPs, as illustrated by the increased number of bilateral and multilateral meetings. However, authorities complained about the lack of time for consultation, given the speed with which they had to present the plans. Many regions also highlighted the long delays for the Commission's approval of RDPs, during which time it was difficult to get information from EC officials on progress made. Although the three multi-regional sub-CSFs were directly managed by central government, nine regional sub-CSFs for Objective One were the responsibility of the appropriate regional authority. According to a government official in Madrid, subnational authorities enjoyed complete autonomy in the operationalization of projects within their competencies once the budget had been decided, and were thus free to decide on projects in conjunction with the Commission without the interference of central government.[14]

Despite increased regional involvement, the central state continued to retain control during key stages of the funding process, as illustrated by its responsibility for sending an indicative budget to each regional government. Although authorities then responded with their preliminary programmes and the proposed level of funding, central government had the final say on the use of funding. The formulation of the RDP was still ultimately the responsibility of the Ministry of Economy and Finance, where changes could be made to the regional programmes before their presentation to the Commission (Morata and Muñoz, 1996, p. 206). Furthermore, although the individual negotiation of the CSF with each region facilitated greater involvement, regional participation in the negotiation of the CSF with the Commission remained limited. The Commission and central administration organized separate meetings to discuss overall distribution or major modifications, and the regions were generally excluded from final decisions.[15] The distribution of funding between the Spanish regions, the most politicized stage of the policy process, was determined by the Commission in consultation with the member state government which retained its central moderating role. The criteria used were similar to those used for distribution between member states to maximize objectivity, and the decision was then presented a posteriori to the regions for their approval.

However, the level of regional awareness of the process had increased, and coordination mechanisms sought to ensure that full account was taken of the level of competency at regional level.

Maximizing their access points to the policy process was a key objective for regional authorities. Officially, the Committee for Public Investment, created by the Secretariat of State for Economic Programming within the Ministry of Economy and Finance, is the forum for coordination between central and regional administrative levels. It provides the regions with the opportunity to be fully involved, although the final decision rests with central government. The Committee meets officially only on exceptional occasions, for example when the RDP is presented to the Commission. However, this is only the formal name, which appears in the Official State Gazette, for far more regular meetings coordinated by the Ministry, which essentially involve the same group of representatives although an official meeting is not called under this name. Regional sectoral meetings (see Chapter 3) are the instruments of coordination most often used for determining the level of regional responsibility for OPs within different sectors. Plans can be established in the absence of the Autonomies in policy areas where the state has exclusive competency, but regional authorities are mostly informed of decisions taken. Meetings between central and regional administrations on economic issues, known as Foros de Economía y Política Regional (Regional Policy and Economy meetings), also occur every three to four months, where regional and central governments can exchange information and discuss developments on a range of economic issues including regional policy. Meetings between subnational and central governments existed prior to EC accession, for example a working group of regional and central representatives was created on 21 December 1984 for the formulation of regional plans, but the level of information exchange and discussion has developed considerably during membership.

The evaluation phase of the process provided Spanish regional authorities with the opportunity to develop a greater input in view of the need for their technical expertise. The monitoring committees are a mechanism for facilitating the functioning of the partnership principle at both national and regional levels. Committees meet at least twice a year for each form of assistance, allowing involvement of regional and local partners. The annual report on the structural funds for 1995 (European Commission, 1996b, p. 229) considered that monitoring committees were functioning well, and that their operating procedures permitted regional and local partners to become more involved than previously. Regional authorities could participate in the committees at subnational level for the multi-regional plans for Objectives One and Two. However, despite the increase in regional participation, strict time limits for the monitoring of projects tended to discourage the full participation of all partners. Furthermore, the complexity of procedures, depending on the particular sector and level of cooperation, inhibited full subnational involvement, a view put forward by the Committee of the Regions (1995). Key problems were the lack of strict legal requirements for the membership of committees, which allowed each member state to determine their composition, and a shortage of technical resources, which limited the effectiveness of evaluation at regional level. According to the Commission's first report on economic and social cohesion (European Commission, 1996c, p. 121), the operation of partnership in monitoring committees across the EU was only just beginning to contribute creatively to problem analysis. Furthermore, the concept of evaluation was a far less established aspect of the policy process in Spain than in other member states (Smith, 1995, p. 333).

Single Programming Documents (SPDs), incorporating both the development plan and the relevant financing request, have been increasingly used in EU cohesion policy in an attempt by the Commission to simplify the policy process. The plans may be expected to reduce subnational input in view of lesser access for the Commission and regional authorities to the member state's formulation of the single proposal. However, the view of Spanish central government officials is that its capacity to obtain information on projects from the regions, and thus retain full control of the process, has been diminished by the use of SPDs. The Spanish government thus decided to retain CSFs for Objectives One and Two, which was not strongly opposed by regional authorities.[16] SPDs are viewed by central administration as a threat to central government's autonomy, and a further attempt by the Commission to strengthen the role of both supranational and subnational actors. According to a former official of the Ministry of Economy and Finance, the real interest of the Commission was to decrease the monopoly over the policy instruments held by central administration, and give the regions a decision-making capacity not permitted in the EC Treaty (Lázaro, 1991a, p. 87). The resistance of the Spanish government to the Commission's interference in its domestic arena is reflected in the speech in the Joint Committee for the EU in 1992 by the Secretary of State for the EU, Westendorp, when he questions the Commission's right to decide on the institutional arrangements within each member state (Ministerio de Asuntos Exteriores, 1992, p. 771). During the negotiation of the CSF for the 1994–9 period, central government officials criticized the Commission for insisting on greater contact with the regions than during the previous period.[17]

Despite the gradual inroads made by the Spanish regions into the policy process, the Autonomous Communities, particularly Catalonia and the Basque Country, were still highly critical of the overly centralized funding system. For example, in April 1993, the PNV spokesperson in the Congress, Iñaki Anasagasti, put forward a proposal in the parliament for greater subnational input to EU regional policy, criticizing the financial centralization of the state (Congress, Series D, no. 400, 2 April 1993, pp. 11–12). PNV representatives proposed regional CSFs, as well as direct financial relations between the Commission and regional administrations, claiming that subnational authorities had a far better knowledge of specific projects than central government. Demands for more regional participation were also frequently articulated by the CiU which, in the Joint Committee for the EU in February 1995, called for greater account to be taken of regional competencies in the management of funding, and criticized decisions taken in advance by the state on quotas for each level (Congress, no. 63, 13 February 1995, pp. 1276–7).

Comparison of the 1989–93 and 1994–9 funding cycles

Taking into account both the criticism of the lack of access to key points of the policy process highlighted by regional authorities, and the advances made towards fuller articulation of the partnership principle, the two cycles of structural funding, 1989–93 and 1994–9, can usefully be compared with a view to drawing conclusions on the extent to which the nature of the policy process has changed in the case of Spain. The Regional Plan for Spanish Objective One regions for the period 1989–93 was presented to the Commission on 30 March 1989, and the Commission approved the CSF on 31 October 1989 following a tense period of negotiation from 26 May to 5 September. Although the plans for each of the Objectives were finally presented by central government, the regions were able to have an input to the priorities drawn up. However, many regions still considered that the plan presented in March 1989 lacked adequate regional participation because of the speed with which the 1988 reform had to be implemented, although the Director-General of Planning in the Ministry of Economy and Finance denied that the decision on the destiny of the structural funds was carried out in Spain in a centralized way (*El País*, 4 August

1989). Despite the Commission's pressure on the Spanish government to involve the regions more (it delayed signing Spanish CSFs in 1989 as Spain had not permitted sufficient regional involvement), the regions obtained little input at the CSF negotiation stage (Marks, 1996, pp. 402–3). Analysts of partnership arrangements consider that the concept has far more chance of being put into effect where EU regions have the competencies and capacity to play a full role; despite calls for greater subnational participation, 'some local authorities, notably in Objective One member states, admitted privately that the implementation of structural fund policies required skills and competencies that exceeded their resources' (Wishlade, 1996, p. 45).

The plan for Objective One regions for the 1994–9 funding cycle was approved by the Spanish government and presented to the Commission on 20 October 1993. The Autonomous Communities were fully involved in the elaboration of the RDP and the setting of priorities, culminating in the meeting on 23 July 1993 of the Committee for Public Investment in which all regional representatives were present. Considerably more bilateral and multilateral meetings with regional authorities took place during the formulation of the RDPs for the 1994–9 funding cycle, partly because more time was allowed for the elaboration of plans. The preparatory negotiations for the CSF began at the start of 1994, and the framework for Objective One for 1994–9 was approved by the Commission on 1 June 1994, and was definitively adopted on 1 July 1994. The Economy Minister affirmed in the Senate Committee of Economy and Finance in June 1994 that the amount of funding received directly by the Autonomous Communities represented a significant proportion of the regional budget (Senate, no. 119, 27 June 1994, p. 6). Furthermore, the Ministry of Economy and Finance made a greater effort in the 1994–9 period to indicate, a priori, the distribution of the multi-regional financing initially received by central government, a significant development considering the conflict with regional authorities caused by its reluctance to regionalize the funding in the previous cycle. The operationalization of the programmes involved greater direct regional contact with the EU level; regular transfers of information between regional authorities and the Commission were not always sent via Madrid, and meetings between regional and EU officials became more common, although a representative from central government would, generally, also be present.[18]

Access to the policy process was still limited for subnational authorities, one illustration being the reluctance of Spanish central government to allow regional participation in monitoring committees for the

Interreg programme, despite the active subnational role in its implementation and the fact that national funding only amounted to around 35 per cent of the total.[19] Nonetheless, an evaluation by the Commission (European Commission, 1996b, p. 229) indicated a broader level of regional participation than during the previous programming period, which was also the opinion of the Committee of the Regions (1995). However, despite some consolidation of the partnership principle, a comparison of the two funding cycles does not reveal a transformation of the process in the Spanish case, or a considerably reduced role for the central state, but highlights some advances made by Spanish regions towards having a greater input to tł e policy process. The transfer of structural funds is still essentially a centralized operation, but the central state's full control of all stages of the process is no longer guaranteed.

As well as these general findings, the distribution of resources between central and regional authorities could be expected to act as a more concrete indicator of the potential increase in regional participation during the 1994–9 funding cycle. This can be illustrated by comparing the distribution of Objective One funding between the levels of Spanish administration during the two funding periods. The CSF for Objective One during 1989–93 (including ESF and EAGGF as well as ERDF) indicates that approximately 33 per cent of the funding was earmarked for programmes under the competency of the Autonomous Communities (Conejos i Sancho, 1993, p. 336). During 1994–9, the CSF for Objective One granted around 33.75 per cent of the total of structural fund resources to regional governments (Ministerio de Economía y Hacienda, 1995, p. 89), thus indicating that the distribution of funding between regional and central authorities has not changed significantly between the 1989–93 and 1994–9 periods. Similarly, Andalusia obtained approximately 10.5 per cent of the total of Objective One funding for the 1989–93 period, and around 10.6 per cent in the 1994–9 cycle. This is supported by a study by Marks et al. (1996b), which finds no evidence for a resource pull hypothesis whereby the active lobbying of subnational governments at EU level can influence the distribution of funding.

The case of Andalusia

The formulation of the regional plan at domestic level for Andalusia for 1987–90 was carried out in very different circumstances from that drawn up in 1984–6, according to an evaluation of Andalusia's regional policy for the Commission by the Instituto de Desarrollo

Regional (Institute for Regional Development) (1997a, p. 56) in Seville. Not only were the economic circumstances more favourable, but considerable adaptation to EC norms was compulsory following accession to the Community. Furthermore, in 1986, most competencies in the Statutes of Autonomy had been transferred to the regions. The Economic Development Plan for Andalusia for 1991–4 was again formulated in a different context, given the added knowledge of the funding process, the learning experience within the EC and the expansive economic cycle. International economic changes and the creation of the Single Market were realities to which Andalusia was forced to adapt, the key objective being greater economic growth in order to catch up with other regions. A report in 1997 by the Instituto de Desarrollo Regional (1997a, p. 59) concluded that the plan was produced by a mature administration which enjoyed wide competencies, and had long experience of government.

In the case of Andalusia, regional reform was particularly urgent because of the extent of its economic crisis, which had been exacerbated by the lack of action to combat key problems by central government (Instituto de Desarrollo Regional, 1997a, p. 53). The Andalusia government considered the development of an administration with the capacity to deal with the region's underdevelopment to be a key priority, including the management of European funding. Only a relatively small number of officials are responsible for EU funding at subnational level, although the regional administration relies on the expertise of a large number of external analysts to monitor and evaluate projects effectively. The new DG for European Funding (see Figure 5.3), created in 1996, did not expand the division significantly, but its creation reflected the increased priority given to the management of the structural funds.

Despite greater organization at regional level, contradictions between the finalized regional plan and the economic priorities highlighted by regional government were used by Andalusia government officials to demonstrate the lack of collaboration between central and regional levels of administration (Rodríguez de la Borbolla, 1989, p. 570). However, evidence exists for some development of a division of labour between central and regional governments, as a consequence of both decentralization and the impact of the EU on policy formation. The Ministry of Economy and Finance in Andalusia is responsible for formulating its RDP and the regional sub-CSF, fixes the financial priorities and is responsible for the coordination of programmes in conjunction with central administration. However, officials in Madrid stressed the key role they played in the coordination of EU funding for Andalusia, given that mechanisms at regional level remained inadequate.[20] Furthermore, despite evidence of greater regional input, interviews at subnational level suggested that the partnership principle had a limited impact on the nature of the policy process. An administrator in the DG for European Funding in Andalusia was sceptical of 'concepts such as partnership used in Brussels which are very distant from the reality of the process in the regions', considering that central government's continued control of the process was accepted by the Andalusia administration.[21]

The establishment of Andalusia's regional office in Brussels as an official delegation in 1995 (Law 164/1995 of 27 June), managed since its creation in February 1991 by the regional development agency Instituto de Fomento de Andalucía (IFA) was symbolically important. It was the first region to apply the outcome of the May 1994 Constitutional court decision on the external representation of the Autonomies (see Chapter 3). However, in general, an economic, more functionally oriented rationale seemed to dominate Andalusia's concept of European policy. The conclusion drawn by Morata and Muñoz (1996, p. 210) that 'administrative "partnership" was mainly financial instead of effective or operational' thus seems relevant for the case of Andalusia. The issue of participation in EU policy-making was more politicized in other Spanish regions, whose level of regional identity and political activity led them to exploit further the opportunities at EU level. The greater lobbying capacity of regions such as Catalonia and the Basque Country even resulted in moves towards regionalization of the Cohesion Fund, which was initially intended to be controlled purely by central government. The achievement of subnational involvement in EU funding earmarked for central government provides an important illustration of the impact on the policy process of regional demands for greater participation.

Regional participation in the Cohesion Fund

The Commission regulation establishing the Cohesion Fund took effect on 26 May 1994, replacing the cohesion financial instrument established on 1 April 1993, which had been a provisional measure in view of the delay in the ratification of Maastricht.[22] Nowhere in the interim instrument or in the Cohesion Fund regulation was reference made to the concept of partnership, and regional participation was similarly absent from guidelines established for the assessment and monitoring of projects. The Spanish government lobbied hard for the establishment of the Fund at intergovernmental level, its link to the EMU criteria lending it a clearly state-centred perspective in contrast to structural funding. Any evidence of a regionalization of the Fund would thus represent a significant evolution.

The Fund is based on three major principles. It provides a financial contribution to member states with a per capita GDP of less than 90 per cent of the EC average; assistance is restricted to the part-financing of projects in the fields of the environment and trans-European transport networks; and it assists member states which have drawn up a programme complying with the conditions on excessive public deficits linked to the implementation of EMU (Article 104c). Funding is conditional on the macro-economic situation, aiming to act as a restraint on lack of budgetary discipline, and to promote continued economic growth. It was argued that the focus on interstate instead of regional cohesion was necessary in the context of EMU, whereby member states lost a large degree of freedom in determining their economic policies[23] (Elorza, 1994, p. 320). The Secretary of State for the EU explained in the Joint Committee for the EU on 12 March 1992 that the Cohesion Fund was an interstate fund which, in keeping with Spanish constitutional arrangements, took regional opinions into account (Ministerio de Asuntos Exteriores, 1992, p. 731). The Economy Minister, Solbes, refused to present the regional distribution of the Cohesion Fund in the Joint Committee for the EU as requested by parliamentary groups in 1994, considering that the 'territorialization' of the Fund should be avoided (Congress, no. 52, 11 October 1994, pp. 1076–7). While the sub-DG for Compensation and Cohesion Funding within the Ministry of Economy and Finance (see Figure 5.2) has responsibility for the coordination and evaluation of the Cohesion Fund, the Autonomous Communities would be expected to have limited participation both in setting priorities, and in the direct management and financing of projects. However, despite the fact that little potential existed for interadministrative collaboration, the contradiction between a nationally oriented fund without a territorial basis, and the level of decentralization of the Spanish state remained. This was particularly the case in policy areas where the regions enjoyed full competencies, for example in the field of the environment.

The Annual Report of the Cohesion Fund (European Commission, 1995a, pp. 92–3) referred to concerns within the Economic and Social Committee and the Committee of the Regions regarding low levels of consultation of local and regional authorities, and key socio-economic actors. The lack of objective criteria for the distribution of funding was repeatedly criticized by regional authorities. Although the regions were initially relatively uninformed about the Cohesion Fund, the considerable amount of funding available led increasingly to written requests for information from the Ministry of Economy and Finance, particularly from the more active regions.[24] A document sent to the regional government in Catalonia by the Ministry of Economy and Finance in 1994 established that projects selected by Autonomous Communities could now be financed by the Fund in agreement with central government (*El País*, 5 July 1994), although it warned against a process of 'territorialization'. However, according to a central government official responsible for the Cohesion Fund, it was intended from the outset that regional authorities would become more involved in the process in an increasingly decentralized state, although the central administration had full control during the first year.[25]

In 1994, central government was obliged to accept a greater recognition of regional competencies in priority areas of the Commission, although the financial allocation was still transferred initially to the national budget. Regional demands for greater participation came to a head in a meeting of the Council for Fiscal and Financial Policy on 21 September 1994, when a decision was taken on subnational participation in the Cohesion Fund. The most active regions in the September meeting were the Basque Country, Navarre and Catalonia, who managed to obtain a common regional agreement on the issue to the effect that the Autonomous Communities would manage 40 000 million pesetas of the funding received from the Cohesion Fund in 1995; 11 000 million pesetas would be set aside for infrastructure projects, and 29 000 million for the environmental field. The agreement was approved in October 1995, and was generally regarded as a first positive step towards greater regional involvement, although Solbes stressed that subnational participation could not continue to increase so that it became detrimental to the central state budget (Congress, no. 52, 11 October 1994, p. 1077).

The impact of the domestic political situation on EU policy is clearly illustrated by the Cohesion Fund. The 21 September 1994 decision can be interpreted as the result of increased leverage of key regions following the 1993 elections (see Chapter 3). The regions most active in their demands for greater participation were also those in receipt of relatively small amounts of Objective One structural funding, namely Catalonia and the Basque Country, which both obtained financing from the Cohesion Fund for a significant number of projects in

1995–6. Other regions have criticized the fact that the most economically advanced regions receive a disproportionately large share of the Cohesion Fund, viewed as a political payment from the government for the support of Catalonia and the Basque Country. Central government's capacity to manipulate its use of the Fund is facilitated by the fact that its guidelines do not highlight the concept of additionality, thus allowing member states to disregard the principle without risk of penalization.

Regional authorities are involved in the Cohesion Fund at a relatively late stage in the process, namely the implementation and evaluation stages. However, demand for greater regional involvement in the earlier planning stages is inevitable according to a DG XVI administrator,[26] even if little potential for further involvement exists. According to a national expert in DG XVI, 'at the end of the day, there is a single interlocutor in the Cohesion Fund for the Commission: the member state'.[27] The largest Cohesion Fund projects are still managed by central government, although the regions try to prioritize environmental projects to maximize their input in areas where they enjoy a higher level of competency.[28] Regional and local participation does not occur in a systematic way, and the Commission is mainly in contact with central administration, as stipulated in the Cohesion Fund regulation. However, the September 1994 agreement facilitated greater regional involvement and direct contact with EU officials. Although welcoming this, Commission officials recognize that it can be more time-consuming and complicated in view of the frequent lack of knowledge of EU funding procedures at subnational level. This particularly caused problems in the first year of participation in 1995, as subnational authorities expected the Cohesion Fund projects to work in a similar way to the ERDF programmes.[29]

Socio-economic actors in Spain have not obtained access to policy-making in the area of the Cohesion Fund. They have made little contact with central government officials regarding the Fund, while the Economic and Social Council has not requested information on projects.[30] A central government official responsible for the Fund denied his opposition to their participation, but considered that, in view of the areas financed by the Fund being in the public sector, their full involvement in the process would indicate participation, and even co-decision, in the state budget;[31] their consultative role via the Economic and Social Council at national level was thus considered adequate. The input of socio-economic actors to EU funding other than the Cohesion Fund may be expected to be greater, given that the priorities of structural funding are more relevant to their interests. However, many institutional obstacles continue to exist at domestic level. This analysis of the level of access to policy-making of trade unions and employers provides a useful contrast with the case of regional authorities.

Access of socio-economic actors to the policy process

Socio-economic actors consider that they have been sidelined from the EU policy-making process during membership (see Chapter 3). The shift towards greater regional participation has not been accompanied by a similar shift in the participation of actors such as trade unions, despite the fact that Article 7 of the Spanish Constitution refers to the role of socio-economic actors in defending and promoting social and economic interests (García Díaz, 1995, p. 79). Although the 1993 reform of the structural funds was generally seen as a fine-tuning of the 1988 reform, one of its innovations was the recommendation of enhanced partnership with socio-economic actors. The 1988 reform had left open the possibility for their inclusion in the principle of cooperation, but their presence was not usual in practice, particularly as the relatively short time within which the CSFs had to be approved meant that consultation, even with regional and local actors, was limited.

The absence of detailed rules defining the nature of participation meant that their involvement was contingent upon the political will of member states (Scott, 1995, pp. 33–4). In one of the final Commission drafts of the reform, the clause on 'institutional norms', which encouraged governments to interpret the cooperation principle restrictively, was omitted, but was then reintroduced following pressure from member states at European Council level.[32] Furthermore, the fact that the type of funding was not clearly specified made it likely that their participation would still be reduced to membership of ESF monitoring committees (CCOO, 1993a, p. 1). The Economic and Social Committee (1994a,b) at EU level criticized the lack of measures established for socio-economic participation, and stressed the need for the support of relevant public authorities at local, regional and national levels. However, the influence of the Committee on the policy process is limited; proposals such as the creation of a single consultative committee for all the funds were largely ignored by the Council and Commission (Economic and Social Committee, 1988, p. 1). Although the Commission expressed willingness to support the participation of key trade unions and employers, their input was largely reduced to its annual obligation to consult them on the EU's structural policy, which clearly indicates the closed nature of the EU opportunity structure for socio-economic actors. However, some advances have been made. A working group, established in 1995, made it possible to bypass the strictly annual nature of the consultation procedure, and turn it into an 'ongoing cooperative process' (European Commission, 1996b, p. 238) and, in 1996, the Commission (European Commission, 1996b) recognized that recent trends indicated a greater willingness to involve socio-economic partners. This was illustrated by the representation of social partners on Objective Three and Four committees in most member states, although participation varied considerably between Objectives and countries.

In Spain, socio-economic actors are not members of the monitoring committees for Objectives One and Two CSFs and OPs. Any formal representation is generally limited to the ESF evaluation committees and, in 1995, the Commission persuaded the Spanish authorities to inform socio-economic partners of the conclusions of the committee evaluating the Objective One CSF. Socio-economic actors were concerned that regional plans, which strongly conditioned the content of the CSFs, were determined by central government priorities, over which they had little, if any, influence (García Díaz, 1995, p. 77). The plans were presented to the Economic and Social Council at national level, where they were discussed by union and business representatives. However, delay in the presentation of plans and the complexity of operational procedures meant that little time was allowed for any in-depth analysis or genuine input to the debate. Socio-economic actors complained of the lack of discussion of the social implications of projects, claiming that their participation was mostly reduced to an informative role when decisions had already been taken. This has also been the criticism of regional evaluation committees, such as the one set up in Andalusia by the pact signed by the regional government, the UGT and CCOO, and the Confederación de Empresarios de Andalucía (Confederation of Andalusia Business Organizations, CEA) in February 1995 (Junta de Andalucía, 1995). However, consultation is considerably more advanced than in other regions, and the Economic and Social Committee (1994b, p. 13) refers to the goodwill shown by the Andalusia regional authority which 'does not seem to have rubbed off on the national authorities as regards the central funds allocated to Andalusia'. The participation of socio-economic actors is dependent on the existence of a tradition of consensus and social dialogue and, even in Andalusia, the influence of socio-economic actors remains limited when major political decisions are taken (Porras Nadales, 1994, pp. 89–90).

The presence of socio-economic actors in Objective One evaluation committees was considered largely unnecessary in view of their minimal involvement in the formulation of regional plans, and their lack of technical expertise in such projects.[33] Evidence would thus seem to suggest a general resistance in the Ministry of Economy and Finance to socio-economic participation. A similar reticence can be found within many regional authorities, for example, in Catalonia, little evidence exists of participation of socio-economic actors in the ERDF Objective Two monitoring committee (Morata and Muñoz, 1996, pp. 211–12). The Commission's 1996 report on economic and social cohesion (European Commission, 1996c, p. 121) proposes distinguishing between decision-making and consultative partners, the former being authorities responsible for co-financing, and the latter being mainly the social partners and interest groups, which 'might allow the political authorities responsible to take a more objective and constructive view of the latter and embrace their involvement more whole-heartedly'.

Although some progress has been made since the 1993 reform of the structural funds, the outcome is uneven, and socio-economic actors remain largely peripheral to the process. Socio-economic participation depends, to a great extent, on the level of commitment to their input at regional and national levels, determined by the institutional norms and practices of each region and member state. A study of the role of trade unions in a regional context, carried out by DG XVI between September 1991 and November 1994, concluded that the subnational level should be seen as an important field of action for trade unions (European Commission, 1996d). The Economic and Social Committee (1994b, p. 17) confirmed this view when it referred to the 'regional authorities' greater amenability to the implementation of Article 4, in contrast with the wariness displayed by the national governments'. However, key socio-economic actors, such as the CCOO (1993a, p. 2), continue to emphasize the importance of direct contact with central government, given that it defines the main lines of economic policy, and has the final say on the formulation of RDPs. The lack of political will to implement the partnership principle in member states remained a major obstacle to the full participation of socio-economic actors. In Spain, the Economic and Social Committee (1994b, p. 12) concluded that 'the national authorities have hitherto taken an extremely centralizing approach to regional development policies'.

Conclusions

During the first years of EC membership, regional participation in the structural funds was limited in Spain, and central administration retained full control of the funding process. However, information exchange and coordinating mechanisms between central and regional authorities have developed during membership. This is a result of the Commission's initiative to encourage subnational participation, greater awareness and capacity at regional level and less resistance within central administration to greater regional input. According to Keating (1997, p. 35), 'regional institutions are important in defining the issues, in mobilizing resources, in providing differential access, in mediating interests and in implementing policy'. Smith (1995, p. 355) concludes that EU funding programmes have had considerable influence on the structure of territorial relations in Spain, describing the funds as 'catalyseurs de la fédéralisation du système politique' (catalysts of the federalization of the political system). Despite the lack of change in distribution of resources between central and regional authorities, the difference between the 1989–93 and 1994–9 funding cycles is essentially one of much enhanced experience, increased resources and greater opportunities for regional participation, most importantly during the implementation stage. The increase in regional involvement was partly the result of the extended time scale for negotiations, and the larger amount of available resources, but the decision rules established at EC/EU level also significantly enhanced the role of regional authorities. This indicates the opening of the opportunity structures at both EU and domestic levels, encouraged by the partnership principle in the 1988 reform. Keating (1997, p. 26) concludes that central states are no longer the privileged arena for all policy areas as they 'may not be able to control the processes they have set in train. New actors and networks may emerge to create a new political game.'

This chapter has sought to capture key elements of a constantly changing policy process where a range of actors other than central government can gain opportunities to participate in a specific policy area.

Changing relations between groups of actors at different administrative levels are illustrated below:

1. *Relations between regional and central government.* Information exchange and more developed coordination mechanisms in the implementation of structural funding enhanced collaboration between regional and central government during EC/EU membership. However, a high level of subnational variation tended to result in a minority of regions maximizing their involvement in the process.
2. *Relations between regional government and the EU level.* Regional authorities were increasingly able to obtain direct contact with officials at EU level although, at key stages of the process, central government still retained its strong national gatekeeper role. However, increased EU resource dependence on the regional level for implementation and evaluation of projects resulted in a more established collaboration between the two levels.
3. *Relations between socio-economic actors and regional government.* Although the Economic and Social Committee highlighted the regional governments' greater acceptance of socio-economic participation in structural funding, key socio-economic actors rarely exploited the opportunities for greater access to policy-making at regional level. Evidence suggests that consultation between unions, employers and the regional government is more advanced in Andalusia than in other regions, as illustrated by the Pact signed in 1995.
4. *Relations between socio-economic actors and central government.* The absence of rules clearly defining the nature of socio-economic participation in structural funding led to restrictive interpretations of the partnership principle by member states. The involvement of socio-economic actors often remained restricted to membership of ESF monitoring committees.
5. *Relations between socio-economic actors and the EU level.* The proposals of the Economic and Social Committee to enhance socio-economic participation at all levels have largely been ignored by the Council and Commission. Although the Commission expressed its determination to increase socio-economic participation, this was largely restricted to annual consultation on structural funding at EU level.

Actors other than central government have thus been able to have an input to the policy process to varying degrees. The marginalization of socio-economic actors reflects their less developed access points to the policy process at national and EU levels. Although the involvement of regional authorities is far greater, an analysis of subnational mobilization is forced to acknowledge the high level of variation between and within member states. Udo Bullmann (1997, p. 17) refers to the asymmetric course of regionalization processes, arguing that participation depends on the strength of the regional government, and key factors such as their economic functions and their methods of democratic participation. The high level of regional variation in Spain carried the risk that only a 'select subset' would be empowered to obtain maximum involvement in the policy-making process (Marks et al., 1996b, p. 63). This is illustrated by the case of Andalusia, where the level of partnership with central and EU levels was less effective than in more politically active regions, thus underlining the danger that an increase in access to the process will exacerbate tensions over resources and competencies. The Castilla and Leon government criticized Catalonia's bid to play a bigger part in the management of the Cohesion Fund, considering that EU financing was being used to achieve domestic political goals rather than the objectives outlined at EU level (*El País*, 3 September 1994). Similar concerns were voiced regarding the distribution of structural funding. Some regions advocated the selection of projects by central government to maintain greater objectivity, for example as expressed by the mayor of Malaga, Pedro Aparicio, in 1994 (*El País*, 28 August 1994). This can be compared with the tensions resulting from the efforts to attain a common regional position in sectoral meetings, as described in Chapter 3. The moderating influence of central government is thus important in reconciling frequently conflicting regional interests (Bachtler, 1997, p. 89), giving it a key role as the only organ able to mediate between different levels of actors, and represent the regions as a whole in an area of 'overlapping competencies, tensions and conflicts' (Marks et al., 1996b, p. 63).

Chapter 1 considered that it was not only the particular policy area and episode which determined the extent of domestic participation, but also the stage of the policy process. Although regional authorities have become involved in the process, the partnership principle only seems to stand a real chance of realization at the implementation and monitoring stages, given the greater demands on regional knowledge and resources to implement detailed projects on the ground. Hooghe (1996a, p. 15) considers that 'who is dominant varies with the phase of policy-making, the policy instrument, and the particular territorial niche'. Marks (1996) outlines the stages of structural programming, highlighting the lesser dependence on regional input during the formulation of RDPs and the negotiation of the CSF, which contrasts with greater subnational participation in the implementation of the OPs and the evaluation of projects. He concludes that 'this ordinal sequence of decreasing functional reliance on subnational government is reflected without exception in the relative strength of subnational actors... across the stages of structural programming within individual countries' (Marks, 1996, p. 408). His conclusions would seem to be borne out in the analysis of the input of Spanish regions at different stages of the process. Although some analysts have tended to dismiss the implementation stage, Smith (1997) underlines its significance as an intensely political process involving bargaining with a wide range of actors outside the big negotiating 'occasions'.

The institutional structure established in each member state has a major impact on the level of regional participation. Despite the progress made towards greater participation in the 1994–9 funding round, regions such as Catalonia, Navarre and the Basque Country still complained about their absence from the negotiation of the allocation of the funding because of remaining obstacles at national level. Distribution of resources between regions within member states was the initiative of central government in conjunction with the Commission, and ratifying policies in the domestic arena tended to be an explanation and justification of decisions already taken. Morata and Muñoz (1996, p. 217) illustrate the Spanish central government's continued hold on the policy process when they describe how it opted for the presentation of global plans for each of the Objectives instead of specific regional CSFs, and prioritized infrastructural projects to minimize subnational input. They conclude that a national approach has largely persisted in Spain, and even Marks (1996, p. 402) acknowledges that the Spanish regions are 'still struggling to institutionalize their influence in the EU'. It is difficult for multi-level analysts to deny the firm evidence for

> the importance in all countries of central administration in the implementation of Structural Funds. This is because of the Commission's lack of administrative capacity and that of the regions, when these exist.... Central governments and administrations can thus not be considered as marginalized by Community regional policy and indeed they sometimes gain in influence over the regions.
>
> (Balme, 1997, p. 73)

Despite moves towards a greater number of access points for subnational actors, and evidence of increased regional mobilization, the central state agrees to share authority to a limited degree and only at certain stages. Subnational authorities may seek to maximize the level of EU funding obtained by their particular region, and exploit the political opportunity structure to enhance their regional autonomy, but central government ultimately enjoys full capacity to formulate a unified national bargaining position at EU level. The central state's role has thus not been significantly reduced by increasing regional input, although the changing nature of the policy-making process, as illustrated by a comparison of the 1989–93 and 1994–9 funding periods, means that its role in the process has had to adapt to a new context. The progress made towards a more decentralized Spanish state, and the enhanced knowledge of EU policy-making at subnational level, are conditions which encourage a greater impact of regional governments on the role of central government in the area of cohesion policy.

Taking into account an increased number of agendas from a wider range of actors requires the insights of the multi-level game perspective to analyse the implementation of structural funding. Although central government continues to control the articulation between the EU and domestic agendas, it may agree to play a weaker role in the implementation and evaluation stages. This is particularly the case where it is more dependent on expertise at regional level to implement projects, even if it refuses to give up its monopoly at other stages of the process. Marks (1997) considers that political actors may agree to disperse authority to subnational or supranational actors for a variety of reasons, such as the need to attain the support of powerful interest groups in the domestic arena. In the case of Spain, the new domestic context, represented by the dependence of central government on regional parties for the survival of its coalition from 1993 to 2000, has facilitated a greater input from the more active regions. This is illustrated by the government's approval of regional involvement in the Cohesion Fund in 1994. However, although regional parties obtained more seats overall in the Congress in the March 2000 elections (the CiU actually obtained one less), the fact that the PP was no longer dependent on the support of regional parties to govern might well indicate a less direct impact on central government policy in the future. This chapter has highlighted the wide range of participating actors and new interactive processes in a constantly changing policy area, thus allowing a more complete analysis of the developing context. However, it also acknowledges the full capacity of the central state to structure the conditions under which domestic actors participate throughout the policy process. As the role of the central state is expected to vary in different policy settings, the conclusions drawn on cohesion policy may not apply in other areas, a hypothesis which is tested by the case of fisheries in Chapters 6 and 7.

6

The Role of the Spanish Central State in the Negotiation of the EU–Morocco Fisheries Agreement

The Spanish government was a key protagonist at EU level in the policy area of fisheries. It played an important role in the renegotiation of the fisheries agreement between the EU and Morocco in 1995, seeking to maximize the defence of its national interests in view of the potentially negative impact of the accord on its fishing sector. Former Agriculture and Fisheries Minister Luis Atienza (1996, p. 12) recognizes the considerable importance of fisheries agreements with non-EU or third countries for the Spanish fishing sector, but also acknowledges that the negotiating process 'no está exento de tensiones de carácter periódico' (is not free from periodic tensions). This chapter focuses on the series of talks in 1995 to renegotiate the 1992 EU fisheries agreement, which caused a high level of tension in the Spanish domestic arena. Central government sought to obtain the optimal deal to present to its fishing sector at domestic level, while being obliged to accept the EU's overall control of the negotiating process. At EU level, Spain had to justify its tough bargaining position *vis-à-vis* Morocco to fellow member states and to the Commission, while seeking to preserve its role as a leading player in the area of Mediterranean policy. The aim is, therefore, to examine the extent to which, in view of the prominent role played by the central government in Spain, an approach which focuses merely on its role seems most appropriate for the analysis. Chapter 7 will then consider the input of key regional and sectoral actors in the domestic arena to the EU bargaining position, and their relations with central government. Conclusions assess the level of participation of key domestic actors, and the capacity of Spanish central government to retain its autonomy during the negotiating process while meeting demands at both domestic and EU levels.

Development of fisheries at EC/EU level

Prior to evaluating the negotiation of the 1995 agreement, an examination of EC/EU fisheries policy, relations between Spain, Morocco and the EC/EU, and previous fishing agreements with Morocco sets the context for the analysis.

Common Fisheries Policy: Spain in the EC/EU

The doubling in size of the Community fishing sector, and an increase of 75 per cent in fishing capacity and 45 per cent in fish consumption, was one result of the accession of Spain and Portugal in 1986. The Accession Treaty set out transitional arrangements, valid until the end of 2002, which guaranteed mutual access to selected fishing areas for EC countries. The CFP focuses on four major areas, namely conservation of stocks, organization of markets, structural measures, and international agreements. Provisions for a CFP were already made in 1957 in the EEC Treaty of Rome and it was established in a transitory form in 1983 before Spain joined the EC (Regulation EEC 170/83 and 171/83), with a view to consolidating it in 1986 on the accession of Spain and Portugal (Regulation EEC 3094/86). The Spanish government considered that the quotas established in the 1983 agreement, negotiated in the absence of Spain, had an extremely negative effect on its fishing sector. EC entry terms have been viewed by one Spanish analyst as 'extraordinariamente duro, largo e irracional' (extraordinarily tough, long and irrational) (Díez-Hochleitner, 1995, p. 15). It was not until eight years after entry that it was agreed that the arrangements for incorporation of the two new members into the CFP should be adjusted by the Council of Ministers,[1] bringing forward the end of the transitional period to 31 December 1995.

Multi-annual guidance programmes, enforcing reductions of up to 20 per cent in fishing effort on member states, were established for the periods 1983–6, 1987–91, 1993–6, and 1997–2002, and measures to assist fisheries were incorporated into the structural fund arrangements in the 1993 reform of the funds (Regulation EEC 2080/93). The various fishery finances available were grouped into one fund, the Financial Instrument for Fisheries Guidance (FIFG), which aims to achieve the objectives of the CFP, while contributing to strengthening economic and social cohesion under Article 130a of the Treaty on European Union (see Chapters 4 and 5 on cohesion policy, and Chapter 7 on regional involvement in FIFG funding). Despite increased measures to assist fisheries, the EU fleet is dependent on agreements with other coastal nations to provide vital access to fishing grounds.

Relations between the EC/EU, Spain and Morocco

Although the Moroccan government feared a deterioration in its relationship with Spain when the Socialists gained power in 1982 (de Larramendi, 1997, p. 405), the PSOE made a major effort to normalize relations. Gillespie (1995, p. 167) argues that the links between Spain and Morocco were diversified and intensified during the Socialist term of office, the beginning of top-level summits from 1990 being one illustration. Two issues, fisheries, and the enclaves of Ceuta and Melilla, were those most likely to cause tensions between Spain and Morocco (Sehimi, 1996, pp. 110–11). The issue of Morocco's claims on Spain's populated enclaves in its territories, the coastal towns of Ceuta and Melilla, caused less tension in the early 1990s, although proposals to grant them Autonomy Statutes in 1994 aroused strong reactions in Morocco.

Spain lobbied in the early 1990s for a restricted free trade agreement between Morocco and the Community. However, Spanish sectors set to lose most from increased competition from Morocco, such as citrus fruit, vegetables and textiles, opposed the agreement. Direct competition between Moroccan and Spanish products led to a deterioration in their relations (de Larramendi, 1997, p. 416). The lobbying power of key Spanish sectors can be illustrated by the final declaration of the EuroMediterranean (EuroMed) conference in Barcelona in November 1995,[2] which was cautious regarding preferential access for fruit and vegetables from non-EU Mediterranean countries, particularly as the overall level of imports from these countries into Spain had tripled over the previous 15 years (Bataller Martín and Jordán Galduf, 1997, pp. 143–8). Morocco feared losing its markets as a result of Spain's EC entry, and therefore reinforced its efforts to establish closer relations with the Community. This was illustrated by its second application for EC membership in July 1987, which was rejected by the Council of Ministers on 15 September (de Larramendi, 1997, pp. 275–6). A protocol was signed by the EC and Morocco referring to Spain and Portugal's accession on 26 May 1988, which ensured the same terms for the entry of Moroccan agricultural products into the EC as for Spanish and Portuguese imports.

In June 1988, a framework agreement for economic and financial cooperation between Spain and Morocco was signed, whereby export credit of 125 000 million pesetas, subsequently increased to 150 000, was provided for purchases of Spanish goods and services (Gillespie, 1995, p. 168). Spanish exports to Morocco increased by a factor of four, partly as a result of the 1988 agreement (de Larramendi, 1997, p. 430). In February 1996, the Spanish government agreed a new economic and financial cooperation agreement for the 1996–2000 period (de Larramendi, 1997, p. 429), and a friendship and cooperation treaty between the two countries came into effect on 28 January 1993 which institutionalized bilateral summits and established measures to increase cooperation in a number of sectoral, financial and cultural fields. At EU level, Spain was the member state most committed to promoting Mediterranean policy (Baixeras, 1996, p. 150), even though it has also been a priority for other countries such as France. Although Spain blocked talks on Moroccan agriculture during the first nine months of membership (de Larramendi, 1997, pp. 416–17), it also played an active role in Mediterranean policy initiatives, as illustrated by the Cooperation Council during the first Spanish Presidency in July 1989 aimed at establishing closer relations with Morocco, and the organization of the 1995 EuroMed conference during its second EU Presidency. However, Gillespie (1997a, pp. 11–12) considers that Morocco has been less prioritized from March 1996 by the new PP government, although the first official trips as PM of both Aznar and González were to Morocco.

Spanish diplomatic efforts successfully promoted the creation of a Euro-Maghreb 'partenariat' at the Lisbon Summit in June 1992, when Morocco was considered by the EU to be a candidate for a special free trade agreement. The Commission's mandate for negotiating an Association agreement was originally approved by the Council of Ministers on 7 December 1993, and Mediterranean policy was given a considerable impulse at the 1994 Corfu Summit when the Commission was asked to write a report on a EuroMediterranean free trade area. The proposal was approved at the Essen Summit in December 1994, and negotiations finally began in 1995. Spanish Commission officials were very eager to organize the EuroMed conference under the Spanish EU Presidency, and direct communication during 1994 and 1995 between Commissioner Marín in Brussels and the Ministry of Foreign Affairs in Madrid enhanced the key role Spain played in the initiative (Baixeras, 1996, p. 159). Morocco's key interest was in increasing the level of economic compensation, and improving the terms for the export of its agricultural products, while Spanish interests in the Association agreement were firmly linked to obtaining fishing rights in Moroccan waters.

The development of EU fisheries was a key source of tension in Spain's relations with Morocco during EC/EU membership.

Third-country fisheries agreements

Without third-country agreements, the general extension of fishing zones to 200 miles,[3] and the resulting substantial reduction in fishing opportunities, would have had serious repercussions for Community fishermen. Over one-quarter of all fish caught by Community boats for human consumption is taken from international waters, or from those under the jurisdiction of non-EU countries, accounting for 40 per cent of total CFP expenditure (European Commission, 1994, p. 29). The Community makes various forms of concessions to the non-member countries with which it negotiates agreements. From 1990, in the so-called second-generation agreements, it sought to promote the mutual development of both parties' fishing industries, and to highlight the opportunities for cooperation (European Commission, 1994, p. 32).

Prior to the negotiations with Morocco, the illegal capture of the Spanish ship *Estai* by Canadian coastguards led to a dispute. Canada's struggle for the control of international waters threatened the Spanish fishing presence in the area, and Spain requested the defence of its fishing rights in its protest against the Canadian action. The fisheries agreement between the EU and Canada was heavily criticized in Spain for the granting of excessive concessions to Canada by the EU, and for not adequately representing Spanish interests. The Spanish fishing sector feared that the EU, having set a precedent with the Canadian dispute, would give in to excessive Moroccan demands. Although Moroccan dependence on the EU distinguished the case from that of Canada, moves by Morocco to establish its own fishing industry led to the questioning of the traditional rights of Spanish fishermen to fish in its waters and, thus, to the protracted renegotiation of the terms of the agreement in 1995.

The Commission has sole power to negotiate EU third-country fishing agreements. The DG for fisheries, DG XIV, under the Commissioner Emma Bonino, was responsible for the negotiations, the chief EU negotiator being the Head of the Latin America, Antarctic and Mediterranean Unit in 1995, John Spencer. The Unit was within Directorate B, which was responsible for international fisheries agreements, as shown in Figure 6.1. Agreements with non-member countries have to be approved by the Council, following consultation of the European Parliament. According to Article 43, the fishing agreement

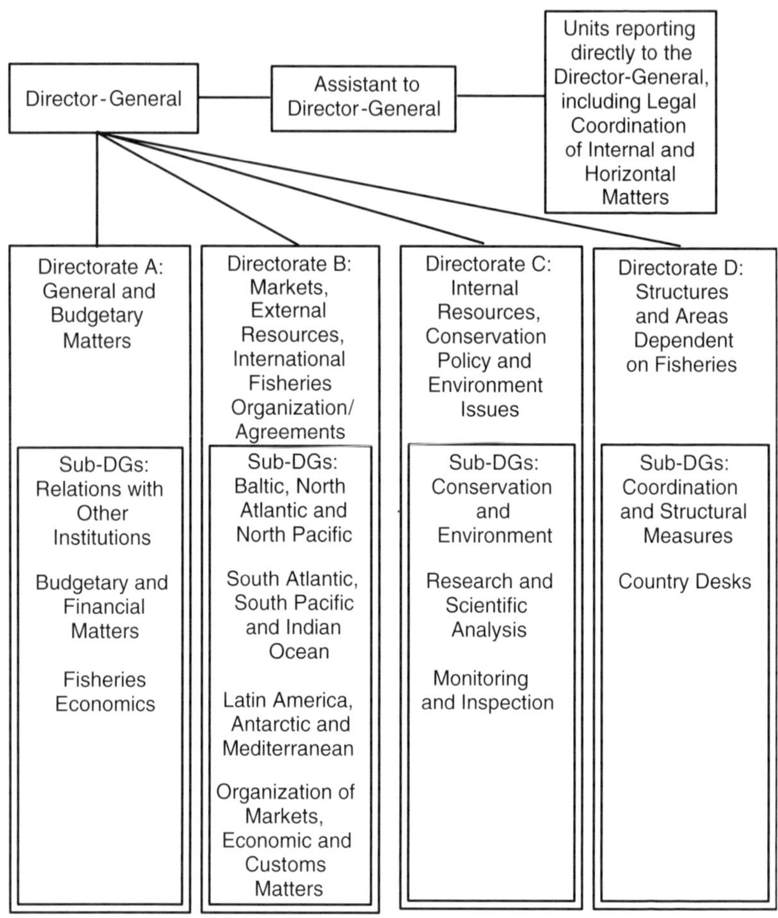

Figure 6.1   Structure of Directorate-General XIV (Fisheries), European Commission, during the 1995 negotiations.

also had to be ratified by the European Parliament, although MEPs were critical of the limitation of their role to the approval of an agreement which had already been negotiated.[4]

Previous fisheries agreements with Morocco

The lack of a well-established legal framework for negotiations in the area of fisheries, the signing of transitory accords in an atmosphere of tension and the relatively high public awareness of the issue make fishing agreements with Morocco particularly problematic for EU negotiators. Morocco can use its pressure on the Spanish government via sensitive or economically weak regions where the fishing sector is dependent on Moroccan resources (Núñez Villaverde and de Larramendi, 1996). The question of fishing rights thus has a high impact on the state of political relations between Spain and Morocco, frequently determining the extent of Spanish concessions to Moroccan demands on political and territorial issues.

Bilateral fishing agreements with Morocco were negotiated by the Spanish administration until 1988.[5] In December 1982, a six-month fishing agreement was signed between Spain and Morocco, but it was not until 1983 that a longer-term four-year accord was agreed, which marked a new period of cooperation. The agreement committed Spain to a 40 per cent reduction in fishing rights and to the protection of fishing stocks, while also seeking to establish a Moroccan fishing industry. The accord was significant as its aim was to end Morocco's use of the non-ratification of agreements as an instrument of political pressure. The Accession Treaty (Article 167) transferred responsibility for managing third-country fisheries agreements formerly negotiated by Spain and Portugal to the EC, and a new EC accord was signed on 25 February 1988 after the former one expired in July 1987. From the beginning of 1988, all EC boats were forced to leave Moroccan waters and, when a new agreement was reached, the Spanish sector, constituting more than 90 per cent of the fishing boats affected, opposed the reduction in fishing quotas imposed. It could be considered that,

> in terms of the fishing negotiation itself, the transfer of responsibility from Madrid to Brussels was an inconvenience, while in broader terms it was advantageous to Spain, bringing an uncoupling of the fisheries issue from political questions (including pressure on Ceuta and Melilla) and various forms of bilateral cooperation, economic, cultural and military.
>
> (Gillespie, 1995, pp. 167–8)

Spain was able to free itself of Moroccan pressures and take advantage of the EC/EU's stronger bargaining position in the negotiations, thus exploiting the opportunities presented by the new EC framework to justify policy decisions in the domestic arena. Some Spanish shipowners were more critical of the Community's defence of their interests, highlighting the greater degree of autonomy in the negotiation of bilateral agreements prior to EC accession.[6] However, the importance of fisheries for Spain was recognized in the EU arena where negotiations were frequently regarded as an essentially Spanish affair, although the Spanish government was often pressurized into making bilateral concessions to attain a new agreement. For example, Spain approved the signing of an accord on 31 March 1988 on the transport of Moroccan citrus fruits through Spanish territory to unblock stalled negotiations on fisheries (de Larramendi, 1997, p. 421).

On 1 May 1992, a new fisheries agreement between the EU and Morocco came into effect, which retained largely the same conditions for EU boats as in the previous accord, while increasing the financial flows to Morocco by 50 per cent. The Commission's offer to begin setting the framework for an Association agreement with Morocco eventually permitted an accord to be reached on fishing rights. The agreement provided for approximately 700 EU fishing boats, more than 90 per cent Spanish, to fish in Moroccan territorial waters for a four-year period in return for a payment of 102 million ECU a year (López García-Asenjo, 1994, p. 338). It was the most important fishing arrangement with a third country that the EU has signed in terms of the potential catch, the number of boats and workers, and the socio-economic impact on regions such as Andalusia, the Canaries and the South of Portugal. The accord involved a mix of finance and easier access for fishery products to the EU market, in exchange for fishing rights and preferential trade terms for selected fish exports. The Commission (European Commission, 1994, p. 32) claimed that the agreement between the EU and Morocco was 'in some ways, a forerunner of the new-style fishing agreements, based more on partnership than price', illustrating its determination to encourage closer economic links and cooperation between the EU and Moroccan fishing industries.

Article 15 of the agreement established that a meeting would be held halfway through the period to examine its functioning. In May 1994, Morocco used Article 15 to request a revision of terms, demanding a substantial reduction in EU fishing rights in its waters, and greater control and inspection of EU fleets, a large proportion of which were Spanish. Morocco withdrew fishing licences from 200 EU boats in 1994 in view of the increasing scarcity of catches. The Spanish delegation, in a communication to the Fisheries Commissioner in 1994, considered that the large reductions in fish quotas proposed by Morocco were totally unacceptable (unpublished letter, 7 September 1994). After five months of tense negotiation, a compromise was reached on 13 October

1994, whereby the 1992 agreement would remain unchanged until 30 April 1995, but its length would then be reduced by one year. Spain was in agreement with Morocco on a full renegotiation of terms for the fishing agreement (unpublished document, 7 September 1994). In November 1994, the Council of Ministers agreed on a negotiating mandate for the Commission and, following a delay which was partly a result of the formation of a new government after the Moroccan elections, negotiations began in March 1995.

Role of the Spanish government in interstate negotiations

The sub-DG for International Fisheries Agreements, in the DG for Fishing Resources within the Ministry of Agriculture, Fisheries and Food (see Figure 6.2) was directly responsible for the negotiations with third countries, its officials acting as key members of the Spanish delegation.[7] Spanish officials were able to have a considerable input to the negotiations as Commission negotiators relied on their high level of

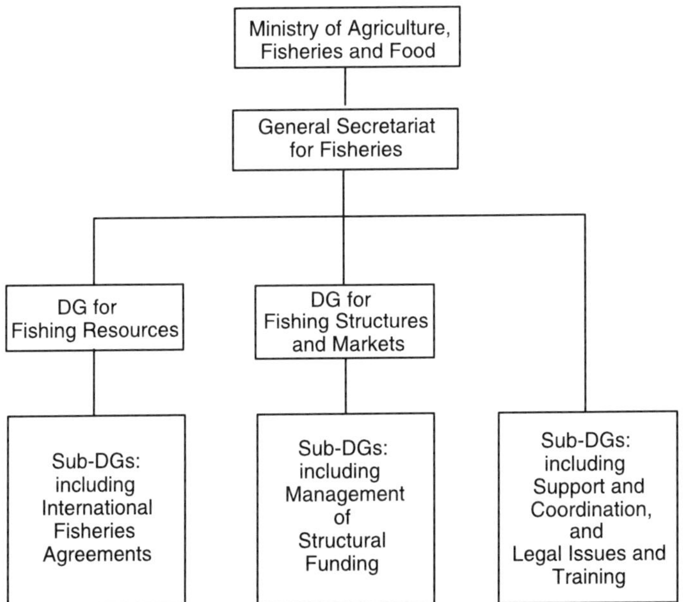

Figure 6.2   Organization of fisheries at central level.

expertise, their past experience of Moroccan negotiating tactics and their close relations with the sector. The renegotiation of the fisheries agreement was expected to be difficult in view of previous negotiations, and the tension caused was intensified by the severe economic crisis in the fisheries sectors of both Morocco and Spain.

Opening positions

According to Abdelmajid Smires, President of the Moroccan shipowners' association, Morocco was determined 'to regain the respect it is owed by exercising its sovereignty over its resources' (*FT*, 1 May 1995), considering that only the surplus stock should be fished by EU fishermen. In the presentation of his programme on Friday, 2 March, PM Abdellatif Filali expressed considerable discontent with the EU's policy towards Morocco for not complying 'with the geopolitical position of the kingdom, its political options and its economic and social achievements' (*Europe*, no. 6435, 8 March 1995, p. 6). The extension of the fishing agreement had been a formality in the past but, according to the President of the Moroccan shipowners' association, it had now become a real negotiation (*FT*, 1 May 1995).

The Moroccan delegation, headed by the Director-General for Fisheries Mohamed Rami, presented a series of tough demands for the new fisheries agreement. They considered that the fishing quotas currently established for EU fishermen should be substantially reduced, the biggest reductions in fishing possibilities being 65 per cent for cephalopods (squid, octopus and cuttlefish) over a three-year period. Furthermore, the delegation demanded that the percentage of Moroccan fishermen on EU fishing boats be raised to 35 per cent (over a certain tonnage, they currently represented about 25 per cent of the crew), and that a partnership between Moroccan and European shipowners be established rather than continue with conventional cooperation measures. A three-year duration was demanded for the fishing agreement, as well as a substantial increase in the payment to Moroccan shipowners. A further controversial demand was for the unloading of catches by Spanish boats partially, or even totally, in Moroccan ports. The Commission considered the reduction in fishing quotas excessive, and proposed a gradual reduction of 25 per cent in cephalopods over three years, and cuts of 5–10 per cent in quotas for other fish types (*El País*, 29 August 1995). However, Moroccan demands regarding the duration of the agreement, the need to ensure conservation of current stocks and the unloading of catches in Moroccan ports were largely approved by EU negotiators.

The Spanish delegation lobbied hard for a tough EU position *vis-à-vis* Moroccan demands throughout the talks. For example, the shortening of the fishing agreement by one year was a Spanish proposal in September 1994 in response to Moroccan demands, which eventually obtained the agreement of other member states. In an interview in June 1995, Bonino considered the strong pressure from the Spanish government on the Commission to be natural in view of the greater implications for its sector (*El Mundo*, 9 June 1995). However, despite acknowledgement at EU level of the implications for the Spanish fishing sector of substantial cuts in quotas, the Spanish government was frequently under pressure from the Commission to compromise its bargaining positions.

Deadlock in negotiations: March–August 1995

Negotiations between the EU and Morocco began in Brussels on 28–30 March 1995, but mainly consisted of setting out the opening positions of the two delegations. A common EU position was reached in coordination meetings between the Commission and member states prior to meeting the Moroccan delegation; bilateral meetings took place when specific problems arose in relation to one member state. The political importance of the agreement in Spain and Portugal was illustrated by the presence of a senior official from the Ministry of Foreign Affairs or the Permanent Representation in the delegation, as well as officials responsible for fisheries.

In the second round on 11–12 April in Rabat, the EU delegation submitted counter-proposals which included less radical reductions in fishing quotas in certain categories, limits to the compulsory biological rest period for some species without discrimination between Moroccan and EU fleets, and optional offloading in Moroccan ports (*Europe*, no. 6466, 22 April 1995, p. 6). However, Morocco did not modify its negotiating position, arguing that the conditions demanded for EU fishermen would be detrimental for its own fishing sector. Negotiations were resumed on 26 April in Rabat but, despite the politically positive talks between Bonino and Moroccan Fisheries Minister Mustapha Sahel prior to the negotiations, the conclusion of an agreement seemed unlikely before the interruption of EU fishing in Moroccan waters on 30 April. The Spanish delegation had shown considerable concern at Bonino's previous optimism regarding the conclusion of negotiations before the end of April, fearful that a rapid agreement would be reached involving terms unacceptable to its sector. However, although the Fisheries Commissioner noted agreement on key principles such as the need to preserve fish stocks, she acknowledged that 'the positions concerning actually putting these principles into the text of an agreement are still far apart' (*Europe*, no. 6469, 27 April 1995, p. 12).

The Commission focused on the importance of partnership arrangements in the fishing industry in the third round of negotiations, including EU–Morocco joint ventures and training schemes. The Spanish delegation was more reticent regarding Commission proposals, stressing the high rate of failure of joint ventures set up since the 1992 agreement. Wide differences remained on the reduction of quotas, resulting in the breakdown of negotiations on 27 April, and the decision to resume talks in May in Brussels. Morocco's intransigent position remained unchanged despite financial incentives offered by the EU, namely over 100 million ECU in annual financing from the Community budget (*Europe*, no. 6471, 29 April 1995, p. 8). The emphasis on a long-term partnership framework continued in the fourth round of negotiations on 15 May, but Moroccan fishing associations criticized arrangements which amounted to sharing the 'pillaging of resources with the Spanish' (*Europe*, no. 6495, 6–7 June 1995, p. 11), and the Moroccan delegation was deeply suspicious of proposals viewed, according to the chief EU negotiator,[8] as an attempt to avoid debate on quota reductions.

The Spanish delegation largely determined the extent of reductions in quotas during each negotiating round. For example, EU negotiators indicated that they would be willing to approve a cut in quotas of up to 30 per cent during the fifth round, while Spain was opposed to what it viewed as a major EU concession, and would only accept a maximum of a 15 per cent global reduction. This made the formulation of a common EU position almost impossible. Nonetheless, Bonino hoped that the fifth round of talks opening in Rabat on 1 June would enable the Commission to take a substantial step towards concluding negotiations (*Europe*, no. 6492, 1 June 1995, p. 10). EU negotiators considered that talks on partnership arrangements would allow a resumption of bargaining on quotas on a case-by-case basis according to the type of fishing. Although Moroccan sources criticized the European delegation for not responding to Moroccan proposals (*Europe*, no. 6495, 6–7 June 1995, p. 11), EU negotiators highlighted their proposals for reaching a common position on quotas following extensive coordination meetings between the Commission and Spanish delegation (*El País*, 3 June 1995).

In June, the Spanish proposal of a cut of only 2 per cent for the cephalopod fleet was immediately rejected by Morocco, and the Commission sought to persuade the Spanish delegation to accept reductions in quotas of 10–30 per cent to convince Morocco to enter the negotiating process. However, the Spanish delegation was aware that the 30 per cent cut in quotas proposed by the Commission would involve a decrease of around 200 Spanish fishing boats, and a loss of 6000 jobs, which would have to be justified in the domestic arena (*Ya*, 3 June 1995). Spain thus refused to compromise its bargaining position any further. The divergences between the EU and Spanish positions were evident and, despite Commission support for the Spanish fishing sector, Spain's demand for a far tougher, less compromising bargaining position was criticized by the Commission and EU member states, particularly when it put short-term gains above more strategic thinking about the future of its sector. For example, Bonino was particularly critical of the Spanish government's postponement of the restructuring of the sector, although acknowledging the difficulty of the task (*El Mundo*, 9 June 1995). Most member states were generally supportive of the Spanish fishing sector, but countries such as France, whose economic interests in Morocco led it to favour Rabat over Madrid at certain stages of the negotiation, were more reticent regarding Spanish interests. The Director-General of DG XIV, Almeida Serra, declared that all 15 member states had to be taken into account (*Industrias Pesqueras*, no. 1636, 15 June 1995, p. 5), indicating his criticism of the predominance of Spanish interests in the negotiations.

Following the failure of the fifth negotiating round, during a visit to Madrid, Bonino highlighted the necessity for further Spanish concessions before a date was set for the resumption of talks. Bonino held bilateral talks whenever political pressure was considered advantageous; her personal interventions in Madrid, Rabat and Lisbon in June were an attempt to establish a more accommodating EU negotiating position (*Europe*, no. 6500, 14 June 1995, p. 12). She sought to maximize political pressure on the Spanish government in meetings with González, attempting to separate high-level political discussions from economic, sectoral issues discussed with officials.[9] The Commission feared that the refusal of the Spanish delegation to approve an unacceptable agreement, in addition to the uncompromising position defended by Moroccan shipowners, would block the negotiations indefinitely (*Europe*, no. 6500, 14 June 1995, p. 12). The Spanish government resented the Commission's criticism of its bargaining terms, and monitored the EU's strategies carefully for fear of becoming the victim of an overly flexible EU negotiating position. Spain was critical of what it viewed as the Commission's attempt to play the role of intermediary between Spain and Morocco, rather than defender of global

EU interests including those of the Spanish fishing sector.[10] No progress was made in reaching a compromise between Spain and Morocco in June (*Europe,* no. 6504, 19–20 June 1995, p. 10), although Morocco was encouraged to return to the negotiating table by the outcome of the Cannes Summit in June 1995, when total funds of 4685 million ECU for the 1995–9 period were approved for the non-EU Mediterranean countries (Khader and Núñez Villaverde, 1996, p. 63). This was partly the result of a deal between Kohl and González, which represented a considerable victory for Spain, even if it meant a 10 per cent reduction in the budget originally proposed by Commissioner Marín (Gillespie, 1997a, p. 10).

In the Spanish parliament on 29 June 1995, the Spanish Agriculture and Fisheries Minister highlighted the importance of relations between Spain and Morocco for improving the climate for the negotiating process, although the EU had exclusive competency as negotiator of the agreement (*El Correo de Andalucía*, 30 June 1995). Actions were taken to improve bilateral relations, for example the visit of Foreign Minister Javier Solana to Rabat in June to hold talks with PM Filali and King Hassan II. The Commission also played a key role in finding a solid base for compromise between the Spanish and Moroccan delegations on areas such as the financial counterpart to be conceded to Morocco.

Towards an agreement: August–November 1995

Fisheries negotiations resumed in Brussels on 11 August. In view of the progress made in high-level political talks, Bonino was hopeful that fishing activity could recommence by 1 September, but when the EU proposal of a global reduction of around 30 per cent in fish quotas was presented on 17 August, it was immediately rejected by Morocco (*El País*, 13 August 1995). The Moroccan delegation demanded as a basis the actual use of fishing possibilities, which were in fact not fully exhausted (until the end of April, the EU had used about 64 000 tonnes out of a possible 82 000), while the EU delegation, under pressure from Spain, insisted on former fishing possibilities as the point of departure. Commission proposals sought a compromise between Moroccan and Spanish demands, for example a system of voluntary offloading of EU catches in Morocco along with financial incentives for EU shipowners. Financial compensation was another outstanding issue (talks were suspended from 19 to 25 August when no compromise could be found) as well as the level of fishing quotas. The plenary session on 25 August ended after 45 minutes following Morocco's refusal to reduce its demands for quotas of 65 per cent for cephalopods and 50 per cent for fish caught by trawlers, while the EU was only prepared to accept cuts of 21 per cent and 10 per cent respectively. The Commission proposal for a 21 per cent reduction in catches of cephalopods represented a major compromise considering it had been preparing to negotiate on the basis of between 30 and 35 per cent according to EU sources (*Europe*, no. 6556, 6 September 1995, p. 8). Fishing of cephalopods represented 30 per cent of Spanish employment directly linked to fishing in Moroccan waters and the Spanish delegation thus needed to stand firm on the issue of quotas. The sixth round of negotiations was suspended when the Moroccan delegation refused concessions made by the EU and demanded a reopening of all issues.

Morocco was reported by a Spanish commentator to have tried to gain support for its position from member states with economic interests in the country when the sixth round failed, but the EU delegation stood firmly by Spanish demands (*Mar*, no. 332, October 1995, p. 8). Spanish government officials were more confident of obtaining an accord in September and October, when Morocco began to export its agricultural products via Spain. However, while welcoming the personal interventions of Bonino, the Spanish delegation remained concerned about her eagerness to reach an agreement which did not fully consider Spanish interests. A comprehensive evaluation of relations between the EU and Morocco was proposed at a meeting of the College of Commissioners on 6 September to discuss the crisis situation. The meeting reaffirmed the EU's determination to conclude negotiations as soon as possible, but highlighted the need for a greater will to negotiate from Morocco (*Europe*, no. 6557, 7 September 1995, p. 8). The Moroccan delegation's refusal to draft a written agreement also caused tension, although some EU officials regarded this as ultimately working to their advantage as it allowed the EU text to become the basis for negotiation.[11] Strengthening relations with Morocco was considered a priority for the EU, but Bonino declared that the Commission was also fully aware of the serious socio-economic problems in Spanish regions most affected by the suspension of fishing activity. An indication of the Commission's support for the sector was the EU's suspension of tinned sardine imports from Morocco. Bonino's personal awareness of the high political importance of the issue was indicated by her statement to the European Parliament that she would speak at any plenary session in September where oral questions on the fisheries agreement were raised (unpublished document, European Parliament, 1 September 1995).

According to negotiators, significant headway had been made by the end of September to reduce differences on the total size of the EU catch, and on financial compensation, to 'a reasonable negotiating zone' (*FT*, 4 October 1995). Talks were held between Bonino and Sahel on 15 September 1995, and González and Bonino met in Madrid on 29 September to discuss potential compromises, particularly on reductions in fish quotas (*El País*, 30 September 1995). A major obstacle to the successful conclusion of negotiations was EU opposition to a significant share of the fish caught by foreign boats passing through Moroccan ports. Morocco proposed a phased changeover as an economic imperative, but the Spanish delegation was reluctant to enforce the condition on more than a 'symbolic' number of vessels (*FT*, 4 October 1995) and favoured a voluntary regime. Spanish officials argued that fishermen could not be expected to unload their catches in Morocco until an adequate infrastructure was in place. Although Morocco's agreement to lower the amount demanded in financial compensation, which was initially three times that obtained in the 1992 agreement, made an agreement in the seventh round starting on 17 October more likely, major differences remained regarding reductions in quotas and unloading in Moroccan ports. The Spanish delegation was prepared to consider a substantial increase in payments to Morocco, in exchange for reductions in fishing quotas, but was aware that other member states would be more reticent about an excessive rise in the EU's financial contribution (*Diario 16*, 14 October 1995). Intensive negotiations at a high ministerial level, where the Spanish delegation played a key diplomatic role, contributed to concessions from both delegations. Following a meeting on 17 October between the Spanish delegation and members of Bonino's cabinet, Atienza declared that he was optimistic for a conclusion to the negotiations which would not be excessively traumatic for the Spanish fishing sector (*El País*, 19 October 1995).

The renegotiation of the fisheries agreement was concluded during the eighth round of negotiations from 10–12 November, when the agreement eventually gained the approval of all delegations. The EU's payment was fixed at 350 million ECU over four years for the right to fish in Moroccan waters, and a gradual 20 per cent decrease overall in the number of EU fishing vessels. The major compromises in the negotiating positions which brought an end to the stalemate were a reduction in fishing possibilities of 40 per cent for cephalopods over the four years, an increase in financial compensation of up to 30 or 35 per cent, compulsory offloading in Moroccan ports only for frozen cephalopods and a suspension period of two to three months a year to enable stocks to reconstitute themselves.[12] As for the controversial issue of unloading in Moroccan ports, most of the fleet were able to continue landing fish in Spain, but some of the larger boats were obliged to unload their catches in Morocco. Morocco also obtained a substantial increase in economic compensation, as well as funding for training and research, in addition to payments from EU shipowners themselves.

A compromise was thus reached between the EU and Moroccan delegations which was acceptable to Spanish officials (*Mar*, no. 332, October 1995, p. 8). Although the Moroccan Fisheries Minister described the four-year accord without mid-way revision as the last agreement of its type (*FT*, 19 December 1995), it was still expected that the EU's needs would be accommodated by Morocco from 2000 through a renegotiation of the agreement. An accord with Mauritania regarding fishing possibilities for 18 additional vessels, mainly Spanish, offset the reductions imposed by the agreement with Morocco, and was described by the Secretary-General for Fisheries, José Loira, as crucial for obtaining the agreement of the Spanish fishing sector, especially in the Canaries, to the reduction in quotas.[13]

Linkage between fisheries and Association agreements

Both the fishing and Association agreements were signed on 26 February 1996. They then had to be ratified by parliaments in all EU member states, Morocco and the European Parliament. The Spanish central government had played a key role in linking the two agreements, and was satisfied with the acknowledgement by EU member states that it was impossible to 'agree a good association agreement with Morocco if Madrid is suffering from concessions on fish' (*FT*, 30 August 1995). Atienza considered that Spain's EU Presidency was not decisive for negotiations with Morocco, but that it gave the Spanish government a privileged position at the centre of the bargaining process, necessitating a full knowledge of the positions of all member states.[14] Although it raised awareness of the crisis situation in its fishing sector during its Presidency, it also had to support the EU's broader strategy of strengthening its Mediterranean policy, for example through Association agreements with Morocco and other third countries (*Europe*, no. 6498, 10 June 1995, p. 4).

The Commission increasingly recognized that additional concessions for sensitive agricultural products of importance to Morocco would reinforce the bargaining power of the fisheries sector, and would thus 'play a determining role in the outcome of negotiations' (*Europe*, no. 6478, 11 May 1995, p. 10). Bonino had initially attempted in April 1995 to separate the two negotiations (*Diario 16*, 27 April 1995), as had the Moroccan PM until strong domestic pressures to obtain increased EU financial aid made talks on the Association agreement more urgent.

Commission officials discussed the possibility of granting Morocco financial support worth one billion ECU over a period of five years in order to restart the fisheries negotiations (*Europe*, no. 6518, 8 July 1995, p. 9), as well as trade concessions including reduced or zero duty tariff quotas for the import of tinned sardines and citrus fruit (*Europe*, no. 6524, 17–18 July 1995, p. 10). Although the proposals met with strong sectoral opposition in the Portuguese domestic arena, Marín considered that the trade concessions were not excessively detrimental to EU sectors, and would make it possible to conclude a good fisheries agreement (*Europe*, no. 6524, 17–18 July 1995, p. 10). Proposals submitted by the Commission at the end of July remained on the table in Council until September due to the stalemate in the fisheries negotiations.

Many Northern EU member states were more concerned about Moroccan agricultural imports than fisheries but, although critical of Spain's overly tough bargaining position and frequently aggressive fleet, largely lent their support to Spanish fishing interests in view of the crisis in its sector. Any support for the Moroccan position from EU member states was skilfully countered by the Spanish delegation. Spanish officials sought to ensure that the interests of its fishing sector were not compromised by the demands of other sectors. However, opposition of some member states to agricultural concessions to Morocco still held up the agreement when the Spanish Presidency submitted the issue to the General Affairs Council for discussion. In the 30 October Council meeting, the Spanish Presidency's attempts to break the deadlock failed, as Germany, Belgium and the Netherlands refused to agree to agricultural concessions on cut flowers, tomatoes and potatoes proposed by the Commission. Westendorp, as Secretary of State for the EU, declared Spain's approval of the limited increases in agricultural imports, and was critical of member states such as Germany, which refused to accept the entry of 5000 tonnes of cut flowers into the EU from Morocco, only 300 of which would reach the German market (*Industrias Pesqueras*, 1 November 1995, no. 1645, p. 5). However, senior government officials suggested that the obstructionist tactics of Northern member states enabled Spain to grant concessions to its own agricultural sector which would have been impossible otherwise.[15] In a Spanish parliament debate on 10 November 1995, parliamentary groups were critical of the agreement on fruit and vegetables, which they considered had been sacrificed to obtain a better deal on fisheries. The weak influence of the parliament on central government's position is illustrated by the fact that the Spanish government largely maintained its negotiating position at EU level despite strong parliamentary support for a PP motion rejecting the agreement (*El País*, 9 November 1995).

Following the deal reached on fishing on 13 November, the Spanish Presidency worked hard to obtain approval of the accord despite continued German, Dutch and Belgian opposition to limited agricultural concessions. Spanish EU ambassador Elorza highlighted the fact that the Spanish delegation would do all they could to obtain a final agreement (*El País*, 30 November 1995). Morocco was reluctant to attend the first preparatory meeting for the EuroMed conference in November, thus causing considerable tension between Morocco and EU member states, particularly Spain. In Morocco, the press hinted at the direct relation between the conclusion of negotiations, and its attendance at the EuroMed conference (*Algeciras Marítimas*, 18 October 1995); the Moroccan presence was problematic if the Spanish fleet was still inactive in its waters. The Association agreement was finally approved in November 1995, a few days before the EuroMed conference began, following 20 days of intensive meetings (*El País*, 11 November 1995). A high degree of coordination between the cabinets of the Commissioners Bonino and Marín, along with strong leadership from the Spanish EU Presidency, had been crucial to the successful conclusion of negotiations, involving last minute adjustments to the terms under which agricultural products could enter the EU.[16]

Interaction between the domestic and EU arenas

The key role of the Spanish central government in negotiations at EU level is clear from this analysis. However, it was not the best moment politically to take up a strategic position as EU President in view of its poor results in the municipal and regional elections in May 1995, particularly in fishing villages affected by the negotiations. The main opposition party used every opportunity to criticize the PSOE government's strategies during the electoral campaign. Political sensitivities surrounding the local elections thus called for an immediate response to regional demands in economically weak areas dependent on Moroccan fishing grounds. Although the vulnerable position of a minority government *vis-à-vis* other domestic actors was denied by officials involved in the negotiations at the time,[17] press reports considered that the Spanish delegation seemed happy to skirt around the toughest problems to avoid concluding an agreement prior to the elections 'para no pagar el precio electoral de sus inevitables concesiones en la negociación pesquera' (in order not to pay the price in the elections for inevitable concessions in the fishing negotiation) (*El País*, 26 April 1995).

The delicate balance between the EU and domestic arenas was clear at the 1995 EuroMed conference, where official Spanish statements on the opportunities presented by closer links with the Mediterranean contrasted with sectoral protest against Moroccan imports. A difficult balance between the demands of fishing and agricultural sectors in the domestic arena, and the need to defend Maghreb interests as a leader in the area of Mediterranean policy at EU level, thus had to be reached.

Domestic responses to the government's negotiation at EU level

A briefing, written by an MEP representing the PP in 1995, enumerated the major criticisms of the PSOE government's negotiation of fisheries agreements with Morocco, including the lack of stricter controls on fish imports into Andalusia from third countries, and the setting of a precedent by renegotiating the 1992 fisheries agreement a year before its expiry without demanding concessions in return (unpublished document, European Parliament, June 1995). The report considered that Spain did not have the influence in the EU to enforce a more global treatment of fisheries issues. It sought to supply ammunition for the opposition during the 1995–6 election campaign. This highlights the constant criticism which the PSOE government had to face throughout the negotiations.

The high level of debate of the fisheries agreement in Spain, which contrasted with the minimal discussion of other EU policy areas, raised the profile of Spanish fishing interests in the EU arena. Despite the key influence on the EU bargaining position exerted by the Spanish delegation, central government faced harsh criticism in the domestic arena for its insufficient defence of national interests and for the low level of concessions obtained from Morocco. The MEP Antonio Gutiérrez Díaz (IU) considered that a key problem for the Spanish fishing sector was the fact that 'la credibilidad y la autoridad de nuestro Gobierno en Europa se encuentra muy degradada' (the credibility and authority of our government in Europe is very low) (*Sur*, 7 May 1995), echoed by the criticism of the MEP Matutes (PP) of the lack of firmness of the PSOE government's negotiating strategy (*El Periódico*, 12 May 1995). The PP accused González of being more concerned about his own personal, pro-European image in Brussels than the defence of Spanish sectoral interests (for example *ABC*, 23, 24, 29 May 1995). The opposition also highlighted the fact that the PSOE government's weakness was exacerbated by its image as a *demandeur* of funding at EU level (see

Chapter 4), which reduced its influence in the decision-making process in key policy areas such as fisheries (*Gaceta de los Negocios*, 19 April 1995). In its defence, government ministers highlighted the PP's approval of the fishing agreement when it won the elections in 1996, the only changes in its terms being negative, namely the longer duration of the suspension period for certain fish types (see Chapter 7).[18] The PSOE considered the majority of the criticism to be politically inspired, as further analysed by the study of the input of key domestic actors in the next chapter.

Conclusions

An analysis of the role of central government in Spain during the negotiations illustrates the importance of its strategies at the EU negotiating table for obtaining the optimal deal for its fishing sector. The Spanish government was frequently criticized by both the Commission and other key EU member states for the predominance of its interests in the negotiations, particularly when short-term sectoral interests were put before more strategic considerations about the future of the sector and the EU's relations with the Mediterranean. Despite overall support for the Spanish fishing sector, key member states, such as France, were critical of the uncompromising Spanish bargaining position, and were unwilling to accept substantial increases in EU payments to Morocco to attain its demands. Considerable evidence exists for Spain's strong influence on the fisheries agenda. It is significant that the former Secretary-General for Fisheries considered in 1996 that the CFP framework which had developed was largely a response to Spain's needs when it joined the Community (Loira, 1996, p. 11).

The negotiation of fisheries agreements with third countries, and particularly Morocco, was a priority for the Spanish government in view of the dependence of its fishing sector on Moroccan waters. Although the chief negotiator of the accord was the Commission, the Spanish government placed considerable pressure on EU negotiators to support its demands, and Spain's EU presidency from July 1995 gave it a central position in the negotiating process. The Moroccan press frequently referred to the uncompromising EU position on fisheries being largely determined by the interests of the Spanish government (*Industrias Pesqueras*, no. 1641, 1 September 1995, p. 5). The Spanish delegation successfully ensured close linkage between the Association and fisheries agreements to increase the pressure on the Moroccan delegation to meet its demands on fishing rights.

Although evidence seems to point to the relevance of an approach to the analysis which focuses merely on the role of the central state, the increasing interaction between the domestic and EU arenas indicates that relations between the Spanish central state and other domestic actors should also be analysed. The Spanish government was able to exploit the high visibility and awareness of the fisheries issue in Spain to explain its intransigent position at EU level to other member states, and to obtain the best deal for the fishing sector, thus 'tying its hands' domestically (Putnam, 1993). Likewise, decisions taken in the EU arena were used to justify to the affected regions the substantial reductions in fishing quotas demanded by Morocco, and the urgent restructuring which was particularly necessary in Andalusia. Central government thus acted as a gatekeeper between the EU and domestic arenas, and used the interaction between them to obtain a balance between sectoral demands at domestic level, and its obligations as an EU member state and EU President from July 1995 to take a leading role in the formulation of a strong EU Mediterranean policy. Spain's role as an 'active state' (Ikenberry, 1986) is thus illustrated by its manipulation of EU and domestic demands to enhance its autonomy. Before assuming that the central state retained its full control of the interface between the domestic and EU arenas throughout the negotiations, Chapter 7 considers the input of other key sectoral and regional actors, some of whom had considerably developed their capacity to gain access to the policy process at both domestic and EU levels.

7
The Input of Other Domestic Actors to the Fisheries Agreement

The focus of the chapter is on the input of key sectoral and regional actors other than the central state to the negotiation of the 1995 EU–Morocco fisheries agreement. Chapter 6 highlighted the framework-setting role of the central state at EU level. The analysis of the mobilization of sectoral and regional actors throughout the negotiating rounds in this chapter provides a more complete analysis of the policy process. The Spanish government was expected by Commission officials to act cautiously over an issue which was far more explosive domestically than the dispute with Canada because few of the boats fishing in Moroccan waters were suitable for operating further afield. The focus is on the case of Andalusia, which is the region most economically dependent on the agreement in view of its lack of alternative fishing grounds, even if other regions such as the Canary Islands have larger fishing quotas in Moroccan waters.

The substantial reductions in fishing quotas proposed by Morocco in 1995 distinguished the negotiations from those of previous accords, and the sector thus sought to maximize the defence of its fishing interests, aware of the serious crisis in affected regions if Morocco's demands were met. In view of the lack of analytical studies of the negotiation of EU fishing agreements, the starting point for the analysis is less clear than in the study of cohesion policy. The evaluation could be expected to conclude that domestic actors were able to exert a strong influence on central government in view of the highly visible protest reported in the press throughout the negotiations. The relevance of a purely state-centric approach to the analysis cannot be assumed, even if access for non-central state actors to the decision-making phase of the policy process at EU level is far more problematic than their input to the implementation of the agreement at ground level.

This chapter examines the institutional framework at central and EU levels, and then analyses the changing structure and organization of regional government and the fishing sector. This lays the foundation for a detailed study of the input of non-central state actors to the policy process, both through widespread protest, and an enhanced level of dialogue. Conclusions are then drawn on the relations between central government and other domestic actors in the fisheries negotiations.

Institutional framework

The institutional framework at central and EU levels determines the nature of the political opportunity structures for key domestic actors. This framework is examined here prior to evaluating the extent to which key actors had developed a greater capacity to exploit available access points to the policy process during Spain's EC/EU membership.

European Union

In addition to the negotiation of EU agreements with third countries, the role of DG XIV of the Commission (see Figure 6.1 in Chapter 6) is to initiate legislative and policy proposals, to manage and administer the CFP and to monitor compliance with Community law. On the basis of proposals from the Commission, the Council of Ministers passes legislation relating to the CFP. In the European Parliament, fisheries issues were discussed in a subcommittee of the Agriculture Committee until a separate Committee for Fisheries was created in 1994, indicating the increasing importance of the policy area. The first two Presidents, both Spanish, have been able to influence the agenda to maximize discussion of contentious issues for Spain such as the agreement with Morocco.[1] Bonino declared in 1998 that direct consultation of the EU fisheries sector would be a priority for the Commission prior to revising the CFP after 2002 (*Pesca Info*, DG XIV Newsletter, no. 13, 1998, p. 3). The European Parliament has also acted as an effective mediator between key regional and sectoral actors, and EU institutions. However, in view of its inability to participate directly in the negotiations, it was not prioritized by key sectoral actors but was, rather, an important additional channel for influencing policy.

Central government

Central government is responsible for the basic regulation of the fishing sector, international relations and the monitoring of international waters. Despite the importance given to fisheries, a relatively small number of people deal with the policy area. One official has responsibility for fisheries in the Spanish Permanent Representation in Brussels, who has a single interlocutor in the SSEU in Madrid, although contact is frequently made directly with the Ministry during EU negotiations. Around 22 civil servants were based in the sub-DG for International Fisheries Agreements (see Figure 6.2 in Chapter 6) in 1997, approximately five of whom were responsible for Morocco, while a total of around 170 officials in central administration work in the area of fisheries. This is a relatively small number when one considers the Spanish fleet of at least 18 000 fishing boats. Despite the relatively low number of officials, fisheries are politically very important in Spain, especially given the high level of public interest.

Central government sought to maintain a dialogue with key regional and sectoral actors throughout the negotiations, one illustration being the Agriculture and Fisheries Minister's visits to the worst affected regions to speak directly to local representatives at key points of the negotiation. It was the Secretary-General for Fisheries as well as key officials in the International Agreements division who were responsible for maintaining regular contact with the sector through regional seminars and meetings with key representatives.

Regional government

At regional level in Andalusia, the DG for Fisheries in the Ministry of Agriculture and Fisheries in Seville, shown in Figure 7.1, enjoyed close relations with the PSOE government during the negotiations, enhanced by the fact that the PSOE was also the ruling party in Andalusia. An increase in regional influence on the bargaining position of central government was also attributed to a different mentality in the DG following the appointment of a new Agriculture and Fisheries Minister, Paulino Plata, in August 1994. Plata was considered to have exploited more fully the regional capacity to have an input to the talks; less evidence exists for collaboration during the 1992 fisheries negotiations when, according to a key sectoral representative, agricultural interests predominated in Andalusia.[2] The increased input was partly the result of Plata's initiative to set up a working group consisting of representatives of both the regional government and fishing sector, the aim of which was to establish a strong, consensual position to present to Madrid. Sectoral meetings also provided regional government with increased opportunities for collaboration with central government (see Chapter 3). One official in the sub-DG for International Fisheries Agreements in Madrid expressed doubts about a possible increase in

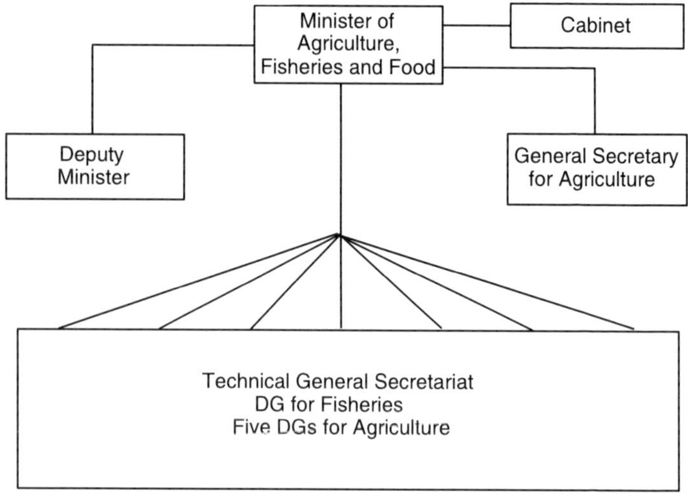

Figure 7.1   Organization of fisheries at regional level.

the influence of regional government as a result of sectoral meetings, but considered their organization a considerable advance given the greater transparency at central level prior to the ratification of agreements in the EU arena.[3]

As well as working-group meetings to decide on a unified bargaining position in the negotiations with Morocco, regional meetings were held to formulate the Modernization Plan for the Andalusia fishing industry in close collaboration with the sector, which thus had a major input to the plan finally approved.[4] According to the plan, proposed on 12 September 1994 and approved by the regional parliament on 13 and 14 December 1994, both the EU's CFP and Andalusia's Statute of Autonomy point to an adequate legal framework at regional level for the planning of its own fishing policy on the basis of a general consensus with key interest groups (Junta de Andalucía, 1997). The Modernization Plan is indicative of the progress made towards greater coordination of fishing policy with the Autonomous Communities, acknowledged by the Agriculture and Fisheries Minister in central government (Atienza, 1996, p. 13).

The greater exploitation of the capacity of regional government to manage FIFG funding is an illustration of the growing collaboration between central and regional levels in the area of fisheries (see Chapter 5 on cohesion policy). The Agriculture and Fisheries Minister from 1996, Loyola de Palacio, proposed institutionalizing a more stable framework for cooperation, as many procedural problems had resulted from the difficulty of maintaining close relations between central and regional government during the first years of funding. The new Secretary-General for Fisheries in the PP government from 1996, Samuel Juárez, feared that the FIFG was being used as a system to assert control over the Autonomous Communities (*Industrias Pesqueras*, no. 1667, 1 October 1996, p. 4). However, in the sectoral meeting on fisheries in Vigo in July 1996, de Palacio highlighted the reliance of the funding system on the cooperation of the Autonomous Communities, claiming that 90 per cent of the competencies in the area of fisheries had already been transferred to regional governments (*Industrias Pesqueras*, no. 1663, 1 August 1996, p. 14). Central administration hoped that an enhanced role for the regional administration would enable more efficient use of the funding, given that only 8 per cent of the money allocated by the EU had been spent by May 1996 (*Mar*, no. 346, January 1997, p. 21). Regional governments considered that developments such as the revision of OPs to adapt them to the demands of subnational authorities, and to ensure improved distribution and use of funding, would lead to their greater input to EU fisheries policy more generally.

Fishing sector

The fishing sector in Andalusia represents a significant proportion of the Spanish fleet, namely 14.9 per cent. The objectives of the Andalusia modernization plan included support for the establishment of organizational structures and the consolidation of existing organizations within the fishing sector to enable the more effective defence of fishing interests, and greater participation of socio-economic actors (Junta de Andalucía, 1997). The successful implementation of the plan sought to establish a more organized fishing sector in Andalusia, particularly in view of its incorporation into the wider EU framework.

Faced with substantial reductions in quotas imposed by Morocco and Mauritania, the fishing sector has been increasingly obliged to organize its interests coherently (Núñez Villaverde and de Larramendi, 1996, p. 54). This is illustrated by the more professional and business-oriented policy developed by key shipowners' associations. In addition to the shipowners' and producers' organizations, fishermen and shipowners have also organized themselves jointly into associations (*cofradías*) in Andalusia, although this is less developed than in other regions. Its lack of unity was particularly problematic during negotiations at EU level. In 1995, a specialist fisheries journal bemoaned the disunity of the fishing sector in Andalusia, the weakness of the Spanish government and the conflicting interests of EU countries which were factors all working in Morocco's favour (*Productos del Mar*, nos. 89–90, May–June 1995, p. 14). The President of the European Parliament Fisheries Committee in 1997, Carmen Fraga Estevez MEP (PP), highlighted the lack of a common position in the sector in Andalusia as largely a result of the fact that its associations of fishermen and shipowners represented very different fish types.[5] Furthermore, many organizations and trade unions were more politically radical in Andalusia, illustrated by the extreme positions of some CCOO representatives, which led to tension with unions in other regions.[6] Andalusia sought to coordinate its interests with other fishing areas opposed to substantial quota reductions imposed by Morocco, but a united position was difficult in view of the existing tensions between groups within the region. In the 1994 renegotiation of the fishing agreement, conflict between groups from Andalusia observing the negotiations was reported, and lobbying actions such as strikes and port closures were rarely well coordinated (*Productos del Mar*, nos. 89–90, May–June 1995, p. 5). Despite attempts to present a united regional position in 1995, representatives of Almeria and Malaga organized joint actions without taking into account the position of other ports.

Despite clear differences in sectoral interests which made a united position highly problematic, coordination of the sector was improving even in Andalusia, as illustrated by the common position reached in the working group created by regional government. Another illustration of the attempt to coordinate regional interests was the creation of the Federation of Shipowners' Associations in Andalusia. It had a clear symbolic importance despite little direct input to the 1995 negotiations and minimal contact with fishermen's associations, and the profile of the Federation was raised by the efforts of its President Pedro Maza to defend acceptable fishing quotas for the sector. In the majority of associations, the management had become more professional, although this was more the case in the larger industrial sector with a higher level of resources, such as cephalopod fishing associations in the Canaries, rather than in the smaller, often family-owned businesses and diverse fishermen's associations common in Andalusia.[7] However, even associations in Andalusia were renovating their organizational structure with a view to creating a representative regional federation which could reduce tensions between the subnational administration and the various associations. One of the central objectives, according to both Rafael Montoya, President of the Andalusia Federation of Fishermen's Associations, and the Director of the DG for Fisheries in Andalusia, Francisco Gómez Aracil, was to present fishermen's demands more effectively to the administration and to shipowners (*Industrias Pesqueras*, no. 1673, 1 January 1997, p. 24). In an interview, Gómez Aracil drew attention to major progress in the restructuring of the sector, including provincial and regional federations of fishermen's associations, and the consolidation of shipowners' associations. He referred to the effective communication between the sector and the fishing administration in Andalusia as evidence of a higher level of organization (*Industrias Pesqueras*, no. 1676, 15 February 1997, p. 7). The former Secretary-General for Fisheries, José Loira, also referred to a more organized fishing sector in the 1990s, although the major task of establishing a single representative association continued to be debated (*Industrias Pesqueras*, no. 1655–6, April 1996, p. 8). The increasing organization of the sector facilitated a greater input to EU-level negotiations, the long duration of the 1995 negotiation and the substantial cuts in quotas demanded by Morocco having particularly encouraged a more coherent articulation of interests.

Trade unions complained about their lack of representation *vis-à-vis* central government (see Chapter 3), although divisions between socio-economic actors often inhibited a common position to present to central government on key issues. Their input to the regional modernization plan was assured through the sectoral meeting on fisheries, which had been set up by the Andalusia Pact on Employment and Productivity of 13 February 1995, for example their presence in monitoring committees (Junta de Andalucía, 1995) (see Chapter 5). Furthermore, an Interministerial Committee was jointly created by the Ministries responsible for Employment and Social Affairs, and Agriculture, Fisheries and Food, to increase discussion of issues affecting workers with union representatives. The CCOO had lobbied hard for the constitution of such a forum, as they considered that the government ignored socio-economic actors in its negotiation of fisheries issues. However, according to trade union representatives, the committee has been of limited effectiveness.[8] The Secretary-General of the CCOO Fisheries Division, FETCOMAR, Jon Azkue, criticized the fact that 'las medidas de la UE eran exclusivamente para los armadores' (EU measures were exclusively for shipowners) (*Gaceta Sindical*, no. 140, October 1995, p. 22).

Opportunities for participation of key regional and sectoral actors

Considerable domestic pressure on central government was inevitable during the negotiations, given the crisis in the fishing sector and the high level of dependence on Moroccan fishing grounds. In previous fishing negotiations with Morocco, central government's bargaining position had also been obliged to take into account key sectoral interests. This is clearly illustrated by a letter in June 1982 from the Spanish Agriculture and Fisheries Minister, José Luis Álvarez, to the Moroccan Economy Minister, informing Morocco that it would not be politically possible to explain greater limitations on the Spanish fleet to the fishing sector, the general public or the Spanish parliament (unpublished letter, Spanish Ministry of Agriculture, Fisheries and Food, Madrid, 14 June 1982). In 1995, the negotiation was potentially more politically sensitive in the domestic arena in view of the greater threat to Spanish fishing rights. Regional authorities lobbied for a greater input to the talks throughout the negotiating rounds, and criticized the lack of transparency of the process.

The PP government in Galicia requested integration into the Spanish delegation of their representatives on the basis of the argument put forward by Juárez, who was a regional government official in 1995, that in addition to requiring the expertise of scientific delegates and central government representatives, there should also be a place for the worst affected Autonomous Communities (*Industrias Pesqueras*, no. 1641, 1 September 1995, p. 10). However, in the Andalusia parliament on 29 March 1995, the regional Agriculture and Fisheries Minister emphasized the limits to the pressure which could be exerted in the negotiations from the regional level (*Ideal*, 30 March 1995). Plata's appearance in parliament had been requested by both the PP and the Andalusia regionalist party who were critical of the weakness of the regional government in the negotiating process. Debates in the regional parliament, although regarded as relatively unimportant by central government, included regular warnings from opposition parties of the disastrous outcome of a weak EU negotiating position. While aware of their limited competencies in the negotiations, regional representatives in affected regions such as Andalusia were extremely critical of the minimal subnational input to talks (*Diario 16*, 19 April 1995), especially when the future of their economy depended on the outcome of the bargaining. Sectoral associations in the Canaries similarly criticized their lack of representation. The President of the main fishing association in the Canaries, José Ramón Fontán, expressed concern that the more visible and violent protest in Andalusia would lead to their demands being prioritized at the expense of regions such as the Canaries (*Industrias Pesqueras*, no. 1641, 1 September 1995, p. 9) (in a similar way to the fears that more active regions would gain higher levels of EU regional funding). Central government in Spain generally considered that established rules did not permit greater representation for subnational governments, as they were not recognized interlocutors at EU level. Government representatives from Andalusia observed negotiating rounds to maximize opportunities to lobby negotiators and, according to central government officials, were always consulted on political issues, while more technical issues were discussed with sectoral representatives directly.[9]

Representatives from the fishing sectors in all affected regions were consulted by central government at negotiating rounds. Although one commentator on the 1994 renegotiation of the agreement considered that the sectoral presence amounted to waiting for minimal information from the Spanish delegation after each session had closed (*Productos del Mar*, nos. 79–80, July–August 1994, pp. 17–19), the sector regarded the opportunity to obtain information first-hand, and defend its specific regional interests, as highly important. Consultation at key points of the negotiation formed an important part of the input of the sector to the Spanish bargaining position.[10] The Spanish delegation was obliged to act as an arbitrator between dispersed regional interests on certain issues, but welcomed observation of the negotiations by representatives from all regions.

The sector was particularly concerned about the agreement with Morocco, as it felt that the conflict with Canada had been resolved without its involvement. For example, the President of the shipowners' association in Cadiz, Arturo Castaño, was highly critical of the concessions made to Canada by the EU delegation, which he considered had placed the EU in a weak, vulnerable position *vis-à-vis* Morocco.[11] The Federación Nacional de Cofradías de Pescadores (National Federation of Fishing Associations) considered direct and permanent contact with officials at central and EU level the most effective mechanism for raising awareness of its demands and lobbying negotiators (*Productos del Mar*, nos. 95–6, November–December 1995, p. 13). Contact with regional government was considered an important accompanying measure, as officials acted as effective mediators with the EU level, assisting in the organization of meetings.[12] DG XIV Commission officials welcomed direct contact with the sector, and considered that this caused minimal tension at national level as central government representatives were generally also present to enhance the articulation of sectoral interests. According to a DG XIV official, 'es normal; no hacemos el acuerdo ni para el gobierno central ni para nosotros, sino para satisfacer los intereses de los armadores' (it is normal; we do not negotiate the agreement for the central government nor for ourselves, but to meet the demands of the shipowners).[13] In addition, the fishing sector lobbied the European Parliament, which sought to increase awareness of regional demands at EU level, and put forward questions raised by the sector to the Commission.[14] In the 1995 renegotiation, the aim of key fishing representatives was to use all potential channels to maximize their influence; the increasing presence of sectoral representatives on EU consultative fishing committees was thus also seen as an important additional channel (*Productos del Mar*, nos. 81–2, September–October 1994, p. 18).

Input of key regional and sectoral actors to the 1995 negotiations

The political opportunity structure may have increased access to the policy process for key regional and sectoral actors during EC/EU membership, but a more established dialogue with government and EU officials did not necessarily ensure their actual influence on the bargaining process. In addition to seeking to formalize dialogue at regional, central and EU levels, the sector in Andalusia thus sought to maximize its pressure on central government and the EU in 1995 via direct measures of protest to show their discontent, such as the boycott of Moroccan goods, strikes and public demonstrations. This is an illustration of both confrontational and assimilative strategies adopted by domestic actors to exploit the domestic opportunity structure, as described by Kitschelt (1986).

Level of protest

Domestic protest raised the visibility of the crisis situation, thus tending to increase the pressure on the Spanish delegation to meet regional demands. The sense of crisis in the Spanish fishing sector was exacerbated by what it regarded as the unacceptable demands of Moroccan fishing industry representatives, for example their refusal to accept increased EU payments in return for more fishing rights (*FT*, 1 May 1995).[15] However, although regional protest may have increased the pressure on central government, particularly during the pre-election period, the lack of coordination of actions reduced their impact. Actions were rarely organized in the region as a whole, and never nationally, so that in May and June 1995, 'por el momento cada puerto afectado parece estar haciendo la guerra por su cuenta' (for the moment each affected port seems to be waging war unilaterally) (*Productos del Mar*, nos. 89–90, May–June 1995, p. 14). However, central government was fully aware of the high visibility and potential impact of sectoral protest in the domestic arena, and considered maintaining calm in Andalusia during the suspension of fishing activity as a key objective. Even during the EC accession talks, one of the key negotiators criticized the fact that the fishing sector was rarely satisfied, illustrated by the fact that 'un pequeño fallo del negociador o una posición menos dura de lo que ellos deseaban los llevaba a protestar con vehemencia' (a minor mistake made by the negotiator or a less tough position than they wanted led to strong protest) (Bassols, 1995, p. 171) (see Chapter 2). The Spanish fishing sector considered that their acts of protest enforced a direct response to their urgent demands, and increased awareness of the extent of the dependence of the Andalusia economy on Moroccan fishing waters.

Central government officials, in regular meetings with representatives of fisheries and agricultural associations, sought to show the negative effects of an illegal boycott and violent acts against Moroccan imports, considering such actions as largely politically inspired, and particularly prevalent during a pre-election period. However, opposition parties highlighted the complacency of central government officials, whose response was described as being limited to verbal criticism of the more violent actions taken. As a result of the Spanish boycott, Morocco was forced to establish new maritime routes to European markets via the Mediterranean ports of France, and the Moroccan press exposed the fear of the authorities that a rise in Spanish protest would prevent the transit of emigrants (for example *Al-Bayane*, 9, 21 June 1995). The Commission considered Spanish acts of vandalism against Moroccan fishing products as harmful to the progress of negotiations (*Europe*, no. 6489, 26–27 May 1995, p. 13), while central government emphasized the importance of the EU's support for its negotiating position to avoid exacerbating domestic tensions. At regional level, the Director-General of Fisheries in Andalusia announced his support of a legal boycott following a meeting with representatives of the Federation of Andalusia shipowners on 19 April 1995, which led to the approval of strict health inspections on Moroccan fish imports; the rigorous nature of controls amounted to an effective boycott. The measure was passed in an attempt to defuse tension in the ports of Algeciras, Malaga and Almeria (*FT*, 16 May 1995). However, in keeping with the demands of negotiators at EU and central levels, violent protest was condemned by regional government, and even some provinces of Andalusia were critical of the more radical actions against Moroccan lorry drivers in ports such as Algeciras. The Moroccan press drew attention to the two-sided nature of the Spanish position, namely the official position adopted by the Spanish delegation at EU level, and its complacency towards illegal acts against Moroccan goods at domestic level for fear of being accused of not fully supporting its fishing sector's demands. This is illustrated by headlines in the Moroccan newspaper *Al-Bayane* on 17 July 1995, which refer both to Madrid's support for increased Moroccan exports of sardines and oranges, and to the pressure placed on the Spanish government by the fishing sector in Algeciras (Ojeda García, 1996, p. 33).

Financial support for the fishing sector, from both the Spanish government and the EU, was a key factor in reducing the rising tension during the suspension of fishing activity. The government highlighted the financial backing in the pre-election period as a clear illustration of its support for the sector, while some press reports cynically linked the speed with which the payments arrived to the PSOE government's need to win votes in the elections (for example *Ya*, 16 May 1995). The Spanish government argued that the European negotiating position *vis-à-vis* Morocco would be strengthened if the EU provided aid to sustain the fishermen for a longer period, but the Commission remained reticent regarding Spanish demands. In the European Parliament Fisheries Committee on 20 March 1995, Bonino ruled out automatic EU payments, and proposed financial backing from the structural funds already allocated to member states (unpublished communication from Spanish Permanent Representation to European Parliament on 14 February 1995). The Spanish cabinet approved a two billion peseta aid package for Spanish fishermen on 28 April 1995 given that the EU–Morocco fisheries agreement represented the livelihood for 28 000 workers in Spain and Portugal, and would affect up to 40–50 000 of the workforce (*Europe*, no. 6471, 29 April 1995, p. 8). A system of monthly individual compensation payments for the crews concerned was established by the Commission, although delays in the transfer of payments caused considerable tension in Andalusia. In addition, FIFG appropriations, already granted to Spain and Portugal under their operational programmes, were partly redirected to compensate shipowners for the temporary inactivity of their vessels (on the basis of Article 14 of Regulation EC 3699/93). During the period, 52 million ECU was made available (48 million for Spain and four million for Portugal), of which 39 million ECU came from EU resources (European Commission, 1996b, p. 99).

Level of dialogue

The Spanish government was fully aware of the sector's reluctance to accept EU legislation which would bring an end to traditional fishing rights in Moroccan waters, claiming from the start of the talks that it would fully support the sector as it had done in previous negotiations. The Secretary-General for Fisheries assured sectoral representatives that the EU would reject conditions which were unacceptable for the Spanish fishing sector,[16] and the Agriculture and Fisheries Minister described Moroccan demands as 'clearly out of proportion and unacceptable' (*FT*, 28 April 1995). After each stage of the negotiation, the Spanish delegation held extensive meetings with sectoral representatives and the Andalusia regional government, considering that direct contact was important for a full awareness of the issues involved, and for maintaining good relations with the sector. The high political importance of the agreement was underlined by the warning of Miguel Arias Cañete MEP (PP) in April 1995, that the agreement could jeopardize 18 000 jobs in Andalusia (*Ideal Granada*, 9 April 1995).

The Andalusia working group set forward its overall position and more specific demands for each fishing type in a document on 27 February 1995 prior to the commencement of negotiations. In March 1995, the Andalusia Agriculture and Fisheries Minister held meetings in Brussels with Commission officials to present the position of Andalusia before negotiations began (*Diario 16*, 21 March 1995). Meetings had been held in January 1995 to inform the Commission directly of specific regional demands, and contact with Fisheries Commissioner Bonino was a priority during the negotiations, including key meetings during the third, seventh and eighth negotiating rounds.[17] Furthermore, regular meetings were held throughout Andalusia in an attempt to formulate a strong position to present to the central and EU levels. One illustration is the presentation to governmental officials of an Algeciras working group document approved by the General Assembly of the Federación Andaluza (Andalusia Federation) on 18 April 1995 which totally rejected Moroccan demands; other provinces applied similar pressure. For example, it was agreed on 19 May, in a meeting of fishing representatives in Barbate, that a document listing demands agreed by the regional government in conjunction with the sector would be presented to central government for its defence at EU level. The fishing village of Barbate is a key example of a locality which is totally dependent on the fisheries agreement with Morocco for its livelihood, and the government was fully aware of the social and economic implications for the community if Moroccan demands were met by the EU (see Appendix for a fuller analysis). Full government support for Barbate was evident in earlier fishing negotiations, as illustrated by a letter in 1981 from the Ministry of Agriculture and Fisheries to the Moroccan Fisheries Minister, where the particular interest of the Spanish government in the Barbate fleet is expressed (unpublished letter, Ministry of Agriculture, Fisheries and Food, Madrid, 1 April 1981).

Despite the different interests of the provinces, the Andalusia fishing sector and regional government sought to maintain a united position, and set out their latest series of demands on 19 June, including an urgent request for meetings with Bonino and Atienza to argue their case directly. The failure of each negotiating round exacerbated domestic tensions at key ports such as Algeciras, and officials from central administration discussed the negotiations with representatives in the worst affected zones whenever another deadlock was reached. Atienza declared that his arguments against violent protest, and for a reasoned defence of fishing interests, were well received by the sector (*Diario de Jerez*, 25 May 1995), although press declarations following the meeting described the dissatisfaction of representatives with his response. Sectoral representatives in Andalusia accused the EU of treating Morocco more like an EU member than Spain (*Industrias Pesqueras*, no. 1636, 15 June 1995, p. 5), and were particularly critical of the notion of partnership which, according to the President of the ASEMAR shipowners' association in Cadiz, was not viable in practice (*Diario de Cádiz*, 6 May 1995). Criticism of the lack of transparency of the policy process was also voiced. However, key sectoral and regional government representatives were given the opportunity to present their demands regarding fishing quotas with major social and economic implications for the region directly to senior officials such as Bonino in Brussels. The close relations between the EU and regional levels are illustrated by Plata's praise of Bonino's sensitivity and in-depth knowledge of the situation experienced in Andalusia (*El Correo*, 30 June 1995).

When negotiations resumed in Brussels on 11 August, tensions were high in the fishing sector in view of the continued suspension of activity. Key sectoral representatives made pessimistic statements about a successful conclusion of negotiations. For example, a key Andalusia representative considered that Spain should veto the signing of a negative agreement, fearing the approval of an accord in the absence of full consultation with the sector (*Algeciras Marítimas*, 9 August 1995). The most contentious issues in the Andalusia fishing sector still held up the negotiations, namely fishing quotas, and the issue of Moroccan fishermen on Spanish boats (see Chapter 6). In a document sent to the Spanish delegation, the CCOO (1995a) highlighted the fact that the Moroccan presence on Spanish ships meant less employment for local fishermen in mainly family-owned businesses, especially in towns in Andalusia such as Barbate and Algeciras. On 30 August, Atienza held meetings with representatives from affected regional governments and the fishing sector to report on all areas of the negotiation. He stressed the importance of a tough Spanish position which was dependent on a unity of action in the sector. A spokesman for the fishermen in Algeciras, Miguel Alberto Díaz, considered that Andalusia's interests were being prioritized for the first time in the negotiations during August (*Algeciras Marítimas*, 10 August 1995).

The lack of agreement on any key issues worked to the Spanish government's advantage in one respect, namely in ensuring unanimous opposition to Moroccan demands as long as no individual region had attained their specific objectives.[18] Despite the criticism of the government, all regional authorities, including those ruled by the PP, were reported to have largely supported the Spanish government's position at EU level (*Mar*, no. 331, September 1995, p. 9). The linkage with the Association agreement, and the EU's commitment to financial aid, were considered effective means of placing pressure on the Moroccan delegation by Andalusia shipowners, who were prepared to accept the inactivity of the fleet rather than an agreement which ignored Spanish interests. Nonetheless, the lack of any concrete results following Bonino's talks in Rabat led to unrest, and demands for greater consultation, exacerbated by the criticism of the main opposition party. According to a spokesperson in Algeciras, where some of the most serious protests had occurred, the breakdown of negotiations at the end of August was 'una auténtica declaración de guerra para el sector' (a genuine declaration of war for the sector) (*El País*, 29 August 1995). Pressure on central government from key fishing representatives was maintained until the final negotiating round in November when, after eight months of suspended activity, tensions were particularly high in the domestic arena.

Reactions to the agreement and implementation

Although the final agreement was, in the view of one Spanish fisheries official, 'the best we could have hoped for' (*FT*, 19 December 1995), the EU's concessions to Morocco in the final negotiating rounds were criticized in the Spanish fishing sector. The Commission's proposals for reducing fishing quotas in August were regarded as an unacceptable concession by representatives from the Canaries in view of Morocco's refusal to make any compromises (*Industrias Pesqueras*, no. 1641, 1 September 1995, p. 9) and the President of the Andalusia Fishermen's Federation, Montoya, declared that Andalusia was not in a position to accept the reduction in its fish catch (*El País*, 13 August 1995). Although the biggest reductions in quotas, namely in cephalopods, had the most impact on the fishing sector in the Canaries, the sector in Andalusia was more dependent on the outcome of the agreement and particularly critical of the accord approved by EU negotiators; this is shown by the widespread protest against the agreement. Central government was accused of not having insisted on a tougher EU negotiating position, but officials responded by highlighting the fact that Morocco did not manage to obtain a number of its initial demands, namely the huge reductions in quotas, the increase in numbers of Moroccans on Spanish ships and obligatory unloading in Moroccan ports.

Many fishing representatives complained of a lack of information. The President of the Andalusia Federation of Fishermen's Associations drew attention to the secretive way in which negotiations were conducted, illustrating this with the lack of awareness of whether an agreement had been reached in the seventh negotiating round. However, it was highlighted at EU level that not even member states could be given the full information on negotiating positions during the talks, the lack of transparency being considered by EU negotiators as a natural part of the bargaining process.[19] Regional government in Andalusia was less critical of central government's negotiating tactics, which was to be expected in view of the PSOE also being the ruling party at regional level. It declared its general satisfaction with the outcome, regarding the input of the regional working group to have been important for the final accord reached. Plata highlighted the fact that the majority of the Andalusia fleet remained active in Moroccan waters, and that the final reductions in fish quotas were less than anticipated.

One key problem in implementing the agreement was Moroccan insistence on a revision of the agreement to permit a suspension of fishing activity in March and April 1997 for cephalopods, in addition to the two months of inactivity in September and October agreed on in the 1995 accord. The demand was at first rejected by Brussels, but was eventually accepted in January 1997. This caused considerable unrest in Andalusia in view of the impact on the fresh fish market, whereas the frozen fish market in the Canaries could adapt more easily to the revised terms. Both regional government and the fishing sector considered that negotiators were at fault for not demanding concessions in return for the extension of the suspension period. However, the revision of the agreement was generally accepted by the sector, particularly in the Canaries where the fact that reciprocity had been accepted by Moroccan fishermen for the first time was welcomed. Despite doubts regarding the willingness of the Moroccan government to renegotiate the agreement, working group meetings organized by the Andalusia regional government in conjunction with the fishing sector formulated their position prior to renegotiation.

Conclusions

Whereas the fishing agreement with Mauritania only affected Cadiz, the agreement with Morocco was of fundamental importance for all the ports of Andalusia. The fishing sector was thus determined to make its demands as visible as possible to regional and central government in 1995. The sub-DG for Fisheries in Andalusia played a key role in keeping central government informed of the sector's demands, and of its response to the Spanish delegation's negotiating terms. The Director-General of Fisheries in Andalusia highlighted the firm position of the regional government throughout the negotiations, following extensive and regular consultation with the sector (*Industrias Pesqueras*, no. 1636, 15 June 1995, pp. 7–9). The Secretary-General for Fisheries affirmed that the Autonomous Communities were consulted throughout the negotiating process;[20] senior government officials thus acted as an important channel between the sector and central government. In the case of Andalusia, good relations between the PSOE Agriculture and Fisheries Ministers at central and regional level aided effective collaboration.

Evidence in this chapter has demonstrated that a range of actors other than central government can gain opportunities to get involved in the policy process. The extensive consultation process between and even during the rounds of negotiations, demonstrates the interaction between actors at all levels during the negotiation of a specific agreement, as outlined below:

1. *Relations between the fishing sector and regional government.* Evidence from the analysis suggests that the Andalusia regional government and the fishing sector enjoyed gradually closer relations during EC/EU membership. Working-group meetings were held at regional level to formulate a bargaining position in negotiations with Morocco, as well as to elaborate the Modernization Plan for the Andalusia fishing sector. Fishing sector representatives considered their participation in the Modernization Plan significant as it set a precedent for future consultation, and especially for the sector's increased input during negotiations with Morocco.[21]

2. *Relations between the fishing sector and central government.* Central government's defence of fishing interests was generally acknowledged in the sector, although sectoral representatives complained about insufficient information, and excessive concessions to the Moroccan delegation. A network of key sectoral representatives and central government officials seemed to be firmly established during the negotiating rounds, which facilitated the direct input of the sector to the Spanish bargaining position. The Agriculture and Fisheries Minister referred to the 'gran coincidencia en el proceso de negociación' (high level of agreement during the negotiating process) between the sector and central administration.[22] Central government officials often relied on data supplied by key fishing organizations to argue the Spanish case at EU level, indicating central government's dependence on the resources of key sectoral actors.

3. *Relations between the fishing sector and the EU level.* The fishing sector managed to obtain direct contact with EU officials even at the highest level, namely with the Fisheries Commissioner. Meetings were often arranged by regional government, and were considered highly important for raising awareness of their interests directly, instead of relying on central government as an intermediary channel. Observation of negotiations at EU level was also a key mechanism for direct consultation with EU officials, when sectoral representatives could provide their expertise and seek to influence the bargaining process.

4. *Relations between regional and central government.* The increased collaboration between regional and central government, for example in the management of FIFG structural funding, and the acknowledgement by the Minister for Agriculture and Fisheries in 1996 that regional government enjoys 90 per cent of competencies in the area of fisheries, fully illustrates the growing capacity of regional government to participate in the policy process and the increasing cooperation between the two levels of government. The crisis situation in affected regions gave regional government a particularly prominent role in representing sectoral interests in the renegotiation with Morocco.
5. *Relations between regional government and the EU level.* Representatives from regional government also observed the negotiations at EU level, and sought to maximize their contact with EU officials, for example Plata's meetings with DG XIV officials prior to, and during, the negotiations. Direct contact was encouraged in Brussels by both the Commission and European Parliament, although central government representatives were usually also present at meetings.

Despite the growing interaction described, key sectoral representatives still voiced their criticism of insufficient support from central government. For example, certain associations felt that central government could have defended the sector at EU level to a greater degree and taken advantage of direct contact with EU negotiators to emphasize further the crisis situation. Some sectoral representatives had similarly complained in 1994 of insufficient meetings with the government, and declared a lack of confidence in both central administration and the EU regarding the negotiation of a fair fishing agreement (*Industrias Pesqueras*, nos. 1620–1, 1 November 1994, pp. 10–11). In 1995, the visibility of the fishing issue was greater in view of the crisis in the sector. It is significant that an informal agreement allowed the EU to resume fishing in Moroccan waters on 25 November to avoid disruption by Spanish fishermen at the EuroMed conference in November. Furthermore, central government officials highlighted the fact that they had repeatedly declared at EU level that the Spanish delegation would not sign an Association agreement while the future of the fishing sector was at risk. The Spanish delegation assured the sector that its bargaining position was firmly based on the demands they had set out. The high impact of fisheries at regional level and the traditionally strong attachment to the fishing industry ensured overwhelming public support for the fishing sector's demands. The PSOE government was thus obliged to pay attention to a dependent sector, faced with huge regional pressures, and the fact that it could not afford to lose face in the domestic arena. A high level of autonomy for central government could thus not be assured.

As illustrated in Chapter 1, certain sets of conditions in the Spanish domestic arena have allowed greater participation of regional and sectoral actors in the EU policy process during EC/EU membership. Key factors are particularly relevant to the case study on fisheries, namely the development of a more advanced lobbying process, illustrated by the increasingly organized fishing sector, greater competencies at regional level as a result of decentralization, and the loss of the PSOE majority in 1993. The loss of majority decreased the government's margin of manoeuvre, which was particularly significant during the pre-electoral period in 1995. Other factors are more specific to the negotiation in question, namely the high tension in the sector caused by the suspension of activity over a long period of time, the potential crisis in affected regions faced with substantial cuts in quotas in Moroccan waters, and a lack of alternative fishing grounds.

An analysis of a one-off negotiation in the area of fisheries allows a study of the relations between actors at the level of the EU, Spanish central and regional government, and key representatives of the Spanish fishing sector. Even if some of the characteristics of the negotiation are unique to the Moroccan case, it provides an illustration of the implication of the increased involvement of domestic actors other than central government in the EU negotiating arena. The negotiations required a delicate balance between tough domestic demands and external EU obligations, which meant a potentially difficult role for central government in Spain. The political rationale for EC entry during the accession negotiations could no longer be used to maintain a clear consensus on European policy, especially as the economic implications of EC/EU membership in areas such as fisheries were increasingly criticized. This is illustrated by a *Eurobarometer* poll in May 1995 which showed that only 20 per cent of Spaniards believed Spain had benefited from EU membership, and 60 per cent, the highest percentage of all EU member states, considered it had not been beneficial (*Eurobarometer*, no. 43, 1995, p. 5). This provides a contrast with the highly pro-European attitude revealed by polls in Spain during the accession negotiations (see Chapter 2).

Although the fishing sector had always sought to maximize its input to talks at EU level, the increased facility with which representatives had direct contact with national and EU officials indicates an opening of the opportunity structure in 1995. This enhanced their input to the negotiating process. Regular contact between central government officials and the sector meant that moves towards the development of an active fisheries 'network' could be noted, involving key representatives of the fishing sector, regional and central government and key informants and negotiators at EU level.[23] The sector was more likely to have confidence in the Spanish delegation's articulation of the national position as a result of this increased contact. One central government official illustrated the complicity between central government and the sector by the fact that it was agreed that the fisheries agreement with Mauritania, in the final stages of the negotiations with Morocco, would be kept secret for a period of time in case it resulted in a weaker EU bargaining position *vis-à-vis* the Moroccan delegation.[24] If the sector's interests were not adequately defended, central government faced domestic protest, increased scepticism about Spain's EU membership and the risk of losing the support of the electorate. The political weight of fisheries in Spain increased the visibility of the sector, and could not be ignored by the PSOE government whose continued power was no longer assured. The strong dependence of the fishing sector, the large number of employees, and the high visibility and public awareness of fisheries ensured that it was prioritized by the PSOE government during the 1995 negotiations. Furthermore, meetings between fishing sector representatives in Andalusia and the EU level were important for the direct representation of sectoral interests, meaning that the central state was no longer relied upon as the sole channel of influence at national level.

The margin of manoeuvre enjoyed by central government was considerably reduced during the negotiating period, the timing of the early rounds ensuring that domestic political factors had a high impact on EU-level negotiations. Although a greater degree of autonomy was possible after the May elections, its minority status and the predicted opposition victory in the 1996 elections still weakened its position *vis-à-vis* the fishing sector. Other key factors, such as the increasingly assertive role of key regional authorities affected by the negotiation and the more organized fishing sector, also increased the pressures on central government. Although this indicates an opening of the political opportunity structure, it does not necessarily indicate a clear impact on policy decisions. Despite regular dialogue between central government and the sector, sectoral representatives still complained that the Commission was making decisions at EU level to which central government in Spain agreed without consulting them. Nonetheless, the analysis clearly demonstrated a growing awareness of the policy process, greater organization of interests and evidence of a network of closely interacting groups. The central state still retained its strong national gatekeeper role as the only recognized negotiator at the EU level. However, in view of the delicate balance to be attained between tough domestic demands and external EU obligations, the analysis should go beyond a focus on the central state as negotiator in the EU arena.

8
Conclusions: Beyond the Spanish State?

The key role played by the Spanish central state in the policy process emerges from the analysis in this book of Spain during its EC accession negotiations and EC/EU membership. The dynamic approach adopted for the study of the Spanish case has made it possible to look beyond the role of the central state and examine new constellations of actors and interactive processes which previous academic work on Spain has tended to underplay. The conclusions of the chapter on the EC accession negotiations supports the general view in the literature that the central state retained a high level of autonomy in the process, while taking into account the input of a range of other domestic actors. However, the analysis also highlights key changes in the institutional framework for policy-making in Spain during EC/EU membership which suggest that a new policy-making context was developing. In view of the greater focus on the central state of existing literature on Spain, detailed empirical work was carried out to explore further relations between the Spanish central state and other key domestic actors in selected policy settings. The case studies of cohesion policy and fisheries illustrate the changing opportunity structures at domestic and EU levels which have enabled other domestic actors to increase their input to the policy process in particular policy areas. Ladrech (1994, p. 85) highlights the importance of differences in the capacity of domestic actors to exploit the opportunities for greater input, 'some fearing a loss of autonomy, others perceiving an opportunity'. This book examines variations in the level of access to policy-making, and in the resources of key domestic actors such as regional authorities and socio-economic groups, as well as the differing degree of control which the central state is able to exert over their involvement.

Although the main objective of this study was to evaluate the nature of the changing relations between the central state and other domestic actors, it did not set out to prove that the central state's role had diminished as a result of key developments at domestic and EU levels. Rather, the aim was to show that it would be obliged to adapt to a new policy-making environment where other domestic actors would have greater potential for enhancing their input. Evidence from the analysis would suggest that this is the case. Although relations between central government and other domestic actors have developed significantly during EC/EU membership, the impact of greater domestic mobilization on the level of autonomy of central government cannot be assumed. Central government appears, rather, to have maintained its key role and autonomy on issues of strategic importance. It has thus conceded power to other domestic actors only where their involvement strengthened its bargaining position at EU level, or where it was dependent on their skills and resources for effective policy implementation.

Evaluation of key findings

This section summarizes key conclusions drawn from the analysis of the role of Spanish central government and other domestic actors during the EC accession negotiations and EC/EU membership followed by key findings from the study of specific policy settings.

EC accession

The study of the EC accession negotiations in Chapter 2 demonstrated the key role of the central state throughout the negotiations. At domestic level, its use of EC-level rationales to justify tough policies, such as the modernization of key sectors, illustrated the level of control it exercised over the interaction between the EC and domestic arenas. At EC level, although the overall pro-European consensus within the country generally strengthened Spain's application for membership, opposition to specific entry terms in vulnerable sectors was also used by central government to gain a better deal. For example, the Spanish delegation sought to negotiate longer transition periods and limits to tariff barriers in the steel sector in the face of strong demands from domestic producers, and the CEOE warned against sacrificing sectoral interests to obtain a political success. However, domestic constraints were of limited use at EC level in view of the high political costs if Spain's integration into the European framework had been jeopardized.

The analysis of the accession period suggests that central government relations with other domestic actors were not developed during the negotiations, although a predictable discrepancy emerged between the claims of UCD and PSOE government officials, and those of key domestic actors regarding the level of information on EC entry available. For example, the CCOO claimed that they only received a posteriori information from central government officials during sporadic meetings while central government, for its part, highlighted the lack of interest shown in the negotiations by the unions. Key lobby groups, such as CNAG representing farmers, were particularly critical towards the end of the negotiations of the lack of consultation with the agricultural sector regarding concrete entry terms. The more active regional authorities were generally better informed than socio-economic actors about the implications of EC entry, although most of the regions were also sidelined from the process. The formulation of the Spanish bargaining position was, perhaps logically, a centralized process, involving a small group of senior civil servants whose autonomy was enhanced by the predominant role played by the executive in the Spanish policy-making process. The unquestioned control of González over the party and electorate from 1982 further centralized the formulation of key bargaining positions.

EC/EU membership

The increasing number and complexity of policy areas, and the growing awareness of EU policy among a wider range of actors, has inevitably changed the nature of policy-making in Spain during EC/EU membership. Key changes include the growing autonomy of key ministries such as Economy and Finance, the greater focus of the SSEU on information exchange, and the higher level of awareness of EU policy among key domestic groups. However, evidence presented in Chapter 3 points to the continued centralization of the process despite these key developments. Until 1993, the majoritarian PSOE government enjoyed considerable autonomy and, even after 1993, it retained a large margin for manoeuvre in the domestic arena although dependent on the support of regionalist parties. The role of an elite of government officials with a high level of expertise in European policy was essential in formulating the Spanish bargaining position. Despite reforms intended to strengthen the role of the Joint Committee for the EU in the Spanish parliament in the process, its actual impact on European policy remained minimal.

The complaint of domestic actors such as unions and employers that they were peripheral to the policy-making process continued to be voiced during EC/EU membership. Fora developed for consultation with socio-economic actors, such as the Economic and Social Council, were found to exert a minimal influence on the Spanish government's position at EC/EU level. Both trade unions and employers have made efforts to enhance their influence on European policy, but progress was limited, particularly when they were faced with the reluctance of central government officials to establish mechanisms for consultation. Union involvement was still largely confined to sending its recommendations to relevant government officials who were under no obligation to take them into account. The CEOE's bargaining strategies in the EU arena remained underdeveloped, and only the most important sectors, who tended to have independent lobbying strategies in the EU arena, seemed to exert any influence on EU policy decisions. Little evidence exists for the development of closer relations between public administration and private interests in the area of EU policy in Spanish society.

Although central government has thus retained its key role during EC/EU membership, the greater input of regional authorities to the policy process should be noted. Sectoral meetings established to increase their participation have enhanced coordination and regional representation, even if only gradually, and in certain policy areas. Although the lack of common agreement between the regions reduced their influence on the negotiating position of central government, the interregional accord on representation in the Council of Ministers in September 1999 is one indication of the potential for further progress although their proposals were not approved by central government. A dynamic approach to the analysis of the policy process thus revealed key changes which could become more significant over time.

Cohesion policy

The case study on cohesion policy clearly indicates the key role played by the Spanish government in interstate negotiation of structural funding. Spanish arguments for budgetary increases at the Brussels, Maastricht and Edinburgh Summits, analysed in Chapter 4, had a significant influence on the policy agenda. Spain had to overcome opposition from net contributors to the Community, who resisted proposals for ambitious resource transfers, by arguing that the development of cohesion policy was in the Community's general interest. Although the 1991 Dutch Presidency initially ignored Spanish demands, Spain ultimately obtained legal guarantees on cohesion within the Treaty. Its voice was strengthened at the Edinburgh Summit by the fact that its support was needed for the acceptance of both the Danish exemptions from Maastricht and enlargement of the Community. The increase in the financial framework from 18.6 to 30 billion ECU by 1999 was regarded as a key victory in the Spanish domestic arena. The Spanish government's intransigent bargaining position was, to a certain extent, a response to the need to present a successful outcome to parliament and the public at large as a means of countering increasing criticism of government reforms, and a less assured consensus on European policy. Key domestic actors increasingly demanded information on policy decisions at EU level, and opposition parties became more critical of central government's negotiation of structural funding. Despite increasing pressures on the PSOE government to negotiate an acceptable deal, evidence of the direct input of domestic actors only emerges during the analysis of the operationalization of structural funding in Chapter 5.

EC funding for Spain was all fed into the national budget during the first year of membership, regarded as an important means of reducing the state deficit of 4.5 per cent of GDP. From 1987, projects that fell within subnational competencies were presented and approved at regional level, although the central state continued to retain control of the process, including the formulation of the RDP. Despite the lack of change in the distribution of resources between regional and central governments between the 1989–93 and 1994–9 funding cycles, the increase in direct transfers of information between the Commission and regional authorities was one of the key developments which indicated that the context for the funding process had changed. However, the level of regional participation depended on the particular stage of policy-making. The CSF was still largely negotiated by the Commission and member states and, even if the partnership principle functioned increasingly effectively in monitoring committees, the Ministry of Economy and Finance maintained that the transfer of resources was the responsibility of central government.

The level of participation was found to vary significantly between different domestic actors. Politically active regions, such as Catalonia and the Basque Country, succeeded in making considerable advances, for example in the area of the Cohesion Fund, where the pressures they exerted on central government in the 21 September 1994 meeting led to their involvement in an initially purely state-run fund. In contrast, in Andalusia, officials were more concerned about maximizing the level of funding received rather than being directly involved in the policy process. The analysis of cohesion policy thus highlighted the high level of variation between regional authorities, to the extent that some even welcomed a key moderating role for the central state to avoid losing out to the more politically active regions. The minimal access to the process for socio-economic actors, despite their inclusion as participants in the 1993 reform of the structural funds, is an indication of central government's greater reluctance to permit the involvement of trade unions and employers. For example, socio-economic actors were not members of the monitoring committees for CSFs and OPs for Objectives One and Two in Spain, their formal representation still being largely restricted to the ESF committees. Even where regional plans were given to the Economic and Social Council for discussion, delay in their presentation and the complex nature of procedures meant that little time was allowed for any input to their formulation. The conclusions of the case study indicate that central government in Spain has permitted greater domestic involvement for a select group of actors, and only at specific stages of the funding process.

Fisheries

The analysis of the renegotiation of the EU–Morocco fisheries agreement in 1995 illustrates the key role of the Spanish delegation in lobbying for a tough EU position *vis-à-vis* Morocco. The extent of reduction in EU fishing quotas was largely determined by the Spanish position, although Spain was sometimes obliged to compromise over its demands. For example, the proposal to cut only 2 per cent of the cephalopod fleet in June 1995, intended to minimize the loss of jobs in the domestic arena, was rejected by the Commission. The evidence examined in Chapter 6 suggests that Spain's EU Presidency enhanced its central role in the negotiations, for example by encouraging a clear linkage between the fisheries and Association agreements in order to obtain the optimal deal for its fishing sector. The Spanish government played an important role in setting the agenda and in influencing the Commission and other member states throughout the 1995 renegotiation of the agreement, which was generally acknowledged by the fishing sector and the regional authority in Andalusia. Sectoral pressures in the domestic arena were used to strengthen the Spanish bargaining position at EU level.

Close interaction between the PSOE government and sectoral and regional actors was evident during the negotiations, particularly as the demands of the fishing sector became a key issue during the municipal and regional elections in May 1995. The high level of protest in affected regions, namely the boycott of Moroccan goods, strikes and high-profile demonstrations, and the public sympathy for the sector's demands, ensured regular consultation between the PSOE government and the sector, although the actual influence on government policy could not be assured. Chapter 7 draws attention to regional governments' increasing participation in EU fisheries policy, for example in FIFG funding, and to the greater organization of shipowners' and fishermen's groups into more representative associations. Whereas the prevalence of smaller, often family-owned businesses in Andalusia was found to have reduced their lobbying capacity, pressure on Spanish negotiators was strengthened in 1995 by the establishment for the first time of a working group by the Andalusia government which sought to reach a common position. Although direct access to negotiators was obtained with increasing facility, for example informal meetings with senior officials such as Commissioner Bonino during the observation of negotiating rounds, the sector still claimed that the EU bargaining position was determined by the Spanish government in conjunction with the Commission and involved minimal dialogue with the sector. The study concludes that the mobilization and strong lobbying capacity of key sectoral and regional actors was evident during the 1995 negotiations, but that its actual impact cannot be overstated in view of the fact that the central state ultimately remained the only recognized negotiator at EU level.

The starting point of this book was that the context for EC/EU policy-making in Spain had changed during membership, affecting the role of the central state and other domestic actors, in both the overall policy process and institutional framework (Chapters 2 and 3) and in specific issue areas (Chapters 4–7). The key findings clearly demonstrate the growing access to the process of non-central government actors, particularly regional authorities, but also show that central government has successfully adapted to the new context and has thus retained a strong role at key policy-making stages.

Changing opportunity structures

As outlined in Chapter 1, the core presumption of a state-centric approach is the continued autonomy of the central state, which may be expected to be largely appropriate for the Spanish case from an analysis of the EC accession negotiations. Even if domestic actors had their own agendas, either the capacity to articulate them was absent, or the Spanish government was sufficiently strong to take little account of them. The central state acted as the exclusive channel for representing domestic interests throughout the period. Despite its dominant role, the consideration of the input of other domestic actors facilitates a fuller explanation of the rationale behind Spanish government strategies during the negotiating period, for example its reaction to opposition to EC entry from key sectors.

The potential for greater domestic input to policy-making during EU membership has been demonstrated in this book, although Chapter 3 also highlighted the key role and autonomy retained by central government. Changes in the institutional framework can be discerned, such as far more direct contact between domestic actors and the EU level, and new channels of participation established by regional authorities. Kitschelt (1986) distinguishes between a substantive impact on policy formulation of key domestic actors, and an impact which merely legitimizes new access points to policy-making, which he describes as procedural. Applying this distinction, Chapter 3 indicated that new channels of participation can be established which, even if not initially influential, may have a greater effect in the long term.

The analysis also explored the role of the central state and other domestic actors in specific policy areas. The study in Chapter 4 of Spain's negotiation of EU funding clearly established an interstate bargaining framework where the Spanish government retained almost exclusive powers of negotiation in policy formulation and the distribution of EU funding. The Brussels and Edinburgh European Councils were state-run operations, largely inaccessible to other domestic actors. The analysis of the negotiation of the 1995 EU–Morocco fisheries agreement similarly provides clear evidence of the key role of the central state in the decision-making process, although a more dynamic framework for exploring the interaction between the EU and domestic arenas allowed a greater focus on new formal and informal channels developed by domestic groups to gain greater input to specific policy areas. Merely focusing on the role played by the central state did not provide a sufficient explanation of the policy process in cases where other actors, for example in the fisheries sector, have developed a high level of expertise and resources. The role of the central state as gatekeeper between two interacting arenas thus affords a more appropriate framework for the analysis at stages in the policy process where involvement of other domestic actors has become more established. The evidence examined in the book strongly suggests that the interstate bargaining framework which emerges from the evaluation of the internal dynamics of key policy areas cannot be examined separately from the domestic negotiating arena.

In the area of cohesion policy, increasingly assertive regional actors and their demands for higher levels of financing were used to strengthen Spain's tough position on structural funding at the Edinburgh Summit in 1992. The Spanish government avoided raising overly high expectations in the domestic arena regarding cohesion, and used the net gains to demonstrate to its domestic constituency the concrete benefits from EU membership. Pressures at EU level also allowed central government to 'sell' policies domestically which would have been difficult to justify otherwise. For example, in the area of fisheries, substantial cuts in fishing quotas in the 1995 EU agreement with Morocco were justified in the domestic arena as the optimal deal for Spain given the pressures of other EU member states, the Commission and the Moroccan delegation. The central state had to strike a delicate balance between the EU and domestic arenas, and its role as national gatekeeper was shown to be crucial throughout the negotiations. The effort required by central government to gain the Andalusia fishing sector's approval of the terms of the EU–Morocco fisheries agreement demonstrates how domestic interests became part of the specification of the bargaining ability of the state. A more demanding domestic ratification process would seem to be in evidence. Sectoral demands were used to justify a tough national bargaining position to counterparts at EU level, while the crisis nature of the issue in the domestic arena made the representation of sectoral interests crucial to the central state's continued hold on power. Central government's manipulation of the EU and domestic arenas was illustrated in selected policy settings, namely the use of a small domestic 'win-set' to increase its autonomy at EU level (the 'tying hands' strategy), and the use of EU-level rationales to justify its policy decisions in the domestic arena.

Although this book has shown that the central state is no longer the exclusive channel for the representation of domestic interests, the lack of a pluralist tradition in Spain has meant that networks of key actors have been slow to develop. The continued marginalization of socio-economic actors from the process provides an illustration of how central government interpreted partnership restrictively, and acknowledged the legitimacy of only a select set of actors in the policy process. The impact of greater access by domestic actors to policy-making depends on their capacity to exploit opportunities, and only a minority of the strongest regional authorities have been able to gain direct access to the EU arena.

Despite evidence of the continued autonomy of central government in Spain, the increasing involvement of regional authorities in the implementation phase of structural funding should be noted. Chapter 5 offered evidence of the development of more elaborate coordination mechanisms and channels for information exchange in the 1994–9 funding cycle. The Commission's promotion of regional involvement, the greater awareness at regional level, and the lesser degree of resistance of central government to subnational involvement have changed the policy-making environment. Considerable evidence exists of increasing regional involvement during the operationalization of structural funding. Marks (1996) refers to the varying functional reliance on regional authorities within the implementation phase, as manifested by the lesser dependence on regional actors during the formulation of RDPs and the negotiation of CSFs, and a much greater dependence on subnational resources for the implementation of OPs and for monitoring. The central state was able to minimize domestic input at key stages in the process when it wished to retain full autonomy, for example by establishing global plans for each of the Objectives, and by ultimately deciding on the destination of funding at regional level, and could encourage more involvement where a greater resource dependency on subnational actors existed. Similarly, in the area of fisheries, mechanisms were established for regular consultation and information exchange between EU and central government negotiators and the fishing sector which indicated an opening of the opportunity structure. However, despite the clear evidence presented in Chapter 7 of a more advanced lobbying process and an increased facility of dialogue at all levels, the input of domestic actors was limited in a context where the central state remained the only recognized interlocutor in the decision-making process.

The limited access to the policy process for domestic actors during the EC accession negotiations, as demonstrated in Chapter 2, was seen to be due to the closed political opportunity structure at domestic level. Unscrambling the autonomous effects of factors at domestic and EU levels is beyond the scope of this study which merely aims to highlight some of the key factors engendering change in a dynamic policy process. Key sets of conditions in Spanish society have been outlined, namely: the political rationale for EC accession, the majoritarian PSOE government, the early stage in the decentralization process, the weak nature of civil society and the low level of demand for information about the EC. The 'game' has changed during EC/EU membership, as illustrated by the changing sets of conditions outlined in Chapter 3, which have allowed a more open political opportunity structure to develop with greater access to policy-making for domestic actors. Although the central state has retained a high level of control over the policy process, central government's monopoly of the interface between the separated EU and domestic arenas can no longer be assumed. The balance in favour of economic over political rationales for membership, the loss of central government's majority, the more advanced stage of decentralization, the development of a stronger civil society, and an increased awareness about EC/EU membership were some of the key changes considered to have encouraged a more open opportunity structure.

Analysis of the changing opportunity structures would seem to indicate that access to the policy process for domestic actors was only enhanced where permitted, and even encouraged, by the central state, and by the nature of the policy setting at EU level. This was illustrated by enhanced regional participation in the implementation of the structural funds. Despite clear limitations to their role, regional authorities were able to obtain direct contact with EU officials, manage their own budgets, and represent their interests in meetings between the Commission and member states. The extent to which the opening opportunity structure at domestic level can be exploited has been shown to depend not only on the resources of domestic actors, but on the particular EU policy area and the stage of the process. Detailed evaluation of the internal dynamics of cohesion policy and fisheries allowed a comparison of the role of the central state and other domestic actors in different policy areas, thus providing a more rigorous test of conclusions on the case of Spain.

Policy areas

The different nature of the two selected policy settings analysed was outlined in Chapter 1 where the localized, crisis management nature of the specific fisheries episode negotiated at EU level was contrasted with the series of negotiating rounds during EU membership in the area of cohesion policy, although both are part of a broader EU negotiating cycle. A further key difference between the policy areas, which was seen to be important in an evaluation of the findings of the cases, was the nature of the most directly implicated domestic actors in each policy setting.

While also examining the access of socio-economic groups to the policy process, the key focus of the study of cohesion policy was on regional authorities, while the most directly involved actors in fisheries were sectoral representatives, even if supported by their regional authority. In the area of structural funding, regional authorities have made increasing input to policy formulation, the management of funding, and the implementation and evaluation of projects. They have used both established mechanisms and their increasing level of skills and resources to gain access to policy-making, particularly in the case of the most active regions. Chapter 3 clearly demonstrated that the access of socio-economic actors to the policy process was more difficult than that of regional authorities, making the input of shipowners' associations and unions to the formulation of a bargaining position in the area of fisheries more problematic. However, given the crisis nature of the negotiations, the fishing sector maximized its pressure on central government in 1995, and was able to establish new channels for dialogue, even if it still complained about the lack of consultation with central government and EU officials.

Despite these key differences, a changed political opportunity structure was evident in both policy areas. In the two cases, the degree to which domestic input was enhanced was found to be dependent on the level of resources of domestic actors, and the extent to which the central state could control their involvement. A study of the interstate negotiating level demonstrates the Spanish government's central role as a strategic actor working to maximize its gains in the EU and domestic arenas in the two policy areas. In the area of cohesion policy, the Spanish government sought to attain a balance between the net gains at domestic level, and its pro-integrationist position at EC/EU level, which highlighted the importance of cohesion for all EU member states. In the area of fisheries, it maintained a delicate balance between domestic gains for its fishing sector, in the form of a satisfactory fishing agreement, and its pro-Mediterranean position in EU-level negotiations which emphasized the importance of strengthening ties with Morocco. Evidence thus points to the active role of the central state as gatekeeper between the domestic and EU arenas in both policy areas.

Stages in the policy process

Relations between the central state and other domestic actors was found not only to be determined by the particular policy area, and the type of domestic actor, but also by the stage in the policy process, as discussed in Chapter 1. The study of cohesion policy offers considerable evidence of increased regional participation during the implementation phase. Policy-shaping decisions frequently required the resources of key domestic actors with a growing capacity to participate, such as regional authorities.

Key decisions determined through interstate bargaining at EU level where the Spanish state enjoyed a high level of autonomy, such as the 1992 Edinburgh decision on financing or the 1995 fisheries agreement, evidently limited awareness of the central state's negotiating tactics, and access to the policy-making process. The study of fisheries focuses on the attempt of regional and sectoral representatives to maximize their influence on central government's bargaining position at inter-state level even though the central state remains the only recognized interlocutor. Key sectoral actors placed considerable pressure on the Spanish delegation during the negotiating rounds, and maximized their input to 'history-making decisions' wherever possible. The implementation of the fishing agreement required direct sectoral involvement, but the sector sought to maximize its pressure on the decision-making phase to avoid the serious economic and social implications of sub-stantial quota reductions, hence the focus in Chapter 7. Despite the factors militating against greater domestic involvement in the fisheries negotiations, its high visibility across the EU, public sympathy for the sector in the domestic arena, and the enormous social and economic implications for specific regions meant that the articulation of domes-tic interests was strengthened, and could succeed in exerting consider-able direct pressure on central government in a pre-election period.

Concluding remarks

The focus on the changing domestic context in the case of Spain has highlighted key conditions which have encouraged greater input of actors other than central government to the policy-making process. This is a result of the impact of both autonomous domestic factors and EC/EU membership. The extent of their relative influence remains an issue for further analysis.

Conclusions point to the continued primacy of the central state in Spain in different policy settings despite the changing nature of the policy process, thus supporting the view of the exalted role of the state in Spanish political culture (Keating, 1993, p. 341). However, this study has gone beyond this assumption, common in existing literature on Spain and the EU, and has taken a more dynamic approach which focuses on the central state's adaptation to a new policy-making con-text. Although the analysis may be criticized for having gone beyond the state-centric view prevalent in previous literature only to return to the primacy of the central state in its conclusions, it has shown the justification for a more dynamic view, which encompasses a wider range of actors in EC/EU policy-making. This is illustrated by the fuller analysis of the decision-making process in the areas of cohesion and fisheries in Chapters 5 and 7, which elaborate considerably on the predominantly statist picture of decision-making portrayed in Chapters 4 and 6. Increasing access to the policy process for other domestic actors does not necessarily mean a reduced role for the central state. The opening opportunity structure does not rule out the possibility that the central state's role has even been strengthened by its adaptation to the changed sets of conditions. However, the journey beyond the Spanish state contributes to a fuller analysis of the policy process and of relations between central government, other domestic actors and the EU.

The key findings of the analysis could have wider significance. The case study on cohesion draws conclusions which are applicable to regions not only throughout Spain, but also across the EU. Although the issues raised by fisheries are more specific to Spain as the member state most affected by the accord, the evaluation of government strategies and access to policy-making of key regional and sectoral actors may be applicable more widely. The conclusions of the book most directly pertain to the case of Spain, but they may, nonetheless, offer insights into the changing nature of the policy process in the broader EU framework.

Appendix: A Study of Barbate

One example of the lobbying capacity at local and regional level is the town of Barbate whose economy depends on fishing agreements reached with Morocco. The port of Barbate lies at the Atlantic end of the strait of Gibraltar. Thirty-nine boats were based there in 1995, representing 550–600 jobs, which would be endangered if Moroccan demands were accepted (the fleet consisted of 170 boats in the 1970s, employing approximately 3000 sailors). The Moroccan proposal to end their fishing rights in Moroccan waters would mean the death of the local economy. The fishing community in Barbate thus fought to retain its fishing rights at the level set in the 1992 agreement. Approximately 70 per cent of the boats are at least 20 years old, which means they have no alternatives to fishing in nearby Moroccan waters.

Barbate felt it had been discriminated against in the 1979 fishing agreement between Spain and Morocco when its historic fishing rights were denied. The agreement reduced the fishing area to one-fifth of the original fishing zone, meaning that only around two-thirds of Barbate's boats had access to Moroccan waters during any one period. A study produced by the ARPEBAR shipowners' association (1995) in Barbate concluded that the 1979 and 1983 agreements gave priority to Ceuta and Melilla (all their boats obtained licences) and discriminated against Barbate. Subsequent agreements have further reduced the fishing zones and the number of licences while the payments to Morocco for fishing rights have increased considerably. Barbate was determined not to accept further reductions in its fishing quotas in 1995. The community felt particularly vulnerable, faced with economic and political decisions at EU level which did not take account of local factors, namely Barbate's exclusive fishing of one fish type. The crisis situation was exacerbated by the scarcity of resources, overfishing by other ports, and a fall in the price of fish, partly a result of an increase in low quality imports.

Key actors and associations

The fishermen's association in Barbate accused central government of ignoring its interests for political reasons, particularly those of the workers, and sought to maximize pressure on the central administration. However, its lobbying strategies were weakened by its lack of collaboration with other associations, for example its refusal to join the National Federation of Fishermen's Associations. ARPEBAR, founded in 1977, represents the majority of shipowners in Barbate and firmly defended the interests of the sector during the 1995 negotiations. The President of the Association attended all negotiating rounds, the aim being to exert direct pressure on negotiators.

The central administration relied on the expertise of such associations to provide detailed information on the sector, on the terms of past agreements and on the prospects for future fishing in Moroccan waters. For example, comparative data provided during the 1995 negotiations demonstrated the high number of jobs dependent on fishing in Moroccan waters in Barbate, and the low cost of maintaining the jobs in comparison with higher costs for other fishing types. This gave the Spanish delegation an important bargaining tool in the negotiation of fishing conditions for Barbate, and clearly illustrates the collaboration between local, regional and central levels in negotiating the optimal deal for the sector.

The President of ARPEBAR was also a member of the Plataforma de Defensa del Sector Pesquero de Barbate (Platform for the Defence of the Fishing Sector in Barbate), consisting of representatives from local government, political parties, trade unions and various other associations. The key objective was to defend local interests, keep the public constantly informed of the current state of negotiations and increase the level of local and regional representation. They considered that the EU delegation was acting weakly and doubted its satisfactory defence of Andalusia's fishing interests. The platform aimed to hold meetings with local and regional government in order to obtain their full support, inform central administration in Madrid of the situation in Barbate, and organize demonstrations to increase public awareness of the implications of the renegotiation. Another committee was established by the IU in Barbate to monitor the negotiations, aiming to make contact with key political and social forces in the area, and keep the local population fully informed of negotiations (*Diario de Cádiz*, 6 April 1995).

Domestic protest

Key actors sought to increase the awareness of the case of Barbate during the negotiations through direct contact with officials at regional, central and EU levels, and through protest which was widely publicized in the press. For example, in April 1995, a demonstration was held in Barbate to show the extent of support for the fishing sector, which was attended by around 7000 people. Demonstrations were organized to publicize their demands whenever negotiations reached another deadlock. In May 1995, the fishermen's association refused to listen to the recommendations of regional government regarding the negative effects of a boycott of Moroccan fish, and continued to block fish imports. Such measures considerably increased the pressure on regional and central government to defend their interests.

Support of regional and central government

Central government officials frequently expressed their determination to defend Barbate's cause. The Secretary-General for Fisheries declared that the Spanish delegation would defend Barbate's cause to the end (unpublished document, local government of Barbate, April 1995), and the Agriculture and Fisheries Minister described Barbate as a symbol of the Spanish fishing sector in his visit there in May 1995. Such statements indicate the strong support for the case of Barbate. Its situation was frequently discussed in meetings in Seville with regional government officials who supported its demand to retain existing quotas.

Strong lobbying at all administrative levels, and the increasingly tense atmosphere as the negotiations continued, made Barbate's fishing quota a key issue during the negotiations. It is significant that its quota was fully retained in the 1995 agreement. However, the problem of the non-recognition of the historical fishing rights of the fleet remains, and it has been estimated that a renegotiation of the agreement could reduce the Barbate fleet by a further three boats, representing a loss of 63 jobs (Junta de Andalucía, 1997). Despite the considerable pressure placed on the Spanish delegation from Barbate representatives, central government could not always fulfil their demands. For example, in meetings between regional and central government during the August negotiating round, a key member of the Spanish delegation explained that, while fully aware of the crisis situation in Barbate, he could not argue for a return to its fishing rights of 1979 at that stage of the talks in view of the negative implications for Spanish interests as a whole (unpublished notes on August negotiating round, ARPEBAR). The sector was critical of the lack of information on negotiations, and considered that agreements with negative implications for the Barbate fleet were hidden for electoral reasons (*El Correo de Andalucía*, 3 May 1995). However, the bargaining tactics of the Spanish delegation were generally praised at local level, and officials acknowledged their reliance on the expertise of Barbate representatives who were present at every negotiating round. This brief study illustrates the high level of contact between local, regional, central and EU levels in the negotiation of the optimal deal for a small fishing village entirely dependent on the EU–Morocco agreement.

Notes

Introduction

1 Allison's concept of using different 'conceptual lenses' has since been used to view the European integration process by other theorists, for example Laura Cram (1997).
2 The centre-right Popular Party is the successor to the Popular Coalition, which lost to the PSOE in the 1982 and 1986 elections, and the Popular Alliance founded in 1976.

2 Relations Between the Spanish Central State and Other Domestic Actors During the EC Accession Negotiations

1 According to the Birklebach report of the European Parliament of 1962, a state without democratic legitimation could not aspire to be admitted into the EC.
2 Interview with former official of Ministry for Relations with the EC, Madrid, 28 May 1996.
3 In six months, only one session at ministerial level took place, on 25 November 1980, compared with five in the previous one and a half years (Bassols, 1995, p. 252). Only six ministerial negotiating sessions were held between February 1981 and October 1982 (Bassols, 1995, p. 261).
4 The Monitoring Committee was formally constituted on 22 January 1985, having been approved by the Catalonia parliament on 27 September 1984 (Ministerio de Asuntos Exteriores, 1985, p. 752).
5 Pacts and agreements became a key element of the policy process during the transition and early 1980s. Agreements included the Inter-confederation Agreement in 1980 between the UGT and the CEOE, the National Agreement on Employment in 1981 between central government, unions and the CEOE, the Interconfederation Agreement in 1983 between employers and unions, and the most far-reaching, and the first tripartite agreement for the González government, the Economic and Social Agreement in 1984.
6 Interview with official of Secretariat of State for Foreign Policy and the EU and former official of Ministry for Relations with the EC, Madrid, 29 May 1996.
7 The full title is Chambers of Commerce, Industry and Navigation whose statutes depend on central government. They date from 1911 and are organized on a provincial basis.
8 Presentation by Calvo Sotelo at Fundación Ortega y Gasset, Madrid, 15 April 1996.
9 Interview with former official of Ministry for Relations with the EC, 28 May 1996, who was adviser to the Secretariat on public information on the EC from 1980 to 1982.
10 Interview with MEP and former member of the UCD, Brussels, 22 February 1996.

11 Interview with member of Senate and former PSOE spokesperson on EC issues 1982–6, Madrid, 27 May 1996.
12 Unpublished letter (CCOO archive, 22 February 1985) from Secretary of State for the EC Marín to the Secretary-General of CCOO, Marcelino Camacho.
13 Seminar given by Calvo Sotelo at Fundación Ortega y Gasset, Madrid, 15 April 1996.
14 A more negative response was recorded when negotiations were delayed, for example 12 per cent fewer Spaniards were in favour of accession in 1983 than three years previously in a Gallup Institute Poll, and only 46 per cent considered that the EC would actually be good for Spain (*The Times*, 15 September 1983).
15 Interview with Spanish MEP (PP), Brussels, 22 February 1996.
16 The Economic and Social Committee was established by the Treaty of Rome in 1957 to enhance the voice of major socio-economic groups appointed by the member states in Brussels.

3 Changing Relations Between the Spanish Central State and Other Domestic Actors During EC/EU Membership

1 While it did not qualify for the fast route option as a historic nationality, widespread support for full autonomy existed in Andalusia and, following a referendum on the issue, the region joined the other three historic nationalities in their accelerated procedure towards full autonomy.
2 The exception is the statute for the Basque Country and Navarre which includes certain tax-raising privileges.
3 Interview with official of CCOO, Madrid, 21 May 1996.
4 Other commentators (such as Colomer, 1995, p. 228) have reported that more than 90 per cent of businesses are affiliated to the CEOE.
5 The 184 federations of the CEOE consist of 17 confederations representing Spanish regions, 37 provincial associations, and 130 sectoral organizations at national or regional level (Newton, 1997, p. 258).
6 The CEOE under Ferrer's leadership enjoyed close relations with the UGT and reached a series of accords with the unions from 1979 (Martínez Lucio, 1991, p. 52). However, the subsequent leader, Cuevas, developed closer relations with the PP, and was less sympathetic to the union cause (Heywood, 1995, p. 255). Although the unions' influence was considered limited, the CEOE was wary of any increase in their standing *vis-à-vis* central government (Heywood, 1995, p. 254).
7 In an interview with an official of the SPR (Brussels, 22 February 1996), the role played by key individuals in EU policy was emphasized, for example the 'free hand' in Brussels of Javier Elorza (Spanish Permanent Representative) and the high level of EU expertise of Westendorp (formerly Secretary of State for the EC). Another illustration was the shift in the decision-making process from Brussels to Madrid in the early 1990s when Elorza and Westendorp moved back to Spain.
8 Interviews with member of the Joint Committee since 1993, Madrid, 28 May 1996, 3 June 1996.

9   The list of sessions is an indication of the increased activity of the committee: 18 November 1996, and 19, 25 February, 4, 18 March, 1, 11, 15,
25 April, and 6, 22, 28, 29 May 1997, with guest speakers including the
Secretary of State for the EU, Ramón de Miguel (18 June 1996), the Spanish
Ambassador in the EU, Elorza (11 April 1997), and Commissioner Oreja (25
April 1997) (Report of the Special Monitoring Subcommittee on the IGC,
Congress, 29 May 1997, pp. 16–17).
10   Interview with former member of the Joint Committee (1986–93), Madrid,
18 June 1996.
11   According to a member of the Joint Committee since 1993 (interview,
Madrid, 28 May 1996), information was obtained with greater facility by
PSOE members during the Socialist term of office up to 1996 than thereafter.
12   Interview with member of the Joint Committee since 1993, Madrid, 28 May
1996.
13   Information supplied by the Clerk to the Joint Committee in a communication to the author in August 1995.
14   In brief, regional authorities were allowed to form part of member states'
delegations in the Council; the Committee of the Regions was created, and
the principle of subsidiarity was incorporated into the Treaty.
15   *Boletín Oficial del Estado* (Official State Gazette, *BOE*), no. 216, 8 September
1992, pp. 30853–4.
16   *BOE*, no. 241, 8 October 1993, p. 28669.
17   *BOE*, no. 257, 27 October 1994, p. 33815.
18   *BOE*, no. 69, 22 March 1995, p. 9037.
19   *BOE*, no. 305, 22 December 1995, p. 36759.
20   The historic Autonomies are Catalonia, the Basque Country and Galicia, so
named because they were the only regions to gain the right to autonomous
government by 1936 during the Second Republic.
21   Interview with official of Ministry of Public Administration, Madrid,
9 October 1996.
22   Interviews with official of the Ministry of the Presidency, Junta de
Andalucía, Seville, 4 October 1996, 19 June 1997.
23   Interview with official of Ministry of Public Administration, Madrid,
12 June 1997.
24   Interview with official of Ministry of Public Administration, Madrid,
12 June 1997.
25   *BOE*, no. 151, 25 June 1994, pp. 68–75.
26   The influence of the CCOO in the Committee was particularly limited as it
was only represented by three out of the 222 members in 1996.
27   Interview with official of CCOO, Madrid, 6 May 1996.
28   Interview with official of CCOO, Madrid, 6 May 1996.
29   Interview with official of UGT, Madrid, 7 May 1996.
30   Interview with SPR official, Brussels, 22 February 1996.

4   The Role of the Spanish Central State in the Negotiation of Cohesion Policy

1   The FCI was put into effect in 1982, its regulations being formally set out in
Law 7/1984 of 31 March, substituted by Law 29/1990 of 26 December.

2 Catalan pressure has continued during the PP's term of office. Following the March 1996 elections, it was agreed that the quota of income tax retained by the region would be increased from 15 to 30 per cent. The accord was viewed by most regional authorities as a concession to the Catalan nationalist party whose support remained essential for the government's parliamentary majority until 2000.

3 The Spanish representatives included the Director of International Relations of the cabinet of the Presidency (José Pons), the Director General of the Treasury (Manuel Conthe), and the Secretary-General for the EC (Elorza), described as the key Spanish spokesman on cohesion.

4 It was agreed that the Cohesion Fund would be extended beyond the Delors II levels to include 3.15 billion ECU for 1998 and 1999. This fell short of the 5.6 billion pesetas originally demanded by Spain, and the Cohesion Fund finally approved amounted to 41 per cent of the amount requested by the Spanish negotiators.

5 Interview with former diplomatic adviser to González on foreign policy, Madrid, 30 May 1996.

6 Interview with former diplomatic adviser to González on foreign policy, Madrid, 30 May 1996.

7 This was suggested by Ugalde Ruiz de Assin of the Popular Coalition party in a question to Foreign Minister Fernández Ordóñez, following his briefing to the Joint Committee for the EC on 13 October 1988 (Ministerio de Asuntos Exteriores, 1988, p. 396).

8 Speech given by González in Brussels, 12 December 1988 (Ministerio del Portavoz del Gobierno, 1988, p. 79).

9 Speech given by González at the German Society for Foreign Policy, Bonn, 17 September 1987 (Ministerio del Portavoz del Gobierno, 1988, p. 39).

10 Speech given by González in the European University Institute, Florence, 19 October 1987 (Ministerio del Portavoz del Gobierno, 1988, p. 62).

11 Speech given by González in the ceremony for the beginning of the academic year at the College of Europe, Bruges, 28 October 1985 (Ministerio del Portavoz del Gobierno, 1988, p. 19).

12 The United Left was formally established in 1986, the Spanish Communist Party being the largest of the member parties.

13 However, the Maastricht Treaty was eventually ratified almost unanimously in the Spanish Parliament with only three *Herri Batasuna* (radical Basque Nationalist) votes against and eight IU abstentions.

14 Interview with former diplomatic adviser to González on foreign policy, Madrid, 30 May 1996.

5 The Input of Other Domestic Actors to Cohesion Policy

1 Regulation 2052/88, *Official Journal of the European Communities (OJ)* L185/9, 1988 (Framework regulation); Regulation 4253/88, *OJ* L374/1 (Co-ordination regulation); Regulation 4254/88, *OJ* L374/15 (ERDF); Regulation 4255/88, *OJ* L374/22 (ESF); and Regulation 4256/88, *OJ* L374/25 (EAGGF).

2 Speech published in European Commission, 1991, *La reconversion des régions industrielles: rencontre des 60 régions éligibles à l'objectif 2 des fonds structurels*, Brussels, 8 July 1991 (Hooghe, 1996b, p. 122).

3 Regulation 2081/93 (Framework regulation), *OJ* L193, 1993.
4 Interview with official of DG XVI/C1, European Commission, Brussels, 17 April 1997.
5 The 1988 reform of the structural funds merely provided for the Commission to present a report on implementation to the Parliament, Council of Ministers, and the Economic and Social Committee. Although the 1993 reform moved towards greater parliamentary involvement, including receiving development plans submitted by the member states, the European Parliament (1996, pp. 30–1) has highlighted its lack of involvement in key policy decisions such as setting the 1994–9 financial perspective, which it describes as being negotiated 'behind closed doors' at the Edinburgh Summit.
6 The Committee consists of 229 representatives of regional and local bodies. The Spanish government showed little enthusiasm for setting up the Committee in the 1991 IGC in view of its aim to strengthen regional representation in Brussels.
7 Interviews with officials of Ministry of Economy and Finance, Madrid, September 1996.
8 Interview with official of DG XVI/C1, European Commission, Brussels, 17 April 1997.
9 Interviews with officials of Ministry of Economy and Finance, Madrid, September 1996.
10 Interview with official of Ministry of Economy and Finance (Adviser, DG for Analysis and Budgetary Programming), Madrid, 23 September 1996.
11 Interview with official of Ministry of Economy and Finance (formerly responsible for Andalusia, Sub-DG for Administration of the ERDF), Madrid, 18 September 1996.
12 Interview with official of Instituto de Fomento de Andalucía (IFA), Seville, 2 October 1996.
13 Interview with former official of Ministry of Economy and Finance, Madrid, 8 October 1996.
14 Interview with official of Ministry of Economy and Finance (Adviser, DG for Analysis and Budgetary Programming), Madrid, 13 June 1997.
15 Interview with official of Ministry of Economy and Finance (Adviser, DG for Analysis and Budgetary Programming), Madrid, 23 September 1996.
16 Interview with official of DG XVI/C1, European Commission, Brussels, 21 April 1997.
17 Interview with official of Ministry of Economy and Finance (official responsible for Andalusia, Sub-DG for Administration of the ERDF), Madrid, 12 June 1997.
18 Interview with official of DG XVI/C1, European Commission, Brussels, 17 April 1997.
19 Interview with official of DG XVI/C1, European Commission, Brussels, 17 April 1997.
20 Interview with official of Ministry of Economy and Finance (official responsible for Andalusia, Sub-DG for Administration of the ERDF), Madrid, 18 September 1996.
21 Interview with official of regional Ministry of Economy and Finance, Seville, 19 June 1997.

22　It was the intention to set up the Cohesion Fund by 31 December 1993 as the second paragraph of EC Article 130d stipulated.

23　Spain was also keen to have an interstate Fund as it meant that the poorest regions of the other eight member states would not be eligible for funding.

24　Interview with official of Ministry of Economy and Finance (Assistant Director-General, Cohesion Fund), Madrid, 23 September 1996.

25　Interview with official of Ministry of Economy and Finance (Assistant Director-General, Cohesion Fund), Madrid, 23 September 1996.

26　Interview with official of DG XVI/E1, European Commission, Brussels, 17 April 1997.

27　Interview with official of DG XVI/E2, European Commission, Brussels, 17 April 1997.

28　All the projects presented by the regions during the first year were in the area of the environment according to an interview with an official of Ministry of Economy and Finance (Assistant Director-General, Cohesion Fund), Madrid, 13 June 1997.

29　Interview with detached national expert of DG XVI/E2, European Commission, Brussels, 17 April 1997.

30　Interview with official of Ministry of Economy and Finance (Assistant Director-General, Cohesion Fund), Madrid, 23 September 1996.

31　Interview with official of Ministry of Economy and Finance (Adviser, DG for Analysis and Budgetary Programming), Madrid, 23 September 1996.

32　Interview with official of CCOO, Madrid, 20 June 1997.

33　Interview with official of Ministry of Economy and Finance (Adviser, DG for Analysis and Budgetary Programming), Madrid, 23 September 1996.

6　The Role of the Spanish Central State in the Negotiation of the EU–Morocco Fisheries Agreement

1　Council Regulation EC 1275/94 of 30 May 1994 on adjustments to the arrangements in the fisheries chapters of the Act of Accession of Spain and Portugal, *OJ* L140, 3 June 1994.

2　The EuroMed conference was the first ever summit between the EU and non-EU Mediterranean countries, held under the Spanish EU Presidency on 27–28 November 1995. It resulted in the Barcelona Declaration, including agreements on the gradual introduction of a free trade area known as the EuroMediterranean Economic Area.

3　Extending the fishing zone towards the 200-mile limit was proposed in 1973. The United Nations General Assembly adopted the 200-mile Exclusive Economic Zone in 1982. The creation of an area around coastal states such as Morocco, within which they had the right to determine access to economic resources, represented a considerable change for the EU fleet.

4　Interview with MEP, President of the Fisheries Committee from January 1997, Brussels, 23 April 1997.

5　From 1975 to 1979, tripartite accords on the administration of the Western Sahara existed between Spain, Morocco and Mauritania.

6　Interview with President of the Professional Association of Shipowners' Firms of Cadiz (Asociación Profesional de Empresas Armadores de Buques de Pesca de Cádiz, ASEMAR), Cadiz, 3 October 1996.

7   Luis de Andres and Rafael Conde of the DG for Fishing Resources were members of the Spanish delegation; Conde presided over the negotiations during Spain's EU Presidency.

8   Interview with chief EU negotiator of fisheries agreement, European Commission, Brussels, 21 April 1997.

9   Interview with former Agriculture and Fisheries Minister, Madrid, 19 July 1996.

10   Interview with former Agriculture and Fisheries Minister, Madrid, 19 July 1996.

11   Interview with chief EU negotiator of fisheries agreement, European Commission, Brussels, 21 April 1997.

12   The number of licensed EU boats was reduced from 600 to 477 over four years, with a gradual increase in fees from the second year. Spanish boats would also take on around 950 Moroccan crew, representing about one in six (*FT*, 19 December 1995). The average reduction in fish quotas was 23 per cent over the four-year period.

13   Interview with former Secretary-General for Fisheries, Madrid, 9 June 1997.

14   Interview with former Agriculture and Fisheries Minister, Madrid, 19 July 1996.

15   Interview with former government official, Madrid, July 1996.

16   Morocco would gradually be allowed to export 5000 tonnes of cut flowers between mid-October and mid-May. The compromise on tomatoes cancelled a 10 000 tonne allowance for April, but increased the total allowance to 150 000 tonnes, permitted to enter the EU between October and March (*FT*, 10 November 1995).

17   Interviews with former Secretary-General for Fisheries, Madrid, 10 July 1996, 9 June 1997.

18   Interview with former Agriculture and Fisheries Minister, Madrid, 19 July 1996.

7   The Input of Other Domestic Actors to the Fisheries Agreement

1   Interview with MEP, former President of the Fisheries Committee, Brussels, 23 April 1997.

2   Interview with President of the Association of Shipowners of Barbate (Asociación de Armadores de Buques de Pesca de Barbate, ARPEBAR), Barbate, 3 October 1996.

3   Interview with official of sub-DG for International Fisheries Agreements, Madrid, 11 June 1997.

4   During the first phase of formulating the plan, 17 fishermen's associations, 4 producers' organizations, 16 shipowners' associations, 2 trade unions and 5 other organizations participated (Junta de Andalucía, 1997).

5   Interview with MEP, President of the Fisheries Committee from January 1997, Brussels, 23 April 1997.

6   Interview with former government official, Madrid, July 1996.

7   Andalusia has 23 fishermen's associations to which around 8000 fishermen are affiliated (*Industrias Pesqueras*, no. 1676, 15 February 1997, p. 28).

8 Interviews with representative of CCOO fisheries sector, Federation of Transport, Communications and Fisheries (Federación Estatal de Transportes, Comunicaciones y Mar, FETCOMAR), Madrid, 10 May 1996, 9 July 1996.

9 Interview with official of sub-DG for International Fisheries Agreements, Madrid, 4 July 1996.

10 Interviews with President of ARPEBAR shipowners' association, Barbate, 3 October 1996, 16 June 1997, and with President of ASEMAR shipowners' association, Cadiz, 3 October 1996.

11 Interview with President of ASEMAR shipowners' association, Cadiz, 3 October 1996.

12 Interview with President of Producers' Organization, Barbate, 17 June 1997.

13 Interview with official of DG XIV, European Commission, Brussels, 18 April 1997.

14 Interview with MEP, former President of the Fisheries Committee, Brussels, 23 April 1997.

15 Evidence from an interview with an official in the SPR (Brussels, 22 April 1997) would seem to suggest that the renegotiation of the accord differed from previous negotiations as the fishing sector in Morocco was far more aware of the implications of the agreement.

16 Interviews with former Secretary-General for Fisheries, Madrid, 10 July 1996, 9 June 1997.

17 Interview with official of regional DG for Fisheries, Seville, 30 September 1996.

18 Interview with former Agriculture and Fisheries Minister, Madrid, 19 July 1996.

19 Interview with chief EU negotiator of fisheries agreement, European Commission, Brussels, 21 April 1997.

20 Interviews with former Secretary-General for Fisheries, Madrid, 10 July 1996, 9 June 1997.

21 Interviews with President of ARPEBAR shipowners' association, Barbate, 3 October 1996, 16 June 1997.

22 Interview with former Agriculture and Fisheries Minister, Madrid, 19 July 1996.

23 Such a network was evident during my fieldwork when sectoral and regional representatives in Andalusia were on familiar terms with key central government and EU officials.

24 Interview with former government official, Madrid, July 1996.

Bibliography

Note: This bibliography includes works which were of general use for the research as well as those directly cited in the text.

Primary sources

Primary document sources

References are made in the text to material from newspapers. The page numbers have not been included as articles were accessed in Spanish press files and in the Chatham House Library, London, where this information was not given.

   Other key sources to which references are made in the text are:

- *Agence Europe* (referred to as Europe);
- *Eurobarometer*;
- *Europe* (1985, 1986);
- *European Trends*;
- *Keesings Contemporary Archives*;
- Spanish parliamentary debates (Congress and Senate).

Chapters 7 and 8 refer to the specialist fisheries journals: *Industrias Pesqueras, Mar, Productos del Mar*, and the DG XIV newsletter, *Pesca Info*.

European Union

European Commission
European Commission (1978a) 'Enlargement of the Community, economic and sectoral aspects', *Bulletin of the European Communities*, Supplement 3/78, 20 April.
European Commission (1978b) 'Opinion on Spain's application for membership', *Bulletin of the European Communities*, Supplement 9/78, 29 November.
European Commission (1982) 'Problems of enlargement: taking stock and proposals', Communication from the Commission to the European Council, Copenhagen, 3–4 December, COM (82) 757 final, 15 November.
European Commission (1987a) 'The Single Act: a new frontier for Europe', COM (87) 100, 18 February.
European Commission (1987b) *Treaties Establishing the European Communities (ECSC, EEC, EAEC), Single European Act, Other Basic Instruments*, Office for Official Publications of the European Communities, Luxembourg.
European Commission (1989a) 'Statement on Spain's term as Council President', *Bulletin of the European Communities*, 1, 22, pp. 84–97.
European Commission (1989b) 'Statement on the Spanish Presidency', *Bulletin of the European Communities*, 7/8, 22, pp. 133–9.
European Commission (1989c) *Guide to the Reform of the Community's Structural Funds*, Office for Official Publications of the European Communities, Luxembourg.

European Commission (1991) 'Report of the Commission to the Council and Parliament on the common fisheries policy', SEC (91) 2288 final, 4 December.

European Commission (1992) 'From the Single Act to Maastricht and beyond: the means to match our ambitions', *Bulletin of the European Communities*, Supplement 1, 11 February.

European Commission (1993) *Community Structural Funds 1994–99, Revised Regulations and Comments*, Office for Official Publications of the European Communities, Luxembourg.

European Commission (1994) *The New Common Fisheries Policy*, Office for Official Publications of the European Communities, Luxembourg.

European Commission (1995a) *Annual Report of the Cohesion Fund*, DG XVI, Brussels.

European Commission (1995b) *Cohesion Financial Instrument, Cohesion Fund, Combined Report 1993–94*, Office for Official Publications of the European Communities, Luxembourg.

European Commission (1996a) *Structural Funds and Cohesion Fund 1994–99, Regulations and Commentary*, Office for Official Publications of the European Communities, Luxembourg.

European Commission (1996b) *The Structural Funds in 1995, Seventh Annual Report*, Office for Official Publications of the European Communities, Luxembourg.

European Commission (1996c) *First Report on Economic and Social Cohesion, Preliminary Edition*, Office for Official Publications of the European Communities, Luxembourg.

European Commission (1996d) *At Regional Level on behalf of Europe's Regions, Developing a New Field of Trade Union Activity*, Study 25, Office for Official Publications of the European Communities, Luxembourg.

European Commission (1996e) *La Notoriété des Politiques Régionales en Europe*, Study 23, Office for Official Publications of the European Communities, Luxembourg.

European Commission (1997) *The Structural Funds in 1996, Eighth Annual Report*, Office for Official Publications of the European Communities, Luxembourg.

European Parliament

European Parliament (1996) 'Resolution on the sixth annual report of the Commission on the structural funds in 1994', *OJ* C277, 5 September, pp. 29–34.

Committee of the Regions

Committee of the Regions (1995) 'Own-initiative opinion no. 234/95 of 20 July 1995 on the role of regional and local authorities in the partnership principle of the structural funds'.

Committee of the Regions (1997) 'Opinion on the sixth and seventh annual reports on the structural funds 1994 and 1995'.

Economic and Social Committee

Economic and Social Committee (1988) 'Fondos estructurales, La indignación del CES', Press release, Brussels, 27 October.

Economic and Social Committee (1994a) 'Own-initiative opinion of the Economic and Social Committee on the involvement of the economic and social partners in Community regional policy', *OJ* C127, 7 May.

Economic and Social Committee (1994b) 'Opinion on the role of the public authorities in the partnership (Article 4 of the Framework Regulation)', CES (94) 1002, 14 September.

Spain

Central government

Ministerio de Asuntos Exteriores (1981, 1982, 1983, 1984, 1985, 1987, 1988, 1992) *Actividades, Textos y Documentos de la Política Exterior Española*, Oficina de Información Diplomática, Madrid.

Ministerio de Economía y Hacienda (1995) *La Planificación Regional y Sus Instrumentos, Informe Anual 1994*, Dirección General de Planificación, Madrid.

Ministerio de Economía y Hacienda (1996) *La Programación Regional y Sus Instrumentos, Informe Anual 1995*, Dirección General de Análisis y Programación Presupuestaria, Madrid.

Ministerio del Portavoz del Gobierno (1988) *La Unidad Europea, Intervenciones del Presidente del Gobierno, D. Felipe González, Brujas, Bonn, Florencia, Bruselas*, Madrid.

Ministerio para las Relaciones con las Comunidades Europeas (1978) *Cómo, Cuándo, Por qué, Informe sobre las Jornadas de Información 'la Adhesión de España al Mercado Común'*, Madrid.

Secretaría de Estado para las Comunidades Europeas (1987) *Balance del Primer Año de la Adhesión de España a la CEE*, Madrid.

Secretaría de Estado para las Relaciones con las Comunidades Europeas (1981) *Dos Años y Medio de Negociaciones para la Adhesión de España a las Comunidades Europeas*, Madrid.

Secretaría de Estado para las Relaciones con las Comunidades Europeas (1982) *Programa de Acción Interior*, Madrid.

Spanish delegation (1991a) 'La cohesión económica y social en la unión política, económica y monetaria: el punto de vista español', Doc: CONF-UP-UEM, 2004/91, Madrid, 5 March.

Spanish delegation (1991b) 'Nota española a la conferencia intergubernamental sobre unión política', Doc: CONF-UP, 1803/91, Madrid, 7 May.

Regional government

Junta de Andalucía (1988) Balance en Andalucía de la Adhesión a las Comunidades Europeas, Consejería de Fomento y Trabajo/Consejería de la Presidencia, Seville.

Junta de Andalucía (1994) *La Agricultura y la Pesca en Andalucía, Memoria 1993*, Consejería de Agricultura y Pesca, Seville.

Junta de Andalucía (1995) *Pacto Andaluz por el Empleo y la Actividad Productiva, Texto Integro del Pacto Firmado por la Junta de Andalucía, CEA, UGT y CCOO*, Seville.

Junta de Andalucía (1997) *Plan de Modernización del Sector Pesquero Andaluz*, Consejería de Agricultura y Pesca, Baeza.

Employers
ARPEBAR (1995) 'Estudio de la evolución de la flota de Barbate tras los acuerdos pesqueros con Marruecos', Barbate.
CEOE (1981a) *La Empresa Española ante la Adhesión al Mercado Común*, vol. 1, Madrid, February.
CEOE (1981b) *La Empresa Española ante la Adhesión al Mercado Común*, vol. 2, Madrid, December.
CEOE (1984) 'Le patronat espagnol face à l'intégration européenne', Speech given by the President of the CEOE, Carlos Ferrer, at Fontainebleau on the occasion of the creation of the European Institute for Business Affairs, 4 January.
CEPYME (1981) 'La PYME española y su ingreso en la CEE, Plan de apoyo y coordinación para el desarrollo de un programa conjunto entre la Secretaría de Estado para las Relaciones con la CEE y CEPYME', Madrid.
Círculo de Empresarios (1979) 'La integración de España en las Comunidades Europeas', Draft opinion, Cuenca, 20 October.
Consejo Superior de Cámaras de Comercio, Industria y Navegación de España (1985) *Las Negociaciones para la Adhesión de España a las Comunidades Europeas*, Ministerio de Asuntos Exteriores, Madrid.

Trade unions
CCOO (1984) 'El ingreso de España en la CEE', Document, Madrid, June.
CCOO (1985a) 'Sobre los contactos mantenidos con la Secretaría de Estado para las Relaciones con las Comunidades Europeas y el seguimiento de las negociaciones de adhesión a la CEE', Document, Madrid.
CCOO (1985b) 'Resolución de la Comisión Ejecutiva de CCOO sobre la entrada de España en la CEE', Document, Madrid.
CCOO (1993a) 'Consideraciones de CCOO al documento de la Confederación Europa de Sindicatos sobre la toma de decisiones respecto a la revisión de los reglamentos de los fondos estructurales', Document, Madrid, 22 May.
CCOO (1993b) 'Análisis de las conclusiones alcanzadas en la cumbre de Edimburgo', Document, Madrid, February.
CCOO (1993c) 'Primeras reflexiones sobre el fondo de cohesión', Document, Madrid, 20 January.
CCOO (1995a) 'Negociaciones 1995, Acuerdo pesca con Marruecos', Internal Document 1, Brussels, 13 August.
CCOO (1995b) 'CCOO considera que el empleo y el reforzamiento de la unión política deben centrar la Cumbre Europea', Document, Madrid, 15 December.
UGT (n/d) *La Unión General de Trabajadores ante la Adhesión de España a las Comunidades Europeas*, Madrid.
UGT (1992a) 'El tratado de la unión, Notas sobre los acuerdos de Maastricht', Document, Madrid, 30 June.
UGT (1992b) 'El tratado de la unión de Maastricht a Edimburgo', Document, Madrid, 23 December.
UGT/CCOO (1995) 'Declaración de UGT y CCOO sobre la Presidencia Española de la Unión Europea', Document, Madrid, July.

Economic and Social Council
Economic and Social Council (1995) 'Informe 4, Sobre el principio de cooperación de los interlocutores sociales y económicos en la política estructural

comunitaria, Interpretación y desarrollo en España del articulo 4 del reglamento (CEE) del Consejo no. 2081/93 de 20 de julio de 1993', Madrid, 20 September.

Institutes/foundations

Fundación para la Investigación Económica y Social y Asociación para el Progreso de la Dirección (1980) 'Sondeo de opinión entre las "1500 mayores empresas españolas" sobre "actitud empresarial ante la integración de España en el mercado común" ', Madrid.

Instituto de Desarrollo Regional (1997a) *El Programa Operativo de Andalucía*, Seville.

Instituto de Desarrollo Regional (1997b) *Evaluación Intermedia del Programa Operativo Andalucía 1994–99*, vol. 1, Seville.

Secondary sources

Acuña, Ramón-Luis (1989) 'L'Espagne, en pleine crise de croissance', *Politique étrangère*, 54, 2, pp. 269–77.

Aja, Eliseo (1995) 'Principales líneas de la reforma constitucional del Senado', *Autonomies*, 20, pp. 51–60.

Alda Fernández, Mercedes and López Nieto, Lourdes (1993) 'El parlamento español: 1977–1993, Una revisión de su papel en la transición y en la consolidación', *Revista de Estudios Políticos*, 81, pp. 241–64.

de Aldasoro, Miguel (1995) 'De la pesca española fuera de sus aguas jurisdiccionales', *Política Exterior*, 45, 9, pp. 25–45.

Allen, David (1996) 'Cohesion and structural adjustment', in Wallace, Helen and Wallace, William (eds), *Policy-Making in the European Union*. Oxford University Press, Oxford, pp. 209–33.

Allison, Graham T. (1971) *Essence of Decision: Explaining the Cuban Missile Crisis*. Little/Brown, Boston, MA.

Almarcha Barbado, Amparo (ed.) (1993) *Spain and EC Membership Evaluated*. Pinter, London/St. Martin's Press, NY.

Alonso, Antonio (1985) *España en el Mercado Común, Del Acuerdo del 70 a la Comunidad de Doce*, Espasa Calpe, Madrid.

Alonso Zaldívar, Carlos and Castells, Manuel (1992) *Spain Beyond Myths*. Alianza, Madrid.

Álvarez-Miranda Navarro, Berta (1995) *Los Partidos Políticos en Grecia, Portugal y España ante la Comunidad Europea: Explicación Comparada del Consenso Europeísta Español*, Doctoral thesis no. 8, Centro de Estudios Avanzados en Ciencias Sociales, Instituto Juan March de Estudios e Investigaciones, Madrid.

Andersen, Svein S. and Eliassen, Kjell A. (eds) (1993) *Making Policy in Europe, The Europeification of National Policy-making*. Sage, London.

Anderson, Jeffery (1990) 'Skeptical reflections on a Europe of Regions: Britain, Germany, and the ERDF', *Journal of Public Policy*, 10, 4, pp. 417–47.

Armero, José Mario (1989) *Política Exterior de España en Democracia*. Espasa Calpe, Madrid.

Armstrong, Harvey W. (1995) 'The role and evolution of European Community regional policy', in Jones, Barry and Keating, Michael (eds), *The European Union and the Regions*. Clarendon, Oxford, pp. 1–22.

Atienza Serna, Luis (1989) 'Política regional europea y descentralización: reflexiones desde el Pais Vasco', in Ministerio de Economía y Hacienda, *Política Regional en la Europa de los Años 90*, Madrid, pp. 579–89.

Atienza Serna, Luis (1996) 'Agricultura y pesca: sólidos cimientos para el futuro', *El Boletín* (Ministerio de Agricultura, Pesca y Alimentación), 34, pp. 12–13 (extract).

Bache, Ian (1998) *The Politics of European Union Regional Policy, Multi-level Governance or Flexible Gatekeeping?* Sheffield Academic Press, Sheffield.

Bache, Ian and Jones, Rachel (forthcoming 2000) 'Has EU regional policy empowered the regions? A study of Spain and the United Kingdom', *Regional and Federal Studies*, 10, 2.

Bachtler, John (1997) 'New dimensions of regional policy in Western Europe', in Keating, Michael and Loughlin, John (eds), *The Political Economy of Regionalism*. Frank Cass, London, pp. 77–89.

Baixeras, Juan (1996) 'España y el Mediterráneo 1989–95', *Política Exterior*, 51, 10, pp. 149–62.

Balme, Richard (1997) 'Regional policy and European governance', in Keating, Michael and Loughlin, John (eds), *The Political Economy of Regionalism*. Frank Cass, London, pp. 63–76.

Bar, Antonio (1988) 'Spain', in Blondel, Jean and Müller-Rommel, Ferdinand (eds), *Cabinets in Western Europe*. Macmillan, London, pp. 102–19.

Bar, Antonio (1989) 'Contenido y dinámica de la estructura gubernamental en España', *Revista de Derecho Político*, 29, pp. 37–113.

Barbé, Esther (1995) 'European political co-operation: The upgrading of Spanish foreign policy', in Gillespie, Richard, Rodrigo, Fernando and Story, Jonathan (eds), *Democratic Spain: Reshaping External Relations in a Changing World*. Routledge, London, pp. 106–22.

Barbé, Esther (1996) 'De la ingenuidad al pragmatismo: 10 años de participación española en la maquinaria diplomática europea', *Afers Internacionals*, 34–5, pp. 9–29.

Barón, Enrique (1989) 'Las regiones en la política regional comunitaria', in Ministerio de Economía y Hacienda, *Política Regional en la Europa de los Años 90*, Madrid, pp. 605–13.

Bassols, Raimundo (1995) *España en Europa, Historia de la Adhesión a la CE 1957–85*. Estudios de Política Exterior, Madrid.

Bataller Martín, Francisco and Jordán Galduf, Josep María (1997) 'España y su acción Mediterránea: abogado o competidor?', *Información Comercial Española (ICE)*, 759, pp. 137–52.

Benegas, José María (1985) 'Europa como proyecto socialista', *Leviatán*, 21, pp. 5–17.

Berrocal, Luciano and Stoffel, Nicole (1996) 'L'Espagne et l'Union Européenne: quel avenir après dix ans de profonds changements?', *Politique étrangère*, 61, 1, pp. 73–86.

Bescós Ferraz, Gonzalo (1995) 'La regulación de los "lobbies" y grupos de interés ante las instituciones comunitarias', *Noticias de la Unión Europea*, 127–8, pp. 21–8.

Börzel, Tanja (1997) 'Does European integration really strengthen the state? The case of the Federal Republic of Germany', *Regional and Federal Studies*, 7, 3, pp. 87–113.

Breckinridge, Robert E. (1996) 'Lessons from the European Community and Spanish democracy', European Communities Studies Association (ECSA) newsletter, 9, 1, pp. 15–19.

Brewin, Christopher and McAllister, Richard (1987) 'Annual review of the activities of the European Communities', *Journal of Common Market Studies (JCMS)*, 25, 4, pp. 363–4.

Bullain López, Iñigo (1990) *Las Regiones Autónomas de la Comunidad Europea y Su Participación en el Proceso de Integración*, Instituto Vasco de Administración Pública (IVAP), Bilbao.

Bullmann, Udo (1997) 'The politics of the Third Level', in Jeffery, Charlie (ed.), *The Regional Dimension of the European Union, Towards a Third Level in Europe?* Frank Cass, London, pp. 3–19.

Bulmer, Simon (1983) 'Domestic politics and EC policy-making', *JCMS*, 21, 4, pp. 349–63.

Bulmer, Simon (1986) *The Domestic Structure of European Community Policy-Making in West Germany*, Garland, London.

Burgorgue-Larsen, Laurence (ed.) (1995) *L'Espagne et la Communauté Européenne, L'état des Autonomies et le processus d'intégration européenne*. Université Libre de Bruxelles (ULB), Brussels.

Bustos Gisbert, Rafael (1995) 'Un paso más hacia la participación autonómica en asuntos europeos, El Acuerdo de 30 de noviembre de 1994', *Revista Española de Derecho Constitucional*, 45, pp. 153–72.

Calonge Velázquez, Antonio (1995) 'Ultimos acuerdos de la Conferencia Sectorial para asuntos relacionados con las Comunidades Europeas: pasos en la dirección correcta', *Revista de Estudios Europeos*, 10, pp. 3–14.

Calvo Sotelo, Leopoldo (1990) *Memoria Viva de la Transición*. Plaza y Janés, Barcelona.

Del Campo, Esther (2000) 'Los grupos de interes en España y la Unión Europea', in Closa, Carlos (ed.), *La Europeización del Sistema Político Español*. Istmo-Akal, Madrid.

Capo Giol, J., Cotarelo, R., López Garrido, D. and Subirats, J. (1990) 'By consociationalism to a majoritarian parliamentary system: the rise and decline of the Spanish Cortes', in Liebert, Ulrike and Cotta, Maurizio (eds), *Parliament and Democratic Consolidation in Southern Europe*. Pinter, London, pp. 92–130.

Caporaso, James A. and Keeler, John T. S. (1995) 'The European Union and regional integration theory', in Rhodes, Carolyn and Mazey, Sonia (eds), *The State of the European Community Vol. 3, Building a European Polity?* Lynne Rienner, Boulder, CO/Longman, Harlow, pp. 29–62.

Caramés Viéitez, Luis (1989) 'Descentralización de la política regional', in Ministerio de Economía y Hacienda, *Política Regional en la Europa de los Años 90*. Madrid, pp. 491–7.

de Castro Ruano, José Luis (1994) *La Emergente Participación Política de las Regiones en el Proceso de Construcción Europea*. IVAP, Bilbao.

Cazorla Pérez, José (1990) 'Andalucía en el contexto regional español: desigualdad y solidaridad', in Parlamento de Andalucía, *Comunidades Autónomas e Instrumentos de Cooperación Interterritorial*. Tecnos, Madrid, pp. 11–33.

Cazorla Pérez, José (1991) 'Andalucía y la Comunidad Europea: cultura y valores', in de Faramiñán Gilbert, Juan Manuel, Delgado Cabezas, Manuel, Cazorla

Pérez, José and Figares Romero de la Cruz, María Dolores (eds), *Interdependencia e Identidad Andaluza ante la Integración Europea*. Centro de Estudios Ramón Areces, Madrid, pp. 117–211.

Christiansen, Thomas (1997) 'Review article', *Journal of European Public Policy*, 4, 3, pp. 486–92.

Ciavarini Azzi, Giuseppe (ed.) (1995) *Survey of Current Political Science Research on European Integration Worldwide 1991–94*. International Political Science Association (IPSA), Brussels.

Círculo de Lectores (eds) (1992) *España y la Unión Europea: Las Consecuencias del Tratado de Maastricht*. Plaza y Janés, Barcelona.

Closa, Carlos (1995) 'National interest and convergence of preferences: a changing role for Spain in the EU?', in Rhodes, Carolyn and Mazey, Sonia (eds), *The State of the European Community Vol. 3, Building a European Polity?* Lynne Rienner, Boulder, CO/Longman, Harlow, pp. 293–316.

Closa, Carlos (1996) 'Spain: the Cortes and the EU, A growing together', in Norton, Philip (ed.), *National Parliaments and the European Union*. Frank Cass, London, pp. 136–50.

Closa, Carlos (ed.) (2000) *La Europeización del Sistema Político Español*. Istmo-Akal, Madrid.

Colino, César (2000) 'La integración europea y el estado autonómica: Europeización, estrategias y cambio en las relaciones intergubernamentales', in Closa, Carlos (ed.), *La Europeización del Sistema Político Español*. Istmo-Akal, Madrid.

Colomer, Josep Maria (1995) 'España y Portugal: regimenes de liderazgo de partido', in Colomer, Josep Maria (ed.), *La Política en Europa, Introducción a las Instituciones de Quince Países*. Ariel, Barcelona, pp. 200–43.

Conejos i Sancho, Jordi (1993) 'Los fondos estructurales de las Comunidades Europeas: aplicación en España y participación regional', in *Informe Comunidades Autónomas 1992*. Instituto de Derecho Público, Barcelona, pp. 327–42.

Constantelos, John (1996) 'Multi-level lobbying in the European Union: a paired sectoral comparison across the French-Italian border', *Regional and Federal Studies*, 6, 3, pp. 28–55.

Cortada, James W. (1980) *Spain in the Twentieth Century World, Essays on Spanish Diplomacy 1898–1978*. Aldwych, London.

Cram, Laura (1997) *Policy-making in the European Union, Conceptual Lenses and the Integration Process*. Routledge, London.

Crozier, Michel (1995) 'La posición del estado ante los otros actores', *Gestión y Análisis de Políticas Públicas*, 2, pp. 93–9.

Dastis, Alfonso (1995) 'La administración española ante la Unión Europea', *Revista de Estudios Políticos*, 90, pp. 323–49.

Dehousse, Renaud (1996) *Intégration ou désintégration? Cinq thèses sur l'incidence de l'intégration européenne sur les structures étatiques*, European University Institute Working Paper No. 4, Florence.

Delgado-Iribarren García-Campero, Manuel (1997) 'El control parlamentario de la política gubernamental relativa a la Unión Europea'. Unpublished manuscript, Congress, Spanish parliament, Madrid.

Díez-Hochleitner, Javier (1995) 'La flota española entra en la Europa azul', *Meridiano CERI*, 2, pp. 14–19.

Duff, Andrew, Pinder, John and Pryce, Roy (eds) (1994) *Maastricht and Beyond, Building the European Union*. Routledge, London/New York.

Elorza Cavengt, Francisco Javier (1994) 'La cohesión económica y social', in *España y el Tratado de la Unión Europea*. Colex, Madrid, pp. 311–30.

Evans, Peter B. (1993) 'Building an integrative approach to international and domestic politics: reflections and projections', in Evans, Peter B., Jacobson, Harold J. and Putnam, Robert D. (eds), *Double-edged Diplomacy, International Bargaining and Domestic Politics*. University of California Press, Berkeley/Los Angeles/London, pp. 397–430.

Evans, Peter B., Jacobson, Harold J. and Putnam, Robert D. (eds) (1993) *Double-edged Diplomacy, International Bargaining and Domestic Politics*. University of California Press, Berkeley/Los Angeles/London.

de Faramiñán Gilbert, Juan Manuel (1991) 'Repercusiones institucionales en Andalucía del ingreso de España en la Comunidad Europea', in de Faramiñán Gilbert, Juan Manuel, Delgado Cabezas, Manuel, Cazorla Pérez, José and Figares Romero de la Cruz, María Dolores (eds), *Interdependencia e Identidad Andaluza ante la Integración Europea*. Centro de Estudios Ramón Areces, Madrid, pp. 21–58.

Featherstone, Kevin (1989) 'Socialist parties in Southern Europe and the enlarged European Community', in Gallagher, Tom and Williams, Allan M. (eds), *Southern European Socialism, Parties, Elections and the Challenge of Government*. Manchester University Press, Manchester, pp. 247–70.

Fernández-Pita González, Rafael (1987) 'La adhesión de España a las Comunidades Europeas, Aspectos organizativos', *Revista de Estudios e Investigación de las Comunidades Europeas*, 1, pp. 61–87.

Fioretos, Karl-Orfeo (1997) 'The anatomy of autonomy: interdependence, domestic balances of power, and European integration', *Review of International Studies*, 23, 3, pp. 293–320.

Friman, H. Richard (1993) 'Side-payments versus security cards: domestic bargaining tactics in international economic negotiations', *International Organization*, 47, 3, pp. 387–410.

García, Carlos (1990) 'Les groupes d'intérêt espagnols et la Communauté Européenne', in Sidjanski, Dusan and Ayberk, Ural (eds), *L'Europe du Sud dans la Communauté Européenne, Analyse Comparative des Groupes d'Intérêts et Leur Insertion dans le Réseau Communautaire*. Presses Universitaires de France, Paris, pp. 115–63.

García, Caterina (1995) 'The autonomous communities and external relations', in Gillespie, Richard, Rodrigo, Fernando and Story, Jonathan (eds), *Democratic Spain: Reshaping External Relations in a Changing World*, Routledge, London, pp. 123–40.

García Díaz, Miguel Ángel (1995) *La política regional comunitaria en la etapa 1994–1999, Su aplicación en España*, CCOO, Working Paper No. 21, Madrid.

García de Enterría, Eduardo (1991) 'La participación de las CCAA en la formación de las decisiones comunitarias', *Revista Española de Derecho Constitucional*, 33, pp. 3–27.

Garrett, Geoffrey and Tsebelis, George (1996) 'An institutional critique of intergovernmentalism', *International Organization*, 50, 2, pp. 269–99.

George, Stephen (1985) *Politics and Policy in the European Community*. Clarendon, Oxford.

Gillespie, Richard (1989) *The Spanish Socialist Party, A History of Factionalism.* Clarendon, Oxford.

Gillespie, Richard (1990) 'The break-up of the "socialist family": party–union relations in Spain, 1982–89', *West European Politics*, 13, 1, pp. 47–62.

Gillespie, Richard (1995) 'Spain and the Maghreb: Towards a regional policy?', in Gillespie, Richard, Rodrigo, Fernando and Story, Jonathan (eds), *Democratic Spain: Reshaping External Relations in a Changing World*. Routledge, London, pp. 159–77.

Gillespie, Richard (1996) 'The Spanish socialists', in Gaffney, John (ed.), *Political Parties and the European Union*. Routledge, London/New York, pp. 155–69.

Gillespie, Richard (1997a) *The Mediterranean Dimension to Spanish Influence in Europe*. Paper given at UACES conference, Loughborough University, 10–12 September.

Gillespie, Richard (1997b) 'Spain and Morocco', unpublished manuscript.

Gillespie, Richard, Rodrigo, Fernando and Story, Jonathan (eds) (1995) *Democratic Spain: Reshaping External Relations in a Changing World*. Routledge, London.

Giner, Salvador and Sevilla, Eduardo (1984) 'Spain: from corporatism to corporatism', in Williams, Allan (ed.), *Southern Europe Transformed, Political and Economic Change in Greece, Italy, Portugal and Spain*. Harper & Row, London, pp. 113–37.

Goldstein, Judith (1996) 'International law and domestic institutions: reconciling North American "unfair" trade laws', *International Organization*, 50, 4, pp. 541–64.

Gómez Fuentes, Ángel (1986) *Así Cambiara España, la Batalla del Mercado Común*. Plaza y Janés, Barcelona.

González, Felipe (1987) 'La Europa que queremos', *Leviatán*, 29–30, pp. 5–14.

González, Felipe (1992) 'El desafio de Europa', *Leviatán*, 49, pp. 5–10.

González, Felipe (1996) 'Pilotar Europa hacia su rumbo', *Política Exterior*, 48, 9, pp. 14–21.

González Sánchez, Enrique (1978) 'Nota sobre la constitución y actuaciones del equipo negociador con las Comunidades Europeas', *Revista de Instituciones Europeas (RIE)*, 5, 3, pp. 78–87.

González Sánchez, Enrique (1980) 'La adhesión de España a las Comunidades Europeas: estado actual de las negociaciones', *RIE*, 7, 3, pp. 1029–41.

González Sánchez, Enrique (1982) 'Las negociaciones para la adhesión de España a las Comunidades Europeas: septiembre 1980 – diciembre 1981', *RIE*, 9, 1, pp. 87–100.

González Sánchez, Enrique (1983) 'Espana-CEE: las negociaciones de adhesión a lo largo de 1982', *RIE*, 10, 1, pp. 95–116.

González Sánchez, Enrique (1984) 'Las negociaciones de adhesión de España a las Comunidades Europeas; enero 1983 – marzo 1984', *RIE*, 11, 2, pp. 477–97.

González Sánchez, Enrique (1985) 'Las negociaciones de adhesión de España a las Comunidades Europeas desde abril de 1984 hasta su conclusión', *RIE*, 12, 2, pp. 439–64.

González Sánchez, Enrique (1986) 'Las relaciones entre España y las Comunidades Europeas a lo largo del periodo de ratificación', *RIE*, 13, 1, pp. 85–104.

González Sánchez, Enrique (1987) 'El procedimiento decisorio comunitario, Participación de las administraciones nacionales, Referencias al caso español', *RIE*, 14, 3, pp. 687–714.

Grande, Edgar (1996) 'The state and interest groups in a framework of multi-level decision-making: the case of the European Union', *Journal of European Public Policy*, 3, 3, pp. 318–38.

Granell, Francesc (1982) 'Las Comunidades Autónomas y la negociación para el ingreso de España en la Comunidad Europea', *RIE*, 9, 3, pp. 815–31.

Granell, Francesc (1984) 'Las Comunidades Autónomas ante la adhesión de España a la Comunidad Europea', Unpublished manuscript for conference at Universidad Internacional Menendez y Pelayo, Santander, 23 July.

Grant, Charles (1994) *Inside the House that Jacques Built*. Nicholas Brealey, London.

Guerra, Alfonso (1989) 'Un proyecto para Europa', *Leviatán*, 38, pp. 97–103.

Guerra, Alfonso (1993) 'Los socialistas y la Unión Europea', *Sistema*, 114–15, pp. 5–11.

Guerra, Alfonso and Tezanos, José Felix (eds) (1992) *La Decáda del Cambio, Diez Años de Gobierno Socialista 1982–1992*. Sistema, Madrid.

Gunther, Richard (1996) *Spanish Public Policy: from Dictatorship to Democracy*, Working Paper No. 84, Centro de Estudios Avanzados en Ciencias Sociales, Instituto Juan March de Estudios e Investigaciones, Madrid.

Gutiérrez Espada, Cesáreo (1994) 'La búsqueda por las Comunidades Autónomas de su "presencia" directa en y ante las Comunidades Europeas', *Gaceta Jurídica de la CE*, D-22, 139, pp. 169–228.

Haas, Ernst B. (1958, 1968) *The Uniting of Europe: Political, Social and Economic Forces 1950–57*. Stanford University Press, Stanford, CA.

Haas, Peter M. (1992) 'Introduction: epistemic communities and international policy coordination', *International Organization*, 46, 1, pp. 1–36.

Haggard, Stephan, Levy, Marc A., Moravcsik, Andrew and Nicolaidis, Kalypso (1993) 'Integrating the two halves of Europe: theories of interests, bargaining, and institutions', in Keohane, Robert, Nye, Joseph and Hoffmann, Stanley (eds), *After The Cold War: International Institutions and State Strategies in Europe 1989–1991*. Harvard University Press, Cambridge, MA/ London, pp. 173–95.

Hannequart, Achille (eds) (1992) *Economic and Social Cohesion in Europe: A new Objective for Integration*. Routledge, London.

Harrison, Joseph (1985) *The Spanish Economy in the Twentieth Century*. Croom Helm, London.

Harrison, Joseph (1992) 'Spain', in Dyker, David A. (ed.), *The National Economies of Europe*. Longman, Harlow, pp. 189–211.

Hayes-Renshaw, Fiona, Lequesne, Christian and Mayor López, Pedro (1989) 'The Permanent Representations of the member states to the European Communities', *JCMS*, 28, 2, pp. 119–37.

Herrero de Miñón, Miguel (1986) *España y la Comunidad Económica Europea*. Planeta, Barcelona.

Heywood, Paul (1991) 'Governing a new democracy: the power of the Prime Minister in Spain', *West European Politics*, 14, 2, pp. 97–115.

Heywood, Paul (1993) *Spain and the European Dimension: the Integrated Market, Convergence and Beyond*, Strathclyde Papers on Government and Politics No. 94, Glasgow.

Heywood, Paul (1995) *The Government and Politics of Spain*. Macmillan, London.

Heywood, Paul (1998) 'Power diffusion or concentration? In search of the Spanish policy process', *West European Politics*, 21, 4, pp. 103–23.

Hildenbrand, Andreas (1987) 'El FEDER y Andalucía: análisis de las primeras acciones de la política regional comunitaria', *Revista de Estudios Andaluces*, 9, pp. 111–48.

Hoffmann, Stanley (1982) 'Reflections on the nation-state in Western Europe today', *JCMS*, 21, pp. 21–37.

Holman, Otto (1996) *Integrating Southern Europe, EC Expansion and the Transnationalization of Spain.* Routledge, London.

Hooghe, Liesbet (1995) 'Subnational mobilisation in the European Union', in Hayward, Jack (ed.), *The Crisis of Representation in Europe.* Frank Cass, London, pp. 175–98.

Hooghe, Liesbet (1996a) 'Introduction: reconciling EU-wide policy and national diversity', in Hooghe, Liesbet (ed.), *Cohesion Policy and European Integration: Building Multi-level Governance.* Oxford University Press, Oxford, pp. 1–24.

Hooghe, Liesbet (1996b) 'Building a Europe with the regions: the changing role of the European Commission', in Hooghe, Liesbet (ed.), *Cohesion Policy and European Integration: Building Multi-level Governance.* Oxford University Press, Oxford, pp. 89–126.

Hooghe, Liesbet (1997) 'A house with differing views: the European Commission and cohesion policy', in Nugent, Neill (ed.), *At the Heart of the Union, Studies of the European Commission.* Macmillan, London, pp. 89–108.

Hooghe, Liesbet and Keating, Michael (1994) 'The politics of European Union regional policy', *Journal of European Public Policy*, 1, 3, pp. 367–93.

Hudson, Mark and Rudcenko, Stan (1988) *Spain to 1992: Joining Europe's Mainstream.* Economic Intelligence Unit, London.

Ikenberry, G. John (1986) 'The state and strategies of international adjustment', *World Politics*, 39, 1, pp. 53–77.

Jeffery, Charlie (1997) 'Conclusions: sub-national authorities and European domestic policy', in Jeffery, Charlie (ed.), *The Regional Dimension of the European Union: Towards a Third Level in Europe?* Frank Cass, London, pp. 204–19.

John, Peter (1996) 'Centralization, decentralization and the European Union: the dynamics of triadic relationships', *Public Administration*, 74, pp. 293–313.

John, Peter (1997) 'Europeanization in a centralizing state: multi-level governance in the UK', in Jeffery, Charlie (ed.), *The Regional Dimension of the European Union: Towards a Third Level in Europe?* Frank Cass, London, pp. 131–44.

Jones, Barry and Keating, Michael (1995) *The European Union and the Regions.* Clarendon, Oxford, pp. 1–22.

Juárez Casado, Samuel Jesús (1997) 'La pesca en España, Cambios en los últimos años y perspectivas', *Papeles de Economía Española*, 71, pp. 2–13.

Keating, Michael (1993) 'Spain', in Keating, Michael (ed.), *The Politics of Modern Europe: The State and Political Authority in the Major Democracies.* Edward Elgar, Aldershot, pp. 311–60.

Keating, Michael (1995) 'Europeanism and regionalism', in Jones, Barry and Keating, Michael (eds), *The European Union and the Regions.* Clarendon, Oxford, pp. 1–22.

Keating, Michael (1997) 'The political economy of regionalism', in Keating, Michael and Loughlin, John (eds), *The Political Economy of Regionalism.* Frank Cass, London, pp. 17–40.

Keating, Michael and Loughlin, John (eds) (1997) *The Political Economy of Regionalism.* Frank Cass, London.

Keohane, Robert and Hoffmann, Stanley (1990) 'Conclusions: Community politics and institutional change', in Wallace, William (ed.), *The Dynamics of European Integration*. Pinter, London, pp. 276–300.

Khader, Bichara and Núñez Villaverde, Jesús A. (1996) 'La asociación euromediterránea: promesas y sombras', *Política Exterior*, 48, 9, pp. 59–74.

Kitschelt, Herbert P. (1986) 'Political opportunity structures and political protest: anti-nuclear movements in four democracies', *British Journal of Political Science*, 16, 1, pp. 57–85.

Kohler-Koch, Beate (1982) *Political Forces in Spain, Greece and Portugal*. Butterworth, London.

Kohler-Koch, Beate (1996) 'Catching up with change: the transformation of governance in the European Union', *Journal of European Public Policy*, 3, 3, pp. 359–80.

Ladrech, Robert (1994) 'Europeanization of domestic politics and institutions: the case of France', *JCMS*, 32, 1, pp. 69–88.

de Larramendi, Miguel Hernando (1997) *La Política Exterior de Marruecos*. Mapfre, Madrid.

Lázaro Araujo, Laureano (1986) *El Espacio en la CEE, La Política Regional*. Trivium, Madrid.

Lázaro Araujo, Laureano (1988) *Transición y cambio en la política regional española*. Ministerio de Economía y Hacienda, Madrid.

Lázaro Araujo, Laureano (1991a) *Política regional comunitaria, Evolución y reforma del FEDER*. Ministerio de Economía y Hacienda, Madrid.

Lázaro Araujo, Laureano (1991b) 'El fondo de compensación interterritorial y la nueva política regional española', *Ciudad y Territorio*, 90, 4, pp. 297–308.

Lehman, Howard and McCoy, Jennifer (1992) 'The dynamics of the two-level bargaining game, The 1988 Brazilian debt negotiations', *World Politics*, 44, 4, pp. 600–44.

Lequesne, Christian (1993) *Paris-Bruxelles, Comment se fait la politique européenne de la France*. Fondation Nationale des Sciences Politiques, Paris.

Lieber, Robert J. (1970) *British Politics and European Unity, Parties, Elites and Pressure Groups*. University of California Press, Berkeley/London.

Lindberg, Leon (1963) *The Political Dynamics of European Economic Integration*. Stanford University Press, Stanford, CA.

Linz, Juan (1981) 'A century of politics and interests in Spain', in Berger, S. D. (ed.), *Organizing Interests in Western Europe: Pluralism, Corporatism, and the Transformation of Politics*. Cambridge University Press, Cambridge, MA, pp. 365–415.

Loira, José Rua (1996) 'Diez años de política pesquera en la Unión Europea', *El Boletín* (Ministerio de Agricultura, Pesca y Alimentación), 30, pp. 6–21.

López Castillo, A. (1993) 'La creación y ejecución del derecho comunitario en España', in *La Comunidad Europea, la Instancia Regional y la Organización Administrativa de los Estados Miembros*. Consejería de la Presidencia de la Junta de Andalucía, Civitas, Madrid, pp. 135–93.

López García-Asenjo, Alberto (1994) 'El sector pesquero', *Boletín Económico de ICE*, 2400–1, pp. 333–8.

Loughlin, John (ed.) (1993) *The Southern European Studies Guide*. Bowker-Saur, London.

McAleavey, Paul and Mitchell, James (1994) 'Industrial regions and lobbying in the structural funds reform process', *JCMS*, 32, 2, pp. 237–48.

McAllister, Richard (1993) 'Developments in member states', in 'The European Community 1992: Annual Review of Activities', *JCMS*, 31, pp. 105–17.

McAteer, Mark and Mitchell, Duncan (1996) 'Peripheral lobbying. The territorial dimension of Euro-lobbying by Scottish and Welsh sub-central government', *Regional and Federal Studies*, 6, 3, pp. 1–27.

Mangas Martín, A. (1987) *Derecho Comunitario Europeo y Derecho Español*. Tecnos, Madrid.

Mann, Michael (1993) 'Nation-states in Europe and other continents: diversifying, developing, not dying', *Daedalus*, 122, 3, pp. 115–40.

Maravall, Jose (1982) *The Transition to Democracy in Spain*. Croom Helm, London/St. Martin's Press, New York.

Marks, Gary (1992) 'Structural policy in the European Community', in Sbragia, Alberta (ed.), *Europolitics: Institutions and Policymaking in the 'New' European Community*. Brookings, Washington, DC, pp. 191–224.

Marks, Gary (1993) 'Structural policy and multilevel governance in the EC', in Cafruny, Alan W. and Rosenthal, Glenda G. (eds), *The State of the European Community Vol. 2, The Maastricht Debates and Beyond*. Lynne Rienner, Boulder, CO/Longman, Harlow, pp. 391–410.

Marks, Gary (1996) 'Exploring and explaining variation in EU cohesion policy', in Hooghe, Liesbet (ed.), *Cohesion Policy and European Integration: Building Multi-level Governance*. Oxford University Press, Oxford, pp. 388–422.

Marks, Gary (1997) 'An actor-centred approach to multi-level governance', in Jeffery, Charlie (ed.), *The Regional Dimension of the European Union: Towards a Third Level in Europe?* Frank Cass, London, pp. 20–38.

Marks, Gary, Hooghe, Liesbet and Blank, Kermit (1996a) 'European integration from the 1980s: state-centric v. multi-level governance', *JCMS*, 34, 3, pp. 341–78.

Marks, Gary and McAdam, Doug (1996) 'Social movements and the changing structure of political opportunity in the European Union', *West European Politics*, 19, 2, pp. 249–78.

Marks, Gary, Nielsen, François, Ray, Leonard and Salk, Jane (1996b) 'Competencies, cracks and conflicts: regional mobilization in the European Union', in Marks, Gary, Scharpf, Fritz W., Schmitter, Philippe C. and Streeck, Wolfgang (eds), *Governance in the European Union*. Sage, London, pp. 40–63.

Marks, Michael P. (1997) *The Formation of European Policy in Post-Franco Spain: The Role of Ideas, Interests and Knowledge*. Avebury, Aldershot.

Martin Martínez, Magdalena María (1995) 'El control parlamentario de la política comunitaria', *RIE*, 22, 2, pp. 445–74.

Martínez Lucio, Miguel (1991) 'Employer identity and the politics of the labour market in Spain', *West European Politics*, 14, 1, pp. 41–55.

Maurer, Lynn M. (1995) *Legislative-Executive Relations in a Newly Consolidated Democracy: The Case of Spain*, doctoral thesis, Ohio State University.

Maxwell, Kenneth and Spiegel, Steven (1994) *The New Spain, From Isolation to Influence*. Council on Foreign Relations Press, New York.

Mayer, Frederick W. (1992) 'Managing domestic differences in international negotiations: the strategic use of internal side-payments', *International Organization*, 46, 4, pp. 793–818.

Milner, Helen (1992) 'International theories of cooperation among nations: strengths and weaknesses', *World Politics*, 44, 3, pp. 466–96.

Milward, Alan S. (1992) *The European Rescue of the Nation-State*. Routledge, London.

Minet, Georges, Siotis, Jean and Tsakaloyannis, Panos (1981) *The Mediterranean Challenge VI, Spain, Greece and Community Politics*. Sussex European Paper No. 11, Sussex European Research Centre, University of Sussex.

Ministerio para las Administraciones Públicas (1995) *La Participación de las Comunidades Autónomas en los Asuntos Comunitarios Europeos*. Madrid.

Moderne, Franck (1987) 'L'administration espagnole et l'intégration européenne', *Annuaire Européen d'Administration Publique*, 9, pp. 137–55.

Molina Álvarez de Cienfuegos, Ignacio (2000) 'La adaptaciòn a la Uniòn Europea del poder ejecutivo español', in Closa, Carlos (ed.), *La Europeización del Sistema Político Español*. Istmo-Akal, Madrid.

Molins, Joaquim M. and Morata, Francesc (1994) 'Spain: rapid arrival of a latecomer', in Van Schendelen, Marinus (ed.), *National Public and Private EC Lobbying*. Dartmouth, Aldershot, pp. 113–30.

Morán, Fernando (1980) *Una Política Exterior para España*. Planeta, Barcelona.

Morán, Fernando (1984) 'La politique européenne de L'Espagne', *Politique Etrangère*, 49, 1, pp. 57–70.

Morán, Fernando (1990) *España en su sitio*. Plaza y Janés, Barcelona.

Morata, Francesc (1993) 'A comparative analysis of four Spanish regions', in Leonardi, Robert (ed.), *The Regions and the European Community. The Regional Response to the Single Market in the Underdeveloped Areas*. Frank Cass, London, pp. 187–216.

Morata, Francesc (1996) 'Spain', in Rometsch, Dietrich and Wessels, Wolfgang (eds), *The European Union and Member States: Towards Institutional Fusion?* Manchester University Press, Manchester/New York, pp. 134–54.

Morata, Francesc (1997) 'Spain and Europe', in Newton, Michael T. (with Donaghy, Peter J.), *Institutions of Modern Spain: A Political and Economic Guide*. Cambridge University Press, Cambridge, pp. 305–43.

Morata, Francesc (1998) 'Spain: modernization through integration', in Hanf, Kenneth and Soetendorp, Ben (eds), *Adapting to European Integration: Small States and the European Union*. Addison Wesley/Longman, Harlow, pp. 100–15.

Morata, Francesc and Muñoz, Xavier (1996) 'Vying for European funds: territorial restructuring in Spain', in Hooghe, Liesbet (ed.), *Cohesion Policy and European Integration: Building Multi-level Governance*. Oxford University Press, Oxford, pp. 195–218.

Moravcsik, Andrew (1991) 'Negotiating the Single European Act: national interests and conventional statecraft in the European Community', *International Organization*, 45, 1, pp. 19–56.

Moravcsik, Andrew (1993a) 'Preferences and power in the European Community: a liberal intergovernmentalist approach', *JCMS*, 31, 4, pp. 473–524.

Moravcsik, Andrew (1993b) 'Introduction: integrating international and domestic theories of international bargaining', in Evans, Peter B., Jacobson, Harold J. and Putnam, Robert D. (eds), *Double-edged Diplomacy, International Bargaining and Domestic Politics*. University of California Press, Berkeley/Los Angeles/London, pp. 3–42.

Moravcsik, Andrew (1994) 'Why the European Community strengthens the state: domestic politics and international cooperation', Unpublished paper.

Moxon-Browne, Edward (1989) *Political Change in Spain*. Routledge, London.

Nanetti, Raffaella Y. (1996) 'EU cohesion and territorial restructuring in the member states', in Hooghe, Liesbet (ed.), *Cohesion Policy and European Integration: Building Multi-level Governance*. Oxford University Press, Oxford, pp. 59–88.

Newton, Michael T. (with Donaghy, Peter J.) (1997) *Institutions of Modern Spain: A Political and Economic Guide*. Cambridge University Press, Cambridge.

Nicoll, William and Salmon, Trevor C. (1994) *Understanding the New European Community*. Harvester Wheatsheaf, Brighton.

Nordlinger, Eric (1981) *On the Autonomy of the Democratic State*. Harvard University Press, Cambridge, MA/London.

Nugent, Neill (1993) 'Editorial: the Treaty on European Union, Looking rather different twelve months on', in 'The European Community 1992: Annual Review of Activities', *JCMS*, 31, pp. 1–9.

Núñez Villaverde, Jesús A. and de Larramendi, Miguel Hernando (1996) *La Política Exterior y de Cooperación de España hacia el Magreb (1982–1995)*. Los libros de la Catarata/Instituto Universitario de Desarrollo y Cooperación, Madrid.

Ojeda García, Raquel (1996) *Relaciones exteriores España-Marruecos: el conflicto pesquero*. Paper given at the Second Congress of Political Science and Administration, Santiago de Compostela, April.

Ordóñez Solís, David (1996) 'Administraciones nacionales e integración europea', *Noticias de la Unión Europea*, 136 (special issue).

Ordovas Blasco, Rafael (1989) 'Los fondos estructurales: un balance social', *Revista de Estudios Sociales y de Sociología Aplicada*, 77, pp. 89–99.

Ortega Álvarez, Luis (1992) 'La coordinación de la administración del estado', *Documentación Administrativa*, 230–1, pp. 31–47.

Osuna, José Luis (1997) 'La pesca en Andalucía', *Papeles de Economía Española*, 71, pp. 117–32.

Payno, Juan Antonio (1983) 'Introduction: the second enlargement from the perspective of the new members', in Sampedro, José Luis, and Payno, Juan Antonio, *The Enlargement of the European Community, Case-Studies of Greece, Portugal and Spain*. Macmillan, London.

Peña, Miguel S. (1997) 'La actividad pesquera en España ante los cambios a escala internacional', *Papeles de Economía Española*, 71, pp. 48–59.

Pérez Calvo, Alberto (1993) 'Participación de las Comunidades Autonómas en la formación de la posicion que el estado ha de trasladar a las instituciones comunitarias', *Documentación Administrativa*, 232–3, pp. 247–70.

Pérez-Díaz, Víctor M. (1987) 'Economic policies and social pacts in Spain during the transition', in Scholten, Ilja (ed.), *Political Stability and Neo-corporatism: Corporatist Integration and Societal Cleavages in Western Europe*. Sage, London, pp. 216–45.

Pérez-Díaz, Víctor M. (1993) *The Return of Civil Society: The Emergence of Democratic Spain*. Harvard University Press, Cambridge, MA/London.

Pérez-Díaz, Víctor M. and Rodríguez, Juan Carlos (1994) *De opciones reticentes a compromisos creíbles, Política exterior y liberalización económica y política: España 1953–1986*, Analistas Socio-políticos Research Paper 3(a), Madrid.

Pérez Tremps, Pablo (1995) 'Comunidades Autónomas, estado y Unión Europea: nuevos pasos hacia la integración descentralizada', in Aja, Eliseo (ed.), *Informe Comunidades Autónomas 1994*. Instituto de Derecho Público, Barcelona, pp. 600–20.

Peterson, John (1995) 'Decision-making in the European Union: towards a framework for analysis', *Journal of European Public Policy*, 2, 1, pp. 69–93.

Petras, James (1993) 'Spanish socialism: the politics of neoliberalism', in Kurth, James and Petras, James (eds), *Mediterranean Paradoxes: Political and Social Structure in Southern Europe*. Berg, Providence, RI/Oxford, pp. 95–127.

Planas, Luis (1985) 'España y la Unión Europea', *Leviatán*, 20, pp. 31–7.

Pollack, Benny and Hunter, Graham (1987) *The Paradox of Spanish Foreign Policy: Spain's International Relations from Franco to Democracy*. Pinter, London.

Pollack, Mark A. (1995) 'Regional actors in an intergovernmental play: the making and implementation of EC structural policy', in Rhodes, Carolyn and Mazey, Sonia (eds), *The State of the European Community Vol. 3, Building a European Polity?* Lynne Rienner, Boulder, CO/Longman, Harlow, pp. 361–90.

Porras Nadales, Antonio J. (1994) 'La administración andaluza entre modernización y clientelismo', *Autonomies*, 18, pp. 81–91.

Powell, Charles T. (1993) 'La dimensión exterior de la transición española', *Afers Internacionals*, 26, pp. 37–64.

Powell, Charles T. (1995) 'Spain's external relations 1898–1975', in Gillespie, Richard, Rodrigo, Fernando and Story, Jonathan (eds), *Democratic Spain: Reshaping External Relations in a Changing World*. Routledge, London, pp. 11–29.

Preston, Christopher (1997) *Enlargement and Integration in the European Union*. Routledge, London.

Preston, Paul and Smyth, Denis (1984) *Spain, the EEC and Nato*. Routledge & Kegan Paul/Royal Institute of International Affairs (RIIA), London.

Pridham, Geoffrey (1991) 'The politics of the European Community, transnational networks and democratic transition in Southern Europe', in Pridham, Geoffrey (ed.), *Encouraging Democracy: The International Context of Regime Transition in Southern Europe*. Leicester University Press/Pinter, Leicester/London.

Pridham, Geoffrey (1995) 'The international context of democratic consolidation: Southern Europe in comparative perspective', in Gunther, Richard, Nikiforos Diamandouros, P. and Hans-Jürgen, Puhle, *The Politics of Democratic Consolidation: Southern Europe in Comparative Perspective*. Johns Hopkins University Press, Baltimore/London, pp. 166–203.

Putnam, Robert B. (1993) 'Diplomacy and domestic politics: the logic of two-level games', in Evans, Peter B., Jacobson, Harold J. and Putnam, Robert D. (eds), *Double-edged Diplomacy, International Bargaining and Domestic Politics*. University of California Press, Berkeley/Los Angeles/London, pp. 431–68.

Recio Figueiras (n/d) 'Consecuencias del proceso autonómico para la integración en las Comunidades Europeas', Manuscript for Third International Seminar on the Social Economy of the Marketplace. Unpublished conference paper, Madrid.

Remiro Brotóns, Antonio (1984) *La Acción Exterior del Estado*. Tecnos, Madrid.

Rhodes, R. A. W., Bache, Ian and George, Stephen (1996) 'Policy networks and policy-making in the European Union: a critical appraisal', in Hooghe, Liesbet (ed.), *Cohesion Policy and European Integration: Building Multi-level Governance*. Oxford University Press, Oxford, pp. 367–87.

Risse-Kappen, Thomas (1991) 'Public opinion, domestic structure, and foreign policy in liberal democracies', *World Politics*, 43, 4, pp. 479–512.

Risse-Kappen, Thomas (1996) 'Exploring the nature of the beast: international relations theory and comparative policy analysis meet the European Union', *JCMS*, 34, 1, pp. 53–80.

Roca, Jordi (1987) 'Neo-corporatism in post-franco Spain', in Scholten, Ilja (ed.), *Political Stability and Neo-corporatism: Corporatist Integration and Societal Cleavages in Western Europe*. Sage, London, pp. 247–68.

Rodríguez de la Borbolla, José (1989) 'Política regional en la Europa de los años 90 y estado de las Autonomías', in Ministerio de Economía y Hacienda, *Política Regional en la Europa de los Años 90*. Madrid, pp. 567–71.

Ross, Christopher J. (1997) *Contemporary Spain: A Handbook*. Arnold, London.

Ross, George (1995) *Jacques Delors and European Integration*. Polity, Cambridge.

Ruesga Benito, Santos M. (ed.) (1989) *1993: España ante el Mercado Unico*. Pirámide, Madrid.

Salas Hernández, Javier and Betancor Rodríguez, Andrés (1991) 'La incidencia organizativa de la integración europea en la administración española, *Revista de Administración Pública*, 125, pp. 495–538.

Salmon, Keith (1995a) *The Modern Spanish Economy: Transformation and Integration into Europe*. Pinter, London.

Salmon, Keith (1995b) 'Spain in the world economy', in Gillespie, Richard, Rodrigo, Fernando and Story, Jonathan (eds), *Democratic Spain: Reshaping External Relations in a Changing World*. Routledge, London, pp. 67–87.

Sampedro, José Luis and Payno, Juan Antonio (1983) *The Enlargement of the European Community: Case-Studies of Greece, Portugal and Spain*. Macmillan, London.

Sánchez-Cuenca Rodríguez, Ignacio (1995) *Las Negociaciones Agrícolas entre la Comunidad Europea y Estados Unidos en la Ronda Uruguay: Un Análisis desde la Lógica de la Elección Racional*. Doctoral thesis no. 9, Centro de Estudios Avanzados en Ciencias Sociales, Instituto Juan March de Estudios e Investigaciones, Madrid.

Sánchez de Dios, Manuel (1995) 'Las Cortes generales', in Román, Paloma (ed.), *Sistema Político Español*. McGraw-Hill, Madrid, pp. 83–109.

Sandholtz, Wayne (1993) 'Choosing union: monetary politics and Maastricht', *International Organization*, 47, 1, pp. 1–39.

Scharpf, Fritz W. (1988) 'The joint-decision trap: lessons from German federalism and European integration', *Public Administration*, 66, pp. 239–78.

Scharpf, Fritz W. (1994) 'Community and autonomy: multi-level policy-making in the European Union', *Journal of European Public Policy*, 1, 2, pp. 219–42.

Scott, Andrew (1993) 'Developments in the European Community economies', in 'The European Community 1992: Annual Review of Activities', *JCMS*, 31, pp. 87–104.

Scott, Joanne (1995) *Development Dilemmas in the European Community: Rethinking Regional Development Policy*. Open University Press, Buckingham.

Sehimi, Mustafá (1996) 'Las relaciones hispano-marroquíes', *Política Exterior*, 49, 10, pp. 110–20.

Shackleton, Michael (1986) *The Politics of Fishing in Britain and France*. Gower, Aldershot.

Shackleton, Michael (1990) *Financing the European Community*. Pinter/Royal Institute of International Affairs (RIIA), London.

Shackleton, Michael (1993) 'Keynote article: the Delors II budget package', in 'The European Community 1992: Annual Review of Activities', *JCMS*, 31, pp. 11–25.

Share, Donald (1989) *Dilemmas of Social Democracy: The Spanish Socialist Workers Party in the 1980s*. Greenwood, Westport, CT.

Sidjanski, Dusan (1991) 'Transition to democracy and European integration: the role of interest groups in Southern Europe', in Pridham, Geoffrey (ed.), *Encouraging Democracy: The International Context of Regime Transition in Southern Europe*. Leicester University Press/Pinter, Leicester/London, pp. 195–211.

Smith, Andy (1995) *L'intégration communautaire face au territoire: Les fonds structurels et les zones rurales en France, en Espagne et au Royaume Uni*. Doctoral thesis, Grenoble.

Smith, Andy (1997) 'The French case: the exception or the rule?', in Jeffery, Charlie (ed.), *The Regional Dimension of the European Union: Towards a Third Level in Europe?* Frank Cass, London, pp. 117–30.

Smith, Martin J. (1993) *Pressure, Power and Policy: State Autonomy and Policy Networks in Britain and the United States*. Harvester Wheatsheaf, Hemel Hempstead.

Smyrl, Marc (1997) 'Does European Community regional policy empower the regions?', *Governance*, 10, 3, pp. 287–309.

Solana, Javier Madariaga (1993) 'España-Europa', *Sistema*, 114–15, pp. 13–23.

Soláns Latre, Miguel Ángel (1995) *Concertación Social y Otras Formas de Neocorporatismo en España y en la Comunidad Europea*. Tecnos, Madrid.

Somers, Frans J. L. (eds) (1991) *European Economies: A Comparative Study*. Pitman, London.

Story, Jonathan (1991a) *Spanish External Policies: Towards the EC Presidency*. Centre for Mediterranean Studies, Occasional Paper No. 2, Bristol.

Story, Jonathan (1991b) 'Spain in the European diplomatic system', *Diplomacy and Statecraft*, 2, 1, pp. 54–73.

Story, Jonathan (1993) 'Spain's transition to democracy', in Story, Jonathan (ed.), *The New Europe: Politics, Government and Economy since 1945*. Blackwell, Oxford/Cambridge, MA, pp. 245–65.

Story, Jonathan (1995) 'Spain's external relations redefined: 1975–89', in Gillespie, Richard, Rodrigo, Fernando and Story, Jonathan (eds), *Democratic Spain: Reshaping External Relations in a Changing World*. Routledge, London, pp. 30–49.

Story, Jonathan and Pollack, Benny (1991) 'Spain's transition: domestic and external linkages', in Pridham, Geoffrey (ed.), *Encouraging Democracy: The International Context of Regime Transition in Southern Europe*. Leicester University Press/Pinter, Leicester/London, pp. 125–58.

Subirats, Joan (1992) *Un problema de estilo, La formación de políticas públicas en España, Exploración sobre los elementos distintivos de nuestro 'policy style' (Una aportación al análisis del sistema político español)*. Centro de Estudios Constitucionales, Madrid.

Subirats, Joan and Gomà, R. (1998) 'La dimensión de estilo de las políticas públicas en España: entremados institucionales y redes de actores', in Goma, R. and Subirats, Joan (eds), *Políticas Públicas en España*. Ariel, Barcelona.

Tamames, Ramón (1986) *Guía del Mercado Común Europeo: España en la Europa de los Doce*. Alianza, Madrid.

Tamames, Ramón (1991) *Estructura Económica de España*. Alianza, Madrid.

Taylor, Paul (1991) 'The European Community and the state: assumptions, theories and propositions', *Review of International Studies*, 17, 2, pp. 109–25.

Taylor, Paul (1996) *The European Union in the 1990s*. Oxford University Press, Oxford.

Tovias, Alfred (1990) *Foreign Relations of the European Community: The Impact of Spain and Portugal*. Lynne Rienner, Boulder, CO/London.

Tovias, Alfred (1995) 'Spain in the European Community', in Gillespie, Richard, Rodrigo, Fernando and Story, Jonathan (eds), *Democratic Spain: Reshaping External Relations in a Changing World*. Routledge, London, pp. 88–105.

Trias i Fargas, Ramón (1989) 'Política regional y estado de las Autonomías: reflexiones desde Cataluña', in Ministerio de Economía y Hacienda, *Política Regional en la Europa de los Años 90*. Madrid, pp. 573–8.

Trillo-Figueroa, Federico (1997) 'El Congreso de los Diputados y el proceso de construcción europea', Unpublished speech, Congress, Spanish Parliament, Madrid.

Tsoukalis, Loukas (1981) *The European Community and Its Mediterranean Enlargement*. George Allen & Unwin, London.

Vázquez, Gonzalo et al. (1996) *El Sector Pesquero Español en la Unión Europea*. Fundación Alonso Martín Escudero, Mundi-Prensa, Madrid.

Wallace, Helen and Young, Alasdair R. (eds) (1997) *Participation and Policy-making in the European Union*. Oxford University Press, Oxford.

Wallace, William (1996) 'Government without statehood: the unstable equilibrium', in Wallace, Helen and Wallace, William (eds), *Policy-making in the European Union*. Oxford University Press, Oxford, pp. 439–60.

Waltz, Kenneth N. (1979) *Theory of International Politics*. Addison-Wesley, London.

Westendorp, Carlos et al. (eds) (1994) *España y el Tratado de la Unión Europea*. Colex, Madrid.

Wigg, Richard (1988) 'Spain: Europeanism in place of socialism', *The World Today*, 44, pp. 115–18.

Wishlade, Fiona (1996) 'EU cohesion policy: facts, figures, and issues', in Hooghe, Liesbet (ed.), *Cohesion Policy and European Integration: Building Multi-level Governance*. Oxford University Press, Oxford, pp. 27–58.

Wright, Vincent (1996) 'The national co-ordination of European policy-making: negotiating the quagmire', in Richardson, Jeremy (ed.), *European Union, Power and Policy-making*. Routledge, London, pp. 148–69.

Youngs, Richard (1996) *The Politics of Economic and Monetary Co-operation in Europe 1986–1993: Britain and Spain Compared*. Doctoral thesis, Warwick.

Zabalza Marti, Antonio (1989) 'La política regional en la España de los noventa', in Ministerio de Economía y Hacienda, *Política Regional en la Europa de los Años 90*. Madrid, pp. 595–604.

Zapico Goñi, Eduardo (1995) 'La adaptación de la administración española a la Unión Europea: un proceso de evolución y aprendizaje permanente', *Gestión y Análisis de Políticas Públicas*, 4, pp. 47–65.

Index